# Purple Golf Cart:

## The Misadventures of an Unconventional Grandma

*A Memoir*
*by*
*Ronni Sanlo*

*Purple Books Publishing*

## Also by Ronni Sanlo

*Working with Lesbian, Gay, Bisexual, and Transgender College Students: A Handbook for Faculty and Administrators*. Greenwood Press

*Identity and Leadership in Academe: Informing Our Lives, Informing Our Practice*. With Alicia Chavez. NASPA

*Unheard Voices: The Effects of Silence on Lesbian an Gay Educators*. Praeger (Greenwood Press)

*Our Place on Campus LGBT Programs and Services* with Sue Rankin and Robert Schoenberg. Greenwood Press

*Gender Identity and Sexual orientation: Research, Policy, and Personal Perspectives*. New Directions in Student Services. Jossey-Bass

Cover design and website by Barbara Gottlieb
www.gottgraphix.com

Library of Congress Number: 1-716207421
ISBN: 978-0-9850986-2-9

Published by Purple Books Publishing
www.purplebookspublishing.com
Palm Desert, CA 92260

Printed in the United States of America

To My Precious Grandchildren…

Come ride with me in my
purple golf cart.

I'll even let you drive.

Now THAT's love!

# CONTENTS

## *Prologue*

Five young girls were bragging about their grandmothers. The first little girl said, "My gramma is kind of big and she wears these weird red hats and flowery dresses. But she makes me laugh a lot. She's pretty cool for a gramma." All the girls nodded in agreement.

The second girl offered, "My grandmother's cool, too. When she visits us, she takes me to the movies and lets me see stuff my mom says I'm not supposed to watch." All the girls heartily concurred, that was definitely cool.

The third girl spoke. "That's nothing. My nana took me on a boat trip last summer and I got to see whales! Lots of them!" Yes, that was very cool, they all agreed.

The two remaining girls were sisters. The younger one, glancing at the older with a knowing smile, announced, "Actually, WE have the coolest grandma." The two sisters high-fived each other as the older one proclaimed, "Yeah! Our grandma's a lesbian and she drives a purple golf cart!"

The other three girls, mouths wide open, just nodded in awe…

# 1. At 63

*M*arch, 2007. I celebrated my 60th birthday every single day that month. Turning 60 seemed so surreal. Was that really me in the mirror? I don't remember aging, and I sure didn't feel 60, whatever that means. And why wasn't I able to know "way back then" what I know now? I suppose we all think those things when we get here. The true gift of aging, after all, is hindsight. Regardless, "60" felt strange rolling off my tongue. To make even more of an issue of turning 60—because I can be *such* a drama queen—it occurred to me that even under the best of circumstances, I've already lived more years than I have left. I intend to make the most of every single day.

I bought myself a purple golf cart for my 60th birthday—purple, with hot pink upholstery and a white roof, my name in white script on the driver's side. I live in a golf community, Palm Desert Greens, for older folks—well, for people over 55 which I am, and mostly retired people, which I'm not. I am a passionate but pathetic golfer, purple is my favorite color, and, really, I just wanted it. When I'm on the streets of the Greens, old men wave to me and their grandchildren think I'm cool in my purple golf cart. But as an aging lesbian, I'm just happy with a girlfriend beside me as we motor through the elder-'hood.

Sixty was a crazy year for me. Following the drama of the age was the trauma of the melanoma diagnosis about six weeks after my birthday. All those years of Florida beaches and boats came back to bite me in the butt, or, rather, on my collar bone, to be site-specific. When I was a teenager in Miami Beach, I made my own suntan potion—a stick of cocoa butter, a good helping of baby oil, and some lemon juice melted together in a jar in the hot Florida sun—then shmeared it all over my body. I fried. Daily. For all the years of my teens. I had the best and darkest tan, and I felt so happy when the Miami Beach sun warmed me from head to toe. I suspect that the years of living on my boat in Key West didn't help my skin much either, but that teenage tan was perfection! Now, decades later, melanoma. I used to say, "If I have to die of something, it may as well be of a good tan." Not so much anymore. Careful what you ask for. The melanoma was caught very early by a smart young dermatologist who noticed the teensy-tiny spot that I completely missed on my routine body check. I was lucky. The surgery got it all. Today my magic sun potion begins with SPF 55.

As if melanoma weren't enough, my sister Sherry, two years younger than I, was diagnosed with Stage III breast cancer. Her diagnosis was far more fearful to my heart than my own melanoma. I couldn't bear to think that either of my sisters would suffer a horrible disease whose treatment is worse than the cancer itself. But Sherry is truly a grand survivor and has become my hero for what it means to be a strong, gracious woman. After the chemo, the removal of both her breasts, and then radiation, she's finally cancer-free. Prayers answered.

As I was settling in to being 60, I received some very sweet and unexpected gifts. I made full professor at UCLA, had several more academic publications, and was recognized as a Pillar of the Profession by the National Association of Student Personnel Administrators (NASPA), my professional organization. In addition, I was invited back to my graduate alma mater, the University of North Florida in Jacksonville, to keynote at their first Lavender Graduation where they honored the lives and achievements of their graduating gay, lesbian, bisexual, and transgender students, an event I founded at the University of Michigan in 1995. They even named a student leadership award after me. I was touched beyond words. At the same time, I was named one of Curve magazine's "Top Twenty Powerful Lesbian Academics" (there are 20???), and identified as one of "Los Angeles' 25 People who Make You Melt" in *Frontiers*, a magazine for young gay men. (How on earth a 60-year-old lesbian grandma melts the hearts of those sweet young men is beyond me but I appreciated the sentiment.)

I chose to write this book for them, for their parents and families, for my own children and grandchildren, and for myself. I needed to finally speak out about the journey I've taken over my 60-some years. I want my children to understand how I yearned for them during our years of separation, and I hope people recognize their own qualities of resilience, passion, survival as they read about mine. Finally, I want to share lesbian and gay history as I lived it so that lesbian, gay, bisexual, and transgender (LGBT) readers and their loved ones learn that our people didn't mysteriously pop out of a gay bar last Thursday night. We have a long and rich history, we LGBT folk, and it's there for the discovery.

While the history in this book is accurate—at least accurate in my own mind—I changed the names of some of the people because this is *my* memoir, not theirs. Their recollections may be—and probably are—much different from mine. I see no need to deliberately piss off people from my past any more than they may have been pissed off originally. You'll know which is which. Pseudonyms are first names only. Real names are first and last. Anyway, others must find voices to tell their own stories. I can tell only mine, and only from my own perspective. In addition, I include a boxed chronology at the beginning of many of the chapters for perspective. I want you, the reader, to understand what was happening socially and politically during those years and how my life—and perhaps yours—was imbedded in and affected by the culture of the day.

I extend my heartfelt thanks to all those folks through the years who encouraged me to write my story. It took a while, but their words stayed with me. I'm grateful to my dear friends Helen Schwartz, Melinda Moore, Jill Harris, Annie Goldman, and my sisters Sherry Horwitz and Barbra Miner, who read much of this work in its early stages, provided feedback, and encouraged me to continue, and to Kristen Snyder who read the almost-final draft. I offer thanks to Peggy Schumacher for her feedback while on our Eco-Arts writing retreat in Costa Rica, and to the women on that trip who listened and offered ideas despite sitting in the humid Costa Rican jungle. I'm also grateful to Dr. Karen Derr who helped me process the painful events and feelings as they captured my attention in my consciousness. Don't do a memoir without your therapist nearby!

Regina Lark, my roommate and best pal, read many iterations of this work as she was building her own businesses. She generously provided tremendous encouragement, marketing tips, and really strong coffee the entire way. Barb Gottlieb, the best web diva ever, guided the technical part when I didn't know there *was* a technical part!

My life could never have been what it was and is without my two precious children, Berit and Erik. They suffered as much as I, yet it didn't stop them from coming "home" to me. Finally, I'm thankful for every person from my past, even the scary ones. Regardless of

## 2.

# From My Jewish Roots, I Rise

---

1947

<u>U.S. President</u>: Harry S. Truman
<u>Best film</u>: Gentlemen's Agreement; Miracle on 34<sup>th</sup> St.
<u>Best actors</u>: Ronald Coleman; Loretta Young
<u>Best TV shows</u>: Kraft Television Theater; Meet the Press; Kukla, Fran & Ollie; Howdy Doody
<u>Popular songs</u>: The Anniversary Song, Heartaches, Peg O' My Heart, White Christmas
<u>Civics</u>: Hollywood "Black List" created
<u>Popular Culture</u>: Microwave oven invented; Jackie Robinson joins Brooklyn Dodgers; *Diary of a Young Girl* by Anne Frank published; *Vice Versa,* the first North American LGBT publication, written and self-published by Lisa Ben in Los Angeles.
<u>Deaths</u>: Henry Ford, Al Capone, race horse Man O' War

---

*"You're almost 25 and you're not married. What are you, funny or something???"*

*T*he words swirled furiously around in my head and landed in my gut like a boxer's powerful punch. My grandfather demanded to know why I wasn't married. I panicked! He *must* know my secret, but how could he? I never told anyone, never acted on it. But he *had* to know or he wouldn't have said it like *that*!

I did the only thing I could think of to deflect his suspicions: I called my old college default date Jake who was now a school band director in Florida. He'd proposed once, just before we graduated from the University of Florida in 1969. He drew a high draft number and didn't

11

want to go to Viet Nam. No need, though. His father bought him a ride in the National Guard.

"Do you still want to get married," I asked even though I hadn't seen or spoken to him in two years, and despite the not-so-insignificant fact that I now lived in Los Angeles.

"Sure, why not?"

We were married three months after my grandfather's words. Eight years later I lost custody of my children.


Though I claim Florida as my home state, I was born in 1947 in the small town of East Liverpool, Ohio. My father's parents, Polly and Saul Ruchelsman, immigrated from Poland in about 1913. From New York they traveled as far west as their money would take them, via Cleveland to East Liverpool, Ohio. East Liverpool is a small town surrounded by pottery and steel mills on the banks of the Ohio River, across from both West Virginia and Pennsylvania, kind of a bend in the river that's easy to miss. Saul had just enough money left of their travel funds to buy a small mom-and-pop grocery but not enough money to change the name on the sign over the door of the store. My grandparents went from being Polly and Saul Ruchelsman to Polly and Saul Lebman because that was the name on the store, Lebman's Grocery.

My father, Sanford Lebman, served in the Army during World War II, in the 42nd Rainbow Division, and came home from Europe with a Purple Heart that signified he'd been injured. He also came home with painful memories of the liberation of Dachau. My father was probably the first American soldier to enter that concentration camp, guns blazing, as his tank tore down Dachau's gates, but it would be another 50 years before he could speak about the atrocities he saw there. He was twenty-two years old when he came home, physically and emotionally wounded. He wanted to be a pharmacist but he went to work for his father in the family grocery store instead.

My mother, Lois Schonfield Lebman, was twenty-one when my father came back from the war. They'd already been married for two years during most of which my father was overseas. My mother was, and still is, a brilliant, beautiful woman. She'd planned to go to college to study journalism but between the war effort and her own mother's serious illness, there was no money for school. She worked as a bank teller instead. She also worked at her parents' shoe store and in Lebman's grocery as the bookkeeper.

While Saul and Polly were classically old-world, my mother's parents, Frances and Schoney Schonfield, were quite modern. Both were born in the U.S. to Russian immigrants and together they operated a shoe store in East Liverpool. Both sets of grandparents had their financial issues, juggling between working-poor and sheer impoverishment. As an unusual result, they all lived together in the same three-story house. My father's parents were on the first floor, my mother's parents on the second, and my parents lived on the third floor while my father built a house for us out in the country, as if East Liverpool were not rural enough.

The concept of family extended over the generations and across many coattails, We were a family who lived and traveled in a pack. Like a flock of birds, in 1954 we all up and shifted from East Liverpool, Ohio, to Miami Beach, Florida. The reason: allergies and hay fever in several of the family members including me. The Jewish migration south had begun. In 1967, the flock migrated again, this time west to Los Angeles.

My mother's parents had actually moved to Miami Beach before the rest of us. I remember flying from Ohio to Miami in one of those old DC-3 tail-dragger airplanes that Pan American World Airways operated. Those planes always smelled like oranges, a Pan Am trademark of squirting citrus fragrance to heighten the anticipation of arrival to Miami, or the attempt to extend a visit if leaving Miami. I also remember the matching leopard-skin-designed bathing suits that my sisters and brother and I had to wear when we went to Miami Beach because some distant Miami-residing cousin-eight-times-removed was the manufacturer.

When my family first moved to South Florida, we stayed with my mother's parents in their brand new home in Miramar, a subdivision near Hollywood, Florida. Within a few months, though, my parents had purchased a newly constructed three-bedroom two-bath house on 181st Street in North Miami Beach for $14,000. I enjoyed living with my Grandma Frances and hated leaving her, but it was time to go, my parents said. North Miami Beach was where hundreds of young Jewish families began to settle, a large modern-day *shtetl*.

My grandmother Frances was modern, powerful, and popular, and president of everything in her community. She was tall and carried herself with an air of authority. She was the most wonderful woman I ever knew, and she loved me fiercely! She was the one person in the entire family who, I remember, just wrapped her arms around me and hugged me tight. I was the first grandchild on both sides of the family. As a precocious, vocal, opinionated little kid, I was the family entertainer. Everyone thought I was pretty terrific, but there was a specialness about the way my grandmother cherished me. I knew without a doubt that no one loved me like she did. Her husband, my grandfather, Schoney, was attractive and debonair. He worked at Abercrombie & Fitch back when it was a "gentlemen's" store and always wore the most current Miami-style pastel slacks and matching shoes and belts.

I missed seeing my grandmother every day after we moved to our own home, but I was glad to be away from my grandfather. Sometimes he just creeped me out. We children were required to kiss the grownups goodnight at bedtime, or kiss them goodbye whenever we left their homes. I didn't like the way my grandfather kissed me, too long and slobbery. I made a million excuses to avoid him. Was I sensing a problem or just imagining something that wasn't real? Everybody seemed to love my grandfather. He died at the age of 87 in 1991, and to this day people remember him fondly. I'm just not one of them. Are there unspoken secrets in the family, those Big Secrets that quietly and insanely form and inform our lives? I don't know. I've never asked. Maybe it was just me...

The other thing that disturbed me about my grandfather was the way he mercilessly harassed my brother about his thumb sucking. While I'm sure many people witnessed my grandfather's unkind words to my brother, no one stopped the old man from saying those things to that little boy, at least not that I remember ever hearing. The harsh teasing started around the time I was discovering my sexual orientation, when I was 11, and continued into my teens. The clear message for me was since no one protected my brother, no one would protect me from such overt and painful judgment. Strangely, when I recently asked my brother about the harassment, he had no recollection of it. Like everyone else, he sang my grandfather's praises. Did I imagine yet another situation with my grandfather way back then? I just don't know...

I knew my Grandmother Frances was very ill. She suffered from non-Hodgkin's lymphoma, and because of ulcerative colitis, she had had an ileostomy. But she never dismissed me because of her health. She'd let me climb into bed with her and hold me close, telling me that I should be a lawyer because I had been "vaccinated with a Victrola needle." Apparently, from the time I was a toddler, I talked incessantly, a trait she thoroughly enjoyed and encouraged. Grandma Frances died in 1958 at the age of 54, three years before my grandfather Saul—my Pop—my father's father passed. Strangely, I have no recollection of my grandparents' deaths or funerals. Children in my family were not supposed to participate in unhappy events. I was in tremendous pain from the loss of my grandmother and had no way to express it so I stuffed it deep down inside of myself.

Several years after my grandmother Frances died, Schoney married Mae Wallace, a woman to whom he remained married until his death in 1991. Mae, who was as loved in our family as if she were a biological member, died 17 years after Schoney, just three months short of her 103rd birthday. A few months before she passed, I visited her in the nursing home near Ft. Lauderdale. I loved Mae and marveled at how articulate she remained despite her physically weakened state. As we shared an ice cream in the dining hall of her nursing home, she said to me, "I'm telling you, Ronni, there's a lot to be said for Alzheimer's. With Alzheimer's, when you live to be this old, you don't know how bad off you are. Wish I had it." Her mind was sharp but her body quit functioning in any meaningful way. She told me she was ready to go. When I kissed her goodbye, I knew it was for the last time. I cried for her, and prayed, as I walked out to my car, into the bright Florida sunshine, grateful that she had been such a sweet part of my life. She and all of my grandparents are buried in the Mt. Sinai cemetery in Miami.

I was never quite sure if my grandparents—Mae and Schoney— knew I was a lesbian until I visited them in Miami one day in about 1984. I had been out as a lesbian for about five years and active in the Florida lesbian and gay civil rights movement. I was taking a light snooze in one of their comfy chairs while they were sitting side by side on the couch. I heard Mae say to my grandfather in a loud whisper to accommodate his hearing, "Aren't you so proud of her?" My grandfather replied, "Yes, except for that, uh, one little thing." Mae responded with what sounded like a whack to his chest—she was only 4'9" and about 110 pounds but powerful in so many ways! "Shut up," she said to him with hushed gusto. "There're lots of people like that!" Thank you, Mae.


When my father's parents, Polly and Saul, moved to Miami Beach in the mid-1950s, they bought a small eight-unit apartment building in the heart of what is now the Art Deco district. They lived in one unit and rented the others. I remember the storage basement in that building, only four steps down but it felt like an immense underground cave. At least that's how I fantasized it. It was my grandfather Pop's domain but he always let me go down there. It was damp and musty-smelling, with only a single hanging light bulb that sometimes swayed and threw eerie shadows on the cement block walls. The room was filled with discarded treasures like clocks and radios and rusted tools. I would go down into that mysterious place where I pretended to be a mad scientist, disemboweling every old electronic thing I could find. I was never frightened there, maybe because my grandfather was always nearby, always enjoying my methodical destruction.

My father's mother, Pauline, or Polly—my Bubba—was typically old-world. Both she and my grandfather came to the U.S. from Poland in the early 1900s and she maintained much of her Polish culture and language. Her claim to family fame was her outstanding meals, plentiful, traditionally Jewish, and always way too much. "Eat more," she would say to already-overweight me. "You like it, yes? Eat more!" I ate. She once said to me, "Someday you will eat peanuts off my head, you're getting so tall." One day, as a teenager, I did! I put a couple of peanuts on top of her black-gray curly hair and nibbled. She loved that!

I'm the oldest of four children, and my sisters and brother are my closest friends. While my siblings were fairly docile as children, I was outgoing, "boisterous," my mother said, though I didn't know what that meant. She also called me "a bull in a china shop." I was never sure if it was because I was clumsy or just a hyperactive kid who was all over the place. I suspect the latter. Sometimes my mother would say, "Walk like a lady. You walk like a football player." I had no idea how football players walked but I knew I certainly preferred footballs to dresses. A tomboy of the highest order!

My mother was the typical 1950s Miami Beach mom, beautiful and tan. Her stylish appearance belied the colitis and the resulting arthritis that tried to overtake her body. She was adamant about the family rules, and just as adamant that our following them would keep us safe and healthy and good. For example, one of her primary rules was "if you can't say anything nice, don't say anything at all." This literally meant that we children could not talk nor feel negatively about people, places, or things. We must always be happy. In theory it's a great and kind idea. In reality, I learned to not trust my feelings, and had no idea how to safely be in natural conflict with people I loved. I would often hear from my parents, "No, you don't feel that way. You feel this way." Or "No, you don't want that toy. You want this toy." Or "No, you don't want to go there. You want to go here." It all came from a place of love, which I never doubted, but it did a hatchet job on my own feelings and desires, which I learned to seriously doubt. It took many years before I realized this, buried along with my inability to feel much emotion. I was oblivious to my wants and needs and desires, and was unable to trust my own judgment. My lack of trust of self and others was profound.


My mother made sure we lived a traditional, though not old-fashioned, Jewish lifestyle, just like everyone else in our community. We went to the synagogue—Beth Torah in North Miami Beach—on Friday nights and Saturday mornings, then Hebrew school on Sunday mornings. We kept a kosher home, which meant, among other things, that we did not mix milk products with meat. Our home remained kosher, in fact, until after the death of my grandfather Saul in 1961. I remember when my mother got a dishwasher, around the same time as everyone else in our neighborhood. It apparently created a huge dilemma among the mothers: since the kosher laws prohibited mixing milk with meat, how should they wash dairy dishes and meat dishes in the same dishwasher? It was a conundrum but Rabbi Lipschitz, of course, had the solution:

wash the dairy dishes, then run an empty cycle with hot water. Wash the meat dishes, then run another empty cycle. That way, dishes don't touch one another, and the hot water sterilizes everything. Oy!

We kept kosher both in and out of the house until Burger King invented the whopper with cheese in the late 1950s. My father became a whopper-with-cheese junkie! The sin of mixing dairy products with meat products became a thing of the past, at least outside of the house, as we began to examine a more modern approach to both our Jewishness and our diets. The early message from this, which served me well for my life, was about change. Change is necessary and inevitable and doesn't have to be bad.

My sister Sherry and I shared a bedroom upstairs—meaning three steps up—in our mid-century modern split-level house with those hard terrazzo floors. The back part of the house was the traditional "Florida room" with floor-to-ceiling jalousie windows on three walls, rattan furniture, and the family television. Jalousie windows: those glass-slat things that never fully shut. I think they were the true signifier of 1950s Miami Beach homes. All of the windows in our house were jalousies.

The dining room, separated from the Florida room by a wall of sliding glass doors, had a large table that seated a small army which is what we were at holidays when all the relatives from Up North descended upon us. Aunt Lil from Pittsburgh used to line us kids up whenever she and Uncle Harry came to town. "Bebe, you're getting to be so pretty. Lenny, you're so handsome. Sherry, you're so beautiful. Ronni, you have such a great personality." Personality?? Screw personality! I wanted to be pretty or handsome or beautiful, too. But I wasn't. I was an overweight tomboy with a great personality. Swell.

My brother Lenny and youngest sister Bebe shared the other upstairs bedroom. Our parents' bedroom was on the opposite side of the house but we were only as far away from them as the intercom system through which they could hear our every word. Sherry and I quickly figured out how to muffle the intercom with towels, and then we'd practice the few four-letter words we knew.

Sherry, two years younger than I, was terribly annoying at times. In the early mornings before I awoke, Sher would get out of her bed, climb into mine, and put her nose almost, but not quite, on top of my nose, with her big eyes open wide and a giant grin on her face. Her breathe always woke me up. "AHHHhhhhhhh!!!!" I'd holler, startled but not frightened, because she did this nearly every day. Or if I had a black-and-blue mark on my leg or arm, Sher would push into it with her index finger and ever-so-innocently ask, "Does that hurt?" Cute. And she always won the fart and burp contests we had when adults weren't around. In fact, she still does!

Len is five years younger than I. He was a genius at creative problem-solving. For example, when he was about nine years old, he had fallen off his bike. The gash on his leg was quite large and bleeding rather profusely. He ran into the house for assistance but no one was immediately available so he went into the bathroom to look for a bandage. He found my box of Kotex, the old kind with the long tail on either end that fit into those hooks attached to the skinny elastic straps. He wrapped the Kotex around his leg and tied the tails. Voila! Satisfied with his bandage, he went back out on his bike. My friends and I were sitting on a nearby street corner in our neighborhood, singing the words from the current *Hit Parade* magazine, when Len peddled by, his leg neatly wrapped in my Kotex. I was mortified!

Bebe, seven years younger than I, was a terrible eater. She hated almost all food except eggs and hot dogs. Her method of operation was to chew her food when our parents were watching, then spit the mouthful into a napkin when they were not. She'd hide the napkin in a shoebox in her bedroom closet. I recently asked her whatever happened to that shoebox full of half-chewed food. She said, "Gee, I don't know. Hamsters? Cockroaches? I don't know." Ick!

My father worked for years as a manager in a paint and hardware store in Hollywood, Florida, then started his own wholesale hardware company called LebCo. (Had he been a visionary kind of guy, we might have become Home Depot. I have forgiven him this.) He worked six days a week but always made time to toss a ball or swim in the pool with us kids in the evenings. I remember one Saturday evening when I had a pool party at our house. About twelve of my high school friends were there, playing in the pool, sliding down the slide, diving from the board, and floating on the inflatable rafts. My father, wanting to know what was going on in the pool lest there be something inappropriate amongst the

19

teen set, decided that my party was the perfect time to clean the tiles that surrounded the pool at water level. That, of course, required his getting into the pool. I was both embarrassed and furious with him, but my father was a favorite with my friends, and ultimately, as usual, he became the life of the party.

I was tremendously excited about going away to the University of Florida in Gainesville in 1965, but my father had serious separation anxiety. My mother, though, championed my leaving, perhaps because she so clearly remembered not being able to go to college herself. My father wanted me to stay home and go to Miami-Dade Community College (*You don't want to go there. You want to go here*), especially since Playboy Magazine had just listed the University of Florida as the top party school in the U.S. But my mother knew it was time for me to leave home, and she made sure my father agreed. Thanks, Mom.

Mine was a good and stable childhood, with a large loving family and strong Jewish roots. The painful events of 1958, however, would guide the choices I made for the rest of my life.

## *3.*
## *The Worst Year of My Life and I'm Only 11!*

---

1958

<u>U.S. President</u>: Dwight D. Eisenhower
<u>Best film</u>: Gigi; Cat on a Hot Tin Roof , Auntie Mame
<u>Best actors</u>: David Niven; Susan Hayward
<u>Best TV shows</u>: Your Hit Parade; Ozzie and Harriet; American Bandstand; The Today Show; The Milton Berle Show; Captain Kangaroo; Leave It To Beaver
<u>Best songs</u>: At the Hop, Great Balls of Fire, All the Way, Short Shorts, Get a Job, Tequila, Poor Little Fool, Purple People Eater, Yakety Yak, Volare, Tom Dooley
<u>Civics</u>: first US satellite launched; NASA formed
<u>Popular Culture</u>: Elvis inducted into Army; *Breakfast at Tiffany's* by Truman Capote, *Exodus* by Leon Uris published; first gay periodical, *One*, distributed through US mail; Barbara Gittings founds Daughters of Bilitis.
<u>Deaths</u>: Alfred Noyes, Michael Todd, W C Handy, Ralph Vaughan Williams, Tyrone Power

---

*I* was the biggest kid in the fifth grade. You can see it in the class photos. Kind of fat, kind of tall, and, well, just sturdy. There was one other girl close to my size but nobody else, not even Big Mike, was bigger than I. In that year:

I started my period almost immediately upon turning eleven, as if that magic age were the ON button for my life. Actually, I think it was, but maybe not so much in a good way;

21

My beloved Grandma Frances died after her battle with colitis and cancer;

I developed ulcerative colitis myself. My mother already had it;

I fell in love with another girl.

*If this is what it's like to be eleven,*
*I'm really scared to be twelve!*

## 4.
## *I Hate That Word!*

*I* was different. So aware at such a young age. My gut felt the horror of the difference but my young head was baffled.

My uncle often talked, no, bragged, about the guy, the *faggot*, he beat up when he was in the Navy. The *queer*. The guy in the dress at the bar who flirted with my uncle, with whom my uncle wanted to have sex until he realized he was about to have sex with a man, not a woman.

And the boys on my block in North Miami Beach, the junior high school boys, and then the high school boys, sometimes called each other *queer*. I always heard them. Whichever boy was the target *du jour* seemed to hate it. Sometimes the boys had a collective target, probably an imaginary person—named Sir Richard—who, as the story goes, pranced around Bayfront Park, that lush green expanse of park with fishing boat docks on the western shore of Biscayne Bay in downtown Miami. (Today it's called Bayside.) Sometimes the boys would tell and re-tell the not-so-funny joke about police putting up a fence around Bayfront Park "to keep the fruits from picking the people." Sometimes the boys would sing the *Puff the Magic Dragon* song but they changed the words:

*Puff the magic faggot lived in Bayfront Park*
*And frolicked with the other queers as soon as it got dark.*

I had no idea what *queer* meant, but I could feel it in my eleven year old gut, the colitis beginning to take charge.

Every time, I heard.
Every time, I felt.
Every time, I knew.

23

I knew, and spent the next twenty years hiding, pretending, agonizing in a sick silent hell. It took twenty years before I could finally...
        Really...
        Know...
        Accept...


*Queer*...it meant me.

# 5.
## *The Jewish Princess*

---

### 1959

<u>U.S. President</u>: Dwight D. Eisenhower

<u>Best film</u>: Ben-Hur; Anatomy of a Murder, The Diary of Anne Frank, Room at the Top

<u>Best actors</u>: Charleton Heston, Simone Signoret

<u>Best TV shows</u>: Twilight Zone; Hawaiian Eye; The Untouchables; What's My Line; This is Your Life

<u>Best songs</u>: Smoke Gets in Your Eyes, Stagger Lee, Donna, 16 Candles, Charlie Brown, Come Softly to Me, Battle of New Orleans, Dream Lover, Sea of Love

<u>Civics</u>: Fidel Castro in power in Cuba; Alaska and Hawaii, 49$^{th}$ and 50$^{th}$ states

<u>Popular Culture</u>: development of first integrated circuit for computers; *Lady Chatterley's Lover* by D. H. Lawrence, *Hawaii* by James Michener and *Doctor Zhivago* by Boris Pasternak published.

<u>Deaths</u>: Lou Costello, Cecil B. De Mille, Frank Lloyd Wright

---

*W*hen my family moved to North Miami Beach, we joined Monticello Park, a little old wooden one-room synagogue in our neighborhood. My Bas (we said *Bas* not *Bat* back then) Mitzvah in 1960 was one of the last services held in that old building. The new synagogue, Beth Torah—meaning House of Torah—was about to open. It was constructed of stone and looked like a giant Jewish Star if you were lucky enough to fly directly over it. The front doors looked like the scrolls Moses held as he came down from Mt. Sinai. (My mother used to reproduce those scrolls every Chanukah on the sliding glass doors in our house, using glass wax and food coloring. Her artistry won the Chanukah decorating contest for

25

years until they got tired of giving it to her. They finally made my mother a judge on the decorations committee.)

My family was immersed in the life of our Jewish neighborhood, surrounded by Jewish culture. I knew very few people who were not Jews. Occasionally I'd meet someone at my school, North Miami Beach Junior High (later to become John F. Kennedy Middle School) who wasn't Jewish because some non-Jews lived south of 163rd Street—the demarcation line.

Beth Torah Synagogue was two blocks south from the junior high. Corky's Deli was a block to the west, and the new 163rd Street Shopping Center was a couple of blocks to the east. We lived about a mile—a short bike ride—to the north of all of those places. It was a great location for young active families, and especially for hyperactive kids like myself.

Like every other Jewish family in our neighborhood, regardless of income, we had a "girl," an African American woman who cleaned our house and who was like a member of the family, sort of. Our "girl" was Mary, who helped my father care for us kids when my mother was so ill. Mary hugged us often and told us she had our pictures on her dresser at home "just like my own children," who I'd never met. But otherwise, we were a very white, very Jewish community and family.

I experienced direct discrimination as a Jewish person only once when I was growing up, though I often saw blatant signs of discrimination against Jews in Miami. (There were many communities, facilities, and hotels in South Florida that were "restricted," which meant only white Protestants were allowed access, even in Miami. In fact, the celebrity Arthur Godfrey owned the big Kenilworth Hotel on Collins Avenue which was a restricted facility—no Jews, no Blacks, no Catholics.) My friends Rosie and Marsha and I were seniors at Miami Norland Senior High School. It was January, 1965, and we had just returned from the winter break. The three of us were musicians in the school concert band which met in a building not connected to the rest of the school. Apparently, while we were in band class, an announcement was made for students to stay out of the main hallway due to 11th grade testing. Since we had not heard the announcement, and since the lunch room was at the far end of the main hall, down the corridor we went, laughing and chatting away as usual. The vice principal, whose name

I've long forgotten, jumped into the hallway and pulled us into the administration office as we passed. He was furious!

"Get in here!" he motioned frantically, his voice a gruff whisper, as we passed by his door. Stunned, we obediently followed him into his office. Strangely, he then walked out, leaving us alone in that inner sanctum. We were frightened, not knowing what rule we'd violated this time, because, well, we inadvertently broke many rules almost daily. Unfortunately for us, whenever Marsha got nervous or scared, she laughed. Her quiet giggling began. When the vice principal returned, he hollered at Marsha for making "snickery" noises. Frightened, Marsha backed away from him, right into the tall wooden stand that held a large metal globe. The globe went crashing down onto the floor and rolled to a stop at the vice principal's feet. We looked up at him in horror! Marsha's giggles became a roar, a loud hysterical roar! Rosie and I were mortified but Marsha's laughter was so contagious that we couldn't contain ourselves any longer. The three of us were at it loudly, unable to stop.

The vice principal screamed something unrecognizable at us, and then made THE HUGE MISTAKE. "You Dirty Jews! Out of here for 10 days!" he bellowed as he suspended us. Dirty Jews? DIRTY JEWS??? Did he really just say that? We couldn't wait to get home to tell our parents! We knew this guy had just crossed a giant line. Our parents conferred with one another then collectively visited the principal that afternoon. The dust settled quickly and we were back in school the next day. The vice principal was gone. Forever.

I felt empowered after that experience, empowered that I had a voice, that I could do something to create change when a bad thing happened. But I also felt sad and confused as well. Why would someone say those things? Why would someone act that way? And why—because for me it was a reminder of the anti-gay words I heard every day at school—do people hate and hurt others? What's the purpose? What's the point? The incident raised more questions than answers for me but I had no one to ask. I remained alone, as always, with my thoughts, and the colitis.

I was actively, religiously Jewish as a young person. During most of my adult life, though, I've been a cultural Jew more than a religious one. For some unknown reason, I've always acknowledged God's presence in my life, even though my relationship with God was on shaky ground for many years. I used to envision God as some external non-gendered entity who sat high above my right shoulder and who really didn't take such good care of me. I felt that God often provided me with choices, knowing I'd select the wrong one, then laugh at me. I was God's entertainment, much like I was as a young child for my family. It was a disturbing vision of God for me. But later, much later, after I had been working a 12-step program for codependency, I gave myself permission to revisit my view of God. Today my God is an internal entity, not an external one. Today my loving God is within me—my intuition, my gut, the voice I consult and heed. I've learned that when I listen to my gut—my God—and trust my intuition—my God—my choice is never wrong. Except, of course, with lottery numbers.

# 6.
## *RSL*

---

### 1960

U.S. President: Dwight D. Eisenhower
Best film: The Apartment; The Alamo, Elmer Gantry, The Sundowners, Sons and Lovers
Best actors: Burt Lancaster, Elizabeth Taylor
Best TV shows: My Three Sons; The Andy Griffith Show; The Flintstones
Best songs: Beyond the Sea, This Magic Moment, Crazy, Wonderful World, The Theme from A Summer Place, Only the Lonely, Cathy's Clown
Civics: Kennedy defeats Nixon; U-2 spy plane shot down over Russia; Adolph Eichmann captured; NASA launched first weather satellite; Greensboro sit-in; Civil Rights Act of 1960
Popular Culture: first working laser built; *To Kill a Mockingbird* by Harper Lee and *Run, Rabbit, Run* by John Updike published.
Deaths: Boris Pasternak, Emily Post, Clark Gable

---

*My* Bas Mitzvah was in April, 1960, *Shabbat HaGadol*, the Great Sabbath, the Friday just before Passover. I was 13 years old. I practiced and prepared for this day with Cantor Kirschenbaum for over a year. Back then, very few girls had Bas Mitzvahs, and females weren't allowed to touch the Torah. We were (and still are in Orthodox Judaism) considered *trafe*, unclean, like ham and shell fish. I studied mightily because I wanted to be a Rabbi. Perhaps, I thought, if I studied hard enough and did all that was required, I would somehow be able to sneak past the laws that said women couldn't be Rabbis. The *trafe* thing again. Thank goodness the rules eventually changed. Today there are many

29

women Rabbis, but not then, not for me.

Back then, 50 years ago, there were a number of traditions associated with boys' Bar Mitzvahs but none yet for girls because Bas Mitzvahs were such new events. For example, the quality of performance for boys was always low. Their voices snapped, crackled, and popped, courtesy of the onset of puberty. Another example: despite the fact that most 13-year old boys were short, the Bar Mitzvah boy was expected to stand as tall as he possibly could in his rented tuxedo with a taller girl on either side of him for the obligatory photos. He had to flex both arms while the girls admired and caressed his non-existent muscles while an unlit cigar hung stupidly from his mouth. Classic! Every boy who ever had a Bar Mitzvah in Miami has that photo.

And there was THE RING, the gold ring with the boy's initials carved into the top of it. Girls received gold necklaces with their first names in script. Boys got The Ring. I wanted The Ring. I knew I was getting the necklace but I wanted The Ring. (*You don't want that. You want this.*) As I began my Bas Mitzvah preparations when I turned 12, I went to the local jewelry store in the 163$^{rd}$ Street Shopping Center and ordered my own ring. Each week I took some of my allowance money to the jeweler to pay a little more on my then-$35 ring. It was a beauty, gold with my initials, *RSL*, carved into the Florentine top. A year later, the week before my Bas Mitzvah, I made the last payment. I was a girl with a Bar Mitzvah ring!

Years later, after I came out as a lesbian, I changed my name. My original name—Ronna Sue Lebman (RSL)—was okay, except no one but a few family members ever called me Ronna. Most folks call me Ronni which I prefer. Ronna Sue sounded so Southern to me, so *Gone with the Wind*-ish. Though I lived in the South, I just didn't identify with the likes of a BobbyJo or JennyMae or BillyBob. RonnaSue. As if that weren't enough, I also have a Hebrew name—Rivkah. Every Jewish kid has a Hebrew name as well as an English name as a remembrance of a deceased family member, preferably someone who lived to be very old. Rivkah. Ronna Sue. Ronni.

When I married, my new last name began with an S. I dropped my middle name of Sue and adopted my maiden or original name, Lebman, as my middle name. My initials became RLS. When I divorced I changed my name again. I didn't want my children to have to deal with the consequences of my public actions or media work by having my same last name, but I didn't want to go back to my original name because it kept getting stuck in my Jewish nose. The b and the m side-by-side in Lebman are really difficult for me to pronounce at times, and I had pretty bad allergies back then.

It was 1979. I came out at the height of the Women's Movement. Many of my friends were adopting their mothers' original names as their own last name. I didn't care for that. Instead, I selected the first syllable of my father's first name—San from Sanford—and the first syllable from my mother's first name—Lo from Lois—to make Sanlo. I kept my original name as my middle name. Actually, I just kept the L. My legal name became Ronni L. Sanlo. The ring—*RSL*—still works, and it's been on my finger for over 50 years. The Florentine design that was scored on top of the initials wore off a long time ago. Yes, I still have my name necklace—*Ronna*—with its Florentine scoring intact because it's been tucked away in my drawer, but my *RSL* ring—The Ring—remains on my finger today, my love gift to my 13-year old self.

1962

<u>U.S. President</u>: John F. Kennedy

<u>Best film</u>: Lawrence of Arabia; To Kill a Mockingbird, The Music Man, Mutiny on the Bounty, The Longest Day

<u>Best actors</u>: Gregory Peck, Anne Bancroft

<u>Best TV shows</u>: The Virginian; The Jetsons; The Beverly Hillbillies; Tonight Show; McHale's Navy; To Tell the Truth

<u>Best songs</u>: Big Girls Don't Cry, Sherry, Telstar, Soldier Boy, Johnny Angel, Breaking Up is Hard to Do, Monster Mash, Can't Help Falling in Love, Sealed with a Kiss, Dream Baby

<u>Civics</u>: John Glen first American to orbit Earth; Cuba Missile crisis; James Meredith registers at the University of Mississippi

<u>Popular Culture</u>: first Telstar transmission; Johnny Carson becomes Tonight Show host; *Another Country* by James Baldwin and *One Flew Over the Cuckoo's Nest* by Ken Kesey published; Illinois first state to decriminalize homosexual acts; Bayard Rustin organizes 1963 civil rights march on Washington.

<u>Deaths</u>: Marilyn Monroe, Eleanor Roosevelt, Ernie Kovacs, William Faulkner

---

*T*he Schwartzbergs (of *course* that's not their real name) lived next door to us in North Miami Beach. Mother, father, two daughters and a son. My sister Sherry was friends with the youngest daughter but the two other Schwartzberg kids, both older than I, rarely ever spoke to us. Sherry's and my bedroom overlooked the Schwartzberg's carport. (Miami Beach houses didn't have garages, only open-air carports.) The Schwartzberg's carport wall had two windows, jalousies, just like ours. One was in the living room, the other in the kitchen. No air conditioners

32

protruded out of the windows yet. Back then, even in summer-steamy Miami Beach, hardly anyone had air conditioning.

Our house and the Schwartzberg's were model homes for the tract in our quiet North Miami Beach neighborhood where kids rode bikes to school, ate fries and drank cherry cokes at Corky's Deli, and chowed down on those tiny burgers at White Castle. Both families moved in around the same time, in the mid-1950s.

When we first moved to North Miami Beach, my family had pool privileges at a little motel on Biscayne Boulevard called the Casa Loma, one of those small drive-in over-night places that dotted highways all over the country. Pool privileges meant we paid a fee for the summer season—Memorial Day to Labor Day—to use the motel's pool to our hearts' delight. Later, and for several years, we rented a summer cabana at the Golden Nugget Motel on Collins Avenue in Sunny Isles along with other families from Beth Torah Synagogue. The Golden Nugget was a typical mid-century Miami Beach motel, turquoise and orange, adjacent to the ocean, with a coffee shop, pool staff, and activities for children. Each family was assigned its own lockable private stall with a shower and changing space. These cabanas were situated side-by-side in a long row under a shared roof, and each had a table and chairs for eating or playing cards or Mah Jong with other cabana-renters who made up the summer pool-and-beach community.

I enjoyed the pool at the Golden Nugget but I truly loved the beach. The lure of the ocean, the rocking of the waves, the feel of the sand between my toes always took me to imaginary far-away places where I felt safe and warm. During my teen years I was an accomplished surfer and went to the beach almost daily, to Haulover Beach just south of Sunny Isles. But for the years before the pool was built in our back yard, my mother took us kids to the Casa Loma later to the Golden Nugget every day of the summer, thanks to the Schwartzbergs.

The Schwartzbergs fought like crazy. They screamed and hollered at each other constantly. My mother visibly cringed when the Schwartzbergs got loud, and even our big sheepdog Rusty moved away from that side of our house. Mom hated hearing such meanness among family members. I was afraid to go into the Schwartzberg's house but my sister Sherry went over there sometimes to play. I remember I had to go

33

get her once, the only time I ever recall entering that house. Mr. Schwartzberg must have been a bookie, I figured, because there was a whole bank of black telephones on a desk in the living room. I never saw so many phones in one place that wasn't the phone company. Bookies, though illegal, were popular in Miami because of all the dog and horse tracks and, of course, Jai Li. My father used to say that it was the ponies that put me through college. He never mentioned it (the bookie code of silence?) but I sometimes wondered if Mr. Schwartzberg had anything to do with my Dad's occasional betting, though I don't recall my parents socializing or even talking much with the Schwartzbergs.

I never could tell what the Schwartzberg fights were about. Sherry and I would sit underneath the jalousie window in our bedroom and listen intently, trying to make out any of their angry words. We just couldn't imagine how and why people treated each other that way.

When the Schwartzbergs got really cranked up, Mom would pile us kids into the station wagon (what else?!) and take us away to the cabana. The fighting occurred daily, which was fine with us because that meant we were quickly hauled off to where we could swim or surf or work on our tans or walk along Collins Avenue or play endless canasta with our friends by the pool. This bliss lasted until the year we got air conditioning. At the same time the AC was installed, my parents put a large in-ground pool in our back yard. Now when the Schwartzbergs fought, my mother just turned on the air conditioner units that sat in our jalousie windows, effectively muffling the battles of the Schwartzbergs. Between our noise-muffling air conditioning and our new in-ground pool, there was no longer a need for a rented cabana.

It was fun to have a big pool in our yard, I admit, but it just wasn't the same for me. I was a serious beach bunny and a dedicated surfer. As soon as I could drive a car, I was at Haulover Beach, surfing with the boys, and ignoring the girls who refused to get wet and mess up their 1960's Gidget hairdos. I easily lost myself in my surfing and, as with my music, I excelled.

Surfing was the best escape for this young Pisces who was personable and popular in school but who preferred alone time to avoid attention or exposure. As long as people saw me as a fine musician or a talented surfer, they didn't notice my short-comings—the colitis or my

34

sexual orientation—both of which often betrayed me. I retreated and hid in my busy-ness. *The best little girl in the world* syndrome. My surfing skills, my grades, my tan, and my music were all I needed.

So air conditioning changed how my family lived. No more spying on the Schwartzbergs through the jalousies and no more fleeing to the beach as a family when the Schwartzbergs got into their daily fights. I missed that.

# 8.
## *All The Girls I've Loved Before*

---

### 1965

<u>U.S. President</u>: Lyndon B. Johnson

<u>Best film</u>: Sound of Music, Dr. Zhivago, Ship of Fools

<u>Best actors</u>: Lee Marvin, Julie Christie

<u>Best TV shows</u>: Lost in Space; Green Acres; The Big Valley; The Dean Martin Show; Wild Wild West; I Dream of Jeannie; Hogan's Heroes; Days of Our Lives; The Dating Game

<u>Best songs</u>: Ticket to Ride, Day Tripper, Back in My Arms Again, Wooly Bully, I Can't Get No Satisfaction, Downtown, Come See About Me, The In Crowd, I Got You Babe, My Girl, Hang on Sloopy, I Feel Fine

<u>Civics</u>: First US troops into Viet Nam; Rev. Martin Luther King Jr. arrested in Selma, AL; Malcolm X killed; Watts riots in Los Angeles: Edward White first American to walk in space; Voting Rights Act; Medicaid and Medicare enacted; Detroit Race Riot

<u>Popular Culture</u>: Bill Cosby in I Spy becomes first African American to headline a TV show; *The Autobiography of Malcolm X* by Alex Haley and *Unsafe at Any Speed* by Ralph Nader published; Mattachine Society leads first gay rights rally at the UN.

<u>Deaths</u>: Winston Churchill, Nat King Cole, T. S. Elliot, Adlai Stevenson

---

*Th*at old Frank Sinatra song *All the Girls I've Loved Before* still rings in my ears. I knew I was a lesbian at a young age but I had no language for it, just crushes. I tried to find reflections of myself in the Sabal Palm Elementary School library, in the North Miami Beach Junior High School library and in the *Encyclopedia Britannica* and the *World Book Encyclopedia* that my parents bought. (One of the ways Jewish parents in my neighborhood showed love for their children was to buy a set of encyclopedias. We had two! ) But I could find nothing. The *H* sections—for *homosexual* because I somehow knew THAT word—in both encyclopedias were well worn with my continued attempts to find myself, hoping that if I kept looking, even in the same place, something would magically appear.

Finally, something did, in the 1962 yearbook of the *Britannica*. There it was: *Homosexual: a man who has sex with another man. See Lesbian.* I went to the Lesbian entry. *Lesbian: a woman from the Greek Isle of Lesbos. See Homosexual.* Swell. I had no idea what any of that meant. The next mention of homosexuality was in the 1969 Reuben book *Everything You Always Wanted to Know about Sex but Were Afraid to Ask.* More about men, nothing about women. I really was queerer-than-queer, I believed. No woman felt the same way I did, and what did the Isle of Lesbos have to do with it anyway? I was terribly confused and felt so alone.

I spent lots of time reading, escaping, seeking. I was always drawn to books about Margaret Meade or Amelia Earhart or Babe Didrikson, strong women who defied society's conventions of...what? Expectations? I was never quite sure why those women spoke to me. They just were different. And the 1960 movie *Spartacus*, so homoerotic! I couldn't identify that homoeroticism back then when I was 12, but that movie called to me. I felt so connected to the relationship between Spartacus and Marcus. I bet I saw it 20 times.

I remember the girls and women in my life from my very first crush: Miss Falloon, my third grade teacher. Maybe it was because I thought she looked like Sophia Loren in that cool convertible in *Yesterday, Today, and Tomorrow*, wearing those leather driving gloves and that big hat and a long silky scarf blowing in the wind. I loved Miss Falloon, never mind that I was eight years old and a girl. That didn't matter to my young heart which broke when Miss Falloon married some really old guy who was maybe 25, but I had another woman waiting in the wings. Even worse than being my teacher though, Mrs. Greenstein was my mom's best friend, with kids MY age! Apparently I was attracted to older women, which wasn't a good idea on several accounts, so I told no one. Ever.

I turned 11 in the spring of my fifth grade, 1958, that awful year, the year it really hit me that I was different. I fell head over heels in love with Annette Funicello, the best Mousekateer EVER, and I got my period that year. So did my friend Olivia who was a year ahead of me in school. Olivia lived on my block and had her own bedroom. She often invited me to spend the night. (Her father was famous in our neighborhood because he had a brand new fire-engine-red-with-white-interior 1958 Cadillac convertible. We Jews in Miami Beach back then LOVED those big-finned babies!)

Olivia and I played a game whenever I spent the night, which was most weekends during the school year. When it was time to go to bed— and there was only one in Olivia's room—we would hug and practice kissing, ostensibly preparing each other for kissing boys. We would cover our mouths with our fingers so it wouldn't be a *real* kiss, just fingers touching in front of our mouths. *Real* kissing was reserved for boys. When the school year was over, Olivia moved on to junior high, and I never spent the night with her again.

This did, however set up a pattern that I would maintain until I graduated from high school. I identified some girl as my "girlfriend" at the beginning of each school year in late August, after a summer of surfing, boating, and vacationing around Florida in the family station wagon. The girl—my girlfriend—never knew how I felt. She just thought we were best friends, and we were! But she was never aware that we were "going together." That was reserved for the secret places of my head and heart. So she also didn't know when we broke up in the spring, which we always did, just prior to the summer vacation from school. Every year, the same story. New girlfriend in the fall; she was clueless. Broke up in the spring; she was still clueless. And while I would secretly be elated in the fall and heartbroken in the spring, I liked the process. Though it became increasingly frustrating as I got older and went on to high school, it was certainly safe. No one knew I was a lesbian. I told no one and never acted on it outside of my pathetic little Walter Mitty brain. Sadly, this routine set in motion my being in and out of many relationships with women later in my life.

But back to the fifth grade: despite my kissy practice with Olivia, and though my heart was reserved for Mousekateer Annette Funicello, I really liked Dana. I made Dana my best friend in the 5th grade so we could spend lots of time together and I could be close to her. That worked. When summer came, we broke up and I rarely ever saw her again.

In the sixth grade, which back then was the last year of elementary school, I had no interest in Dana. I met Kathleen who, of course, became my new best friend. We "went steady" all year long, except, of course, she didn't know, and we, of course, "broke up" when summer came, but she didn't know that, either. And there was another actor that year as well. I was smitten with the character Zelda Gilroy, played by Sheila James on the television program called *The Many Loves of Dobie Gillis.* Zelda was so strong, so smart. Forty-five years later, Sheila James Kuehl and I are friends in real life.

I attended North Miami Beach Junior High School for grades seven, eight, and nine. In the seventh grade, my "girlfriend" was Penny. Penny was a bit dicey in my head because she wasn't Jewish. Oy! We were in band together and sat next to one another in the clarinet section. (I started out on clarinet but switched to the Sousaphone after I broke my clarinet. My mother always called me a "bull in a china shop." The clarinet was way too fragile for me. It's darned hard to bust a Sousaphone!)

Maybe it was because Penny wasn't Jewish that I felt a bit more flirtatious with her than the others. Sometimes I walked her home from school. She lived south of 163rd Street where few Jews lived. Whenever I walked Penny home I felt like I was crossing into the badlands, both geographically and behaviorally. Sometimes I put my arm around her waist when we walked. It seemed to be okay with her. That was as bold as I got. With anyone. Ever.

Eighth grade was Brenda. Ninth grade, Sandra, the most beautiful girl in the school. In fact, years later she was a homecoming queen at the University of Florida. Alas, my method of operation didn't change, even with popular and attractive Sandra. School was out and I was gone.

Miami Norland Senior High School: Linda in the tenth grade, Wendy the eleventh, and Dede in the twelfth. Same thing. Best friends all year long, "going steady" in my head, "breaking up" in June. The Dede thing was reminiscent of Penny in the seventh grade but it felt more dangerous now. Like Penny, Dede wasn't Jewish. It was one thing in the seventh grade when I was 13, but at 18 and a senior, I certainly should know better. I was so confused. Which was worse? Being attracted to a girl or to a *goy* (someone not Jewish)?? Neither was good.

By the time I graduated from high school in 1965, I still had never uttered the words—*queer, lesbian, homosexual*—aloud nor told anyone about my fantasy life. In fact, the only time I even thought the words in my head was when I looked into a mirror and referred to myself in the third person as *that damned queer*. I dated boys as I was expected to do and was even called boy-crazy once by my father. I was thrilled about that because it meant that I was a success at hiding my secret, my truth. That and the colitis were killing me.

I went to the University of Florida in Gainesville in the fall of 1965 as a music major. I was the first woman ever to be in the UF jazz band. I sat in the alto sax solo chair. (I switched from the Sousaphone to the alto saxophone in high school because my band director, Gene Greco, wouldn't allow a girl to play Sousaphone. Sousaphones were made of metal back then and way too heavy for me to carry in the annual Orange Bowl Parade or in weekly football game half-time shows. The sax was perfect and I loved it.) My career goal changed from Rabbi to high school band director.

College was very different for me. My "dating" pattern wasn't the same anymore. In 1964, author Rita Mae Brown had been kicked out of one of the women's residence halls at Florida for being a lesbian, the whispered stories went. I sure didn't want that to happen to me so I laid low. In fact, I intentionally acted to prevent people from ever guessing about me. I didn't become "best friends" with any woman, and, instead, dated another music major, a guy named Jake. I met Jake my first day at Florida. He was at my residence hall, waiting for the new (female) music majors to arrive. He was charming and adorable and welcoming, and he knew we were to be in the jazz and marching bands together. I learned that he played in a nightclub band on the weekends, in a jazz band in the African American community, and in the local pit band when Broadway plays came to Gainesville. He paved the way for me to play in those groups as well. We became great friends and each other's default dates. If a weekend came around and neither of us had a date, we'd go out with each other.

I was dedicated to my music program. I loved playing alto sax whether in the Florida Gator Marching Band, the concert band, and the jazz band. I also had a sax group for which I transcribed string quartets of the old masters, just to see if we could sound like violins. Sometimes we did.

Just to make absolutely sure no one figured me out at college, I deliberately harassed the three gay men I knew in the music school. I didn't really know for sure if they were gay but everyone talked about them, so I assumed they were. (They were.) I was so cruel. I said terrible things to them so that people wouldn't guess that I was just like them. I hated that part of myself. I hated seeing myself—my *queer* self—in those young men. My heart still hurts when I think about what I did and I offer deep apologies to those guys and to the universe. Sadly, I see many students on college campuses today, 45-plus years later, doing exactly the same thing, lashing out at the part of themselves that they detest.

In my junior year at Florida I re-met a woman I had known only peripherally since the third grade. Mitra. She was a pianist and a composer who had transferred to UF from Miami-Dade Community College. Her music moved me to tears every time I heard her play. I would sit outside her practice room, on the floor of the old wooden music building which was originally the first women's gym on campus, listening to her creations. Mitra's music had a hauntingly sad Israeli flavor to it. As an alto saxophone major, I asked her to be my accompanist, but I really wanted to ask her to be my life partner. For the first time—maybe the only time in my life—I was truly in love. She didn't know and I never told her.

Mitra became my accompanist, my roommate, my best friend. We were inseparable for the remainder of our college careers. When we graduated in December of 1969, she moved to Los Angeles with me, to where my family had relocated from Miami two years earlier. Mitra and I lived together for almost two more years, sharing a one-bedroom apartment on Ventura Boulevard in the San Fernando Valley. Though there was nothing at all sexual about our relationship, I thought of us as a couple. Neither of us dated anyone. She and I were family, and I was happy. Mitra didn't know I was in love with her, but our lives were easy and fun.

41

August, 1971. My grandfather's haunting question: *You're almost 25. What are you, funny or something?* My life with Mitra came to an abrupt end, and the colitis once again took hold of my gut.


My grandfather, Schoney, the one who gave me the creeps and who harassed my brother years earlier, questioned why I wasn't married. *What are you, funny or something?* he repeatedly demanded to know. Did he really know? How could he possibly know? But he had to know or he wouldn't have said it like *THAT*! I wracked my brain to recall if I slipped up somewhere along the way, left a hint of some sort. I could think of none. I immediately called my old college default date and friend Jake who was now a school band director in Florida. We hadn't seen or spoken to one another since graduation nearly two years earlier. When I asked if he still wanted to get married—he'd asked me in college to avoid the draft—he responded, "Sure, why not?" Nearly as romantic as my proposal.

We were married three months after my grandfather's comment. I was pregnant several months later.

# 9.
## The Marriage Closet

---

### 1971

<u>U.S. President</u>: Richard M. Nixon

<u>Best film</u>: The French Connection; A Clockwork Orange, Fiddler on the Roof, The Last Picture Show

<u>Best actors</u>: Gene Hackman, Jane Fonda

<u>Best TV shows</u>: All in the Family; McMillan and Wife; The Electric Company; The Sonny and Cher Comedy Hour

<u>Best songs</u>: Joy to the World, It's Too Late, How Can You Mend a Broken Heart, She's a Lady, Just My Imagination, One Bad Apple, Take Me Home Country Roads, Don't Pull Your Love, Knock Three Times

<u>Civics</u>: US Supreme Court unanimously rules in favor of busing to achieve racial desegregation in schools; 26th Amendment to the U.S. Constitution lowers voting age to 18.

<u>Popular Culture</u>: U.S. ping pong team goes to China; All in the Family debuts on TV; Kennedy Center for the Performing Arts in Washington DC opens; University of Michigan Gay Services opens; Gay Activists Alliance adopt lower case Greek lambda as symbol for justice.

<u>Deaths</u>: Jim Morrison, J.C. Penney; Igor Stravinsky

---

The panic was almost more than I could stand. It was my wedding day and I wanted to die. The oldest child, the first grandchild on both sides of the family, the first wedding in my generation of cousins. My parents' house in the Porter Ranch neighborhood of Los Angeles was like an ant farm of hustle and bustle, with everybody, including Mitra (the person I *really* wanted to be marrying), doing last minute chores, preparing for the day. My mother made sure everyone had their clothes just right as she and my step-grandmother Mae put the finishing touches on the dresses. My sisters handled the arrangements at the Odyssey Restaurant

43

in Granada Hills where the wedding would take place. The men wisely kept out of the way.

All of the people attending the wedding were "bride's side" folks. Jake, the man I was marrying, flew in from Florida for our wedding. No one, not even his parents, came with him. But he had comrades in the form of my brother Len and my sister Sherry's fiancé Barry. It was November, 1971.

I remember when I told my mother that I was going to marry Jake. It took me a couple of weeks to muster up the courage to tell her. I knew it wasn't going to be easy for either of us but I was focused on my mission: to hide my true identity—fast!

"Mom, I have wonderful news to share with you," I lied. "Jake and I are going to be married!" She'd met Jake a couple of times when she visited me at the University of Florida.

Silence for a moment. "Jake?" she asked. "That skinny *goy* from Florida? I haven't heard you mention him since you graduated. Married? To a *goy*?"

She was correct on all counts. "Yes. Jake. We've been talking quite a bit since I left Florida (not true), and we miss each other (not true). I'm almost 25. It's time I married." *Oh brother*, I thought. *Did she really believe me?*

Mom was shocked, to say the least. She wasn't happy that I was marrying someone who was taking me all the way back to Florida, and she sure wasn't happy that I was marrying someone who wasn't Jewish. This wasn't the fairy-tale wedding she had in mind for her first-born, though ironically I don't remember ever talking with her, or anyone really, about my getting married or what kind of wedding I might want. But for the first time in my life, my mother stopped talking to me. Luckily, the silence lasted for only a short time, right after she consulted with Rabbi Lipschitz in Miami.

This was awful. I wanted to be marrying Mitra. Jake was the wrong person and I knew it. I was deeply conflicted about my actions and in tremendous emotional pain. I remember weighing my options very carefully when I awoke the morning of my wedding: marriage, or suicide. Either one could have happened that day.

*Oh my God, my God...what am I doing?* I cried, holding myself in my bed, rocking from the power of my sobs. *How can I do this? How can I NOT do this?* My family was downstairs, buzzing and busying with last minute issues for the family's first wedding. *I can't! I can't!* I couldn't breathe, couldn't think, could only cry as the pain of my decision filled my body, filled my soul. My thoughts raced through my head. *How can I do this?* Disappoint everyone? Disappoint Jake who came 3000 miles, to be left at the alter? Embarrass him and my family? Disappoint my Mom who finally got it together enough to want to celebrate? *How can I let them all down?????*

I was in a full-blown panic attack! Like a madwoman, I considered my options. *Mitra, stop all this for me! Tell me you love me. I'll do anything to be with you! Tell me! But you can't. You're not like me. No one is. I'm the only sick one here. I may as well die. I will NOT tell anyone I'm gay. That's it! Die!*

I fell to my knees, out of control and sobbing so hard that my body ached. *I can die. Right here. I can die. I don't want to be here any more. It's too much...too much...*

I had no idea how to go about ending my life. I calmed myself down, working frantically to get a small tenuous grip on my head and my heart. I decided that whether I got married or committed suicide, my life was over. The Big Lie won. I started to breathe again, feeling a bit more calm now. I took my time. I needed time, to pull myself together, to face this day that I dreaded with every fiber of my being, my self-loathing sitting heavily on my heart.

I often felt alone and isolated as a child and a teenager, felt so different from family and friends with the secrets I carried. I trusted no one, not even myself. My heart played tricks on me because I kept falling in love with girls. My body played tricks on me because of the colitis. My mother was too ill with her own colitis and other health issues to be available to me. My father worked full time, and cared for my three younger siblings and me as best he could during my mother's illness. There just wasn't time nor opportunity for extras like dealing with a weird kid. But really, I was just too embarrassed and ashamed to tell my parents how bad I felt and how difficult each day was for me, especially at school. The fecal incontinence caused by the colitis kept me hyper-vigilant about my body, so I kept to myself and hoped and prayed that no one would find out about the truths of my life. Ironically, I was popular in school. The outside appearances completely belied the feelings I had about myself. And now, once again, I felt so isolated and alone on the inside while a giant family event was about to take place in my honor. My wedding.

So this day, in November 1971, was my wedding day, and it was the first time—but not the last—that I seriously thought about suicide. I mused about it occasionally as a teen, but today, my wedding day, I believed if I had the means, I would have followed through. I got married instead. My youngest sister Bebe and I cried together that day. She was crying because I was moving away from her, back to Florida. I was crying because I didn't want to leave my family or Mitra.

This day was surreal. Was I committing emotional suicide, or was this my first survivor moment? Did I die a kind of death that day by marrying Jake the band director, Jake my old friend from college? The only good news for me was that never again would someone ask me if I were *funny or something*. The closet door was nailed shut.

## 10.

# *Ronni and Jake Sitting in a Tree...*

---

1978

<u>U.S. President</u>: Jimmy Carter

<u>Best film</u>: The Deer Hunter; Midnight Express, Coming Home, Heaven Can Wait, An Unmarried Woman

<u>Best actors</u>: Jon Voight, Jane Fonda

<u>Best TV shows</u>: Dallas; 20/20; Taxi; Mork & Mindy; WKRP Cincinnati; Diff'rent Strokes

<u>Best songs</u>: Stayin' Alive, Kiss You All Over, Three Times a Lady, Hot Child in the City, Boogie Oogie Oogie, Grease, Just the Way Your Are, You Needed Me

<u>Civics</u>: balloon angioplasty developed; U.S. Supreme Count in Bakke case bars quota systems in college admissions; Briggs Initiative defeated in CA; Harvey Milk assassinated

<u>Popular Culture</u>: Jim Jones mass suicide in Jonestown, Guyana; Walkman stereo; *And Still I Rise* by Maya Angelou, *The World According to Garp* by John Irving, *The Dream of a Common Language* by Adrienne Rich, and *War and Remembrance* by Herman Wouk published; Rainbow flag designed

<u>Deaths</u>: Hubert Humphrey, Norman Rockwell, John D. MacArthur, John D. Rockefeller III, Carl Betz, Peggy Wood, Will Geer, Totie Fields

---

*J*ake was a good sport about the wedding even though absolutely no one from his family attended. At the last minute his mother announced that she was afraid to fly, so there wasn't enough time for his parents to take a train from Orlando, Florida to Los Angeles for the wedding of their only child. But Jake was as gracious as he could be under the circumstances. Socializing without a tenor sax in his hands was not his strong suit but he managed to get through it all. Immediately after the wedding Jake and I returned to Florida, to a deeply redneck part of the

47

state where he was a high school band director. We had no honeymoon. No time and no money. Jake needed to get back to prepare his band to march in the Ocala Christmas Parade the following weekend. Our wedding night took place in his, now our, apartment in bumfuck Florida, just before the colitis attacked my body with full fury.

The small rural town in which we lived, population 2,000, was about 90 minutes north of Tampa, and not unlike the place where Jake grew up. The next town north from ours was smaller and even more redneck—if that were possible. At the north and south ends of that town on State Road 301—the only way in and out—were signs that read, "Nigger, don't let the sun go down on you here." Being Jewish (and now frightened), I suspected I was about as welcome there as the African American people, many of whom were now my friends. It was late 1971.

The colitis overtook my body with a vengeance immediately after the wedding and I was hospitalized in Orlando for several weeks, from just before Christmas to just after New Year's, 1972. I was living a lie, 3,000 miles from my family and from Mitra, and profoundly miserable, though Jake and his parents were wonderfully attentive and kind. I was very ill and felt terribly alone in the middle of friggin' nowhere. What saved me, I believe, was getting pregnant.

Jake didn't want children, at least not right away. I was too ill to work and desperately needed a distraction. Pregnancy, to my surprise, provided that for me. In fact, it was as if my body said, "Okay, we have an important job to do here so let's not screw this up." The colitis subsided although I was left for a while with the remnants of the accompanying arthritis that attacked my joints. I was downright skinny from the colitis but my knees were the size of grapefruits. My elbows were so swollen that I could barely brush my hair or my teeth, and sitting down on a toilet was extraordinarily painful. Luckily, but slowly, it subsided.

I remember when my mother was so ill with colitis and the arthritis that kept her so debilitated. I tried to suppress that memory but now my body was as wounded as hers had been. I remember my father making cocktails of cod liver oil and orange juice for my mother, something he'd read somewhere or heard. He was convinced it would work. It—or something magical—did work because Mom got better over time.

Nonetheless, I remember its grip on her, and on us as children, and I feared for my own child-to-come. Finally, though, as promised by my doctor, it all subsided and I felt well for the first time in nearly a year.

I loved being pregnant. It gave me a focus. I felt valuable and important. I spent all of my waking hours looking forward to having a child, something I truly never thought about in my entire life. Getting married and having babies just never occurred to me. It's not that I thought they were bad ideas. I just never consciously envisioned myself in that way, as someone's wife and someone's mother.

Jake's disinterest in children was fine with me. He worked with his high school band and flew small airplanes. Both kept him busy enough. He was a good man, treated me well and with great concern, and was not at all demanding about much of anything. We both disliked the town in which we lived and were thrilled when he was hired as the band director at a brand new school near his hometown just north of Orlando. In the summer of 1972 we were able to move away from Redneck Hell, USA, but really, we went from the frying pan to the fire.

Moving to Jake's hometown meant living near Jake's parents. Coming from a large and loving family, I thought this would be a good thing. Jake was an only child. His mother Cynda was born and raised in the same town as Jake, as were her mother and brothers. She was a slender, put-together, stylish  kind of woman with beautiful expensive clothes that she wore well. She was welcoming and caring when I first joined the family, and had genuine deep concern for me when I was so ill.

Jake's father, Big Jake, was a sweet, quiet little guy who had migrated to Central Florida from South Carolina—Suth C'lina—when he was quite young. He was a Southern "cracker" and proud of it. He also had a history of being a fall-down drunk. He would take little Jake to bars with him when Jake was just a toddler, so Jake knew every swizzlin' alcoholic in the county. When Big Jake found 'ligion, he "got saved" and quit drinking. I remember one Sunday afternoon, sitting in a restaurant with the family when some sloshed old drunkard sauntered over to our table, leaned against my father-in-law and slurred, "Hey Big Jake, I liked ya' better, boy, when ya's a sonofabitch." Cynda nearly choked.

When Big Jake got sober he became a land appraiser and made a ton

49

of money evaluating major properties in central Florida. Cynda worked for Big Jake. I quickly discovered that Cynda was downright mean, not satisfied unless she controlled every person in her world. She soon detested me because, I suspected, she was unable to exert much control over me. She stopped at nothing, justifying everything in the name of God. Whether he agreed or not, Big Jake allowed Cynda her reign. Once when a flock of pigeons roosted on the roof of her house, Cynda announced, "Ah prayed really hawd for Gawd to remove those pigins, and lo-and-behold, He did! It was truly a merracle!" It wasn't much of a merracle *or* miracle for the pigeons. They were lying dead in her back yard after having been shot at close range. Either she hired someone to do the deed or she did it herself. Regardless, I seriously doubt it was God's intervention.

Jake's folks were pleased that their son, a practicing atheist at the time and therefore a disappointment to them, married a Jewish woman. They said it "put diamonds in our God crown," or something ridiculous like that. But that honeymoon didn't last very long. I was a disappointment to them on a variety of levels, not the least being my growing need to distance myself from them, especially from Cynda.

I first became suspicious of Jake's parents' politics when they quit the Southern Baptist Church because it had become too liberal, they said. "It started lettin' in the wrong people," declared Cynda. So Big Jake and Cynda bought some land, built a big one-room structure, and formed their own church, the local Bible Church. Jake's mother, now a church owner, informed pastors about what they must preach. If they didn't preach the sermon of her choosing, they were fired. It was many a preacher who moved through those revolving doors of bigotry.

Jake's parents often invaded our house on Sundays after their church service and brought some of their bigoted cronies with them— unannounced, of course, and with conversion on their minds. Jake and I hated when they did that, so one Sunday we answered the door in our bathrobes, looking as if we'd been romping in the hay.

"Well, hey there! Happy to see y'all although we weren't expecting comp'ny, as y'all can see. Come on in! Have some sweet tea and a moon pie?" I was downright cheerful, sporting my best, albeit exaggerated, Southern accent. Horrified, they fled in a fury and never again returned on a Sunday morning without calling first.

During another visit, my daughter, Berit, who was about three years old at the time, was watching Sesame Street. Roosevelt, the African American Muppet, was doing a shtick with Bert and Ernie. Jake's mother pointed to the television and tersely announced, "There, Berit! There's a nigga. You have tuh be careful 'round them."

"Whaaaat???" I was in disbelief! This was over the top, even for Cynda. "Don't tell her stuff like that!"

"Well, ya know it's true, Ronni. If a nigga has one ounce a whaht blood in 'em, they got some hope. He maht even be able to get outta the yard and inta the house. But if a whaht person has an ounce a nigga blood in 'em, he'll always be bad."

"You've GOT to be kidding! Out! Leave my house now! I do NOT want my daughter hearing such bigoted garbage in her own home."

"Jake?" Cynda looked at my husband, her son.

"She's in charge of the house, Mom, just like you're in charge of your house. I'll talk with you later about this." That was the closest I ever heard Jake stand up to his mother. Cynda left but not without swearing to get her vengeance. So much for Christian love.

When Berit was born my step-grandmother Mae graciously came up from Miami for a few days to give me a hand. My grandfather, Schoney, was with her. He had a small tape recorder and recorded his first great-grandchild every time she cried, saying it was the sweetest sound he'd ever heard. And then he'd listen to it! For hours! Every time I'd lie down for a much needed nap, he'd turn on the tape. I'd jump up from my nap because I heard my baby cry. Berit, of course, was fast asleep. So annoying, that tape! But the one funny thing my grandfather did, I have to admit, was to tell Jake's prim-and-proper mother Cynda, who was slim and stylish in a prissy buttons-fastened-up-to-her-neck sort of way, that she could park her stockings by his bedside any time. He was a known womanizer which wasn't funny, but the look on Cynda's face sure was! She was furious but said nothing, just turned on her heels and huffed away. Priceless!

Jake expected and asked little of me. As long as dinner was ready and the beer was cold, he was fine during the week. On weekends we often went camping or spent time with friends from college, many of whom were also band directors in the Central Florida area. Jake was never the doting-father kind of guy and rarely participated with the children. They were solely my responsibility.

I was a great mom. I did not work outside the home for most of my marriage because it would have cost way too much to hire a sitter on Jake's teacher's salary. I did, though, make a few extra dollars occasionally by being the substitute teacher for all of our band director friends. Eventually I got a part-time job at Burdines Department Store, working evenings and weekends, to help supplement Jake's income. But mostly, I was at home with the children.

Berit, to whom I referred as *Treble Clef* throughout my pregnancy, showed early signs of brilliance so I enrolled her in a Suzuki violin class at the age of 16 months, on a 1/10th size violin. She was reading by the age of two so I talked the local pre-school into admitting her even though she was much younger than the other children. They tested her then invited her to enroll. Through that pre-school she took little-kid classes in computers at what was then Florida Technological University in Orlando. She was four. She remained identified as gifted until she graduated from high school. She was offered a full scholarship to the University of Florida but her father's parents shipped her off to a missionary school in bum-fuck Wisconsin. She was kicked out for some sort of bad behavior after the first semester, returned to Central Florida, got a job at Disney World, and married the first guy she dated. But I digress.

Berit was born in 1973, Erik in 1976. As gifted as Berit was intellectually, Erik was the more emotional child, so demonstrably loving and gentle but with occasional flashes of anger. Both children were breast fed, potty trained at the appropriate times, and had darling personalities. Both were good and kind and sweet, and I was a damned fine mom whose children were the center of my universe.

The first time I contemplated leaving Jake—irrespective of my sexual orientation—was during a weekend trip to Disney World in 1977. Berit was four, Erik was almost a year old. Jake didn't care much for the whole Disney World thing. Everything disturbed his senses: the lines, the commercialism, the fact that hundreds of acres of beautiful old Florida scrub had succumbed to a giant mouse, and I understood. We went to Disney World anyway, for the kids and with friends who also had two young children. We'd spent a good portion of the day standing in lines which parlayed Jake's irritation to full blown rage. By the time we went to dinner, he was boiling.

Erik began to cry in the restaurant. Jake believed that children should never be heard in public places and gruffly ordered me to take Erik outside immediately. I did, without dinner. Soon after, Jake emerged from the restaurant, fuming, with Berit in tow.

"It's too much! I can't stand it. We're going back to the hotel." His teeth were clenched. I'd never seen him so angry.

"We need to eat, Jake," I said, fully ignored by him. We rode in silence back to the hotel. When Jake got out of the car, I scooted over into the drivers seat.

"We just passed a Burger King. What do you want?" I tried to keep calm for the children. Erik was asleep in his car seat in back but Berit was sitting straight up, next to me, at attention, eyes wide open, trying hard not to cry.

Jake raged. "If you bring anything back for me I'll smash it in your face!" he screamed. Berit started to cry, and, frankly, so did I. Erik was frightened into wakefulness. In that moment, I knew I was leaving this man. I just didn't know when. I wanted to gun the engine right then and there, drive north on I-75, then west on I-10 to Los Angeles, to my family. I should have, but I didn't. I just drove away, until the children and I were feeling safe and calm again. When we returned to the hotel a while later, Jake was fast asleep, empty beer cans lined up on the dresser. Thank God, he was a mellow drunk. However, over the next several months Jake's rage escalated.

I often worked Saturday evenings at Burdines when Jake could be home with the children. I came home from work on one particular Saturday evening in December of 1977 and found everything as usual. Jake drinking beer and watching television, the children asleep in their respective rooms.

Early the next morning, Berit, who was almost five, came into our room and climbed into bed with me. "Mommy," she said softly. "Derek made me do things yesterday." Derek was the 15 year old boy who lived two doors down from us. I felt a sudden hit of nausea begin to churn in my gut.

"What things, sweetheart?" I tried to be calm, not knowing what to expect, and yet knowing exactly what I'd hear. She explained in detail what had happened. I felt my anger rise, my patience plummet. I couldn't breathe! I had to find my breath....fast! For her...

"Did you tell Daddy, honey?" I asked, trying hard, so hard to be calm, to not frighten my little daughter.

"Yes, I told him yesterday."

*Yes???? YES????* I couldn't believe what I was hearing, but my daughter, at age 4, didn't know what it meant to lie. With every ounce of gentleness I could muster, I asked her to go play in her room for a few minutes, that I needed to talk privately with Daddy.

"What in hell just happened?" I was seething. I asked Jake if what I heard was accurate. He said Berit told him this last night but he didn't believe her.

"Jake, you ass! Berit doesn't lie. She doesn't know what it means to lie. What happened?" I growled, my body tight, ready to strike.

"But this really couldn't have happened," he said, almost with disinterest.

"Fuck you, Jake. It happened. I'm calling the police."

"Don't, Ronni. You're just asking for trouble."

*Whaaat???* I lost it! "Our daughter was sexually molested, Jake! There's going to be trouble all right! I need the police here or I'm gonna go kill that kid myself, and you should have already done it. DAMN you!"

I called the police, then told Berit that they were coming to talk with us. I told her that what Derek did was bad, that such behavior is reserved for adults who love one another, that she did nothing wrong. Derek did, and he needed to be punished. The police came to our house quickly. I explained what had happened. A female officer talked with Berit in private. Next, a male officer interviewed her. Berit seemed relatively calm throughout the ordeal, unlike her mother who was flipping out between trying to be sane for Berit and wanting to murder both Jake and

54

that kid! Berit's story was consistent in both interviews and credible enough that the officers arrested Derek.

In the meantime, Jake called his parents. Surprisingly—or maybe not—they were appalled that I had the audacity to call the police. "Ronni, you're just draggin' the family name through the muuud," was Cynda's response. I told her I didn't care, that Berit's well-being was far more important than the friggin' family name, that this kid had to get off the streets. Though Derek was charged and found guilty of sexual molestation, my mother-in-law hated me even more than she already did. Jake told his mother he was "at a loss as to how to handle" me. Go handle yourself, Jake, you ass!


I worked with two young men at Burdines Department Store who were openly gay which was rather courageous for 1970s Florida. Tony was 19. His best friend Richard was 22. They identified me as an understanding, open-minded person, not having a clue that my own coming-out was just around the corner. Tony gave me a book entitled *RubyFruit Jungle* by Rita Mae Brown, which, he said, would help me understand him better. That was the first gay-related book I ever read. Tony included a note with the it that read: *You're a wonderful friend and I love you. Thank you for caring about me and for understanding.*

Tony dated older men and was very excited about the new person he was seeing. The man was at least two decades older than Tony and a pilot of a small Cessna airplane. He was coming to Burdines to get Tony to fly him to Miami for dinner. Tony couldn't wait to introduce me to his new lover. When the man arrived, Tony brought him to me. The man froze, clearly not able to decide if he should run or just die on the spot. He was my colitis doctor! I'd known him for seven years, and he, of course, knew me—inside and out. I knew he lived in my town, had a wife and children, and had recently been elected to the local airport authority board. He practically dragged Tony out of the store. While the good doctor was obviously horrified at seeing me, I was elated! I didn't care what he was doing with Tony. I just knew that for the very first time, I had someone with whom I could talk about my sexual orientation. And who better than my apparently gay doctor? I couldn't wait for my next appointment. When I saw him a week later, he was extremely nervous but he calmed down when he realized that I had no intention of blowing his cover. I just needed his help.


By April of 1978, Jake and I were living under a truce of sorts. Tony and Richard invited several straight couples from Burdines to go dancing at the Parliament House, the largest gay bar in central Florida. Jake was to meet me at Burdines after work and we'd go with everyone to the club on South Orange Blossom Trail. The Parliament House was not only the largest gay bar in Florida, it also had a drag show that was immensely popular among straight and gay folks alike.

Jake called about 20 minutes before Burdines closed that evening. "I don't feel like going, but you go ahead. Have fun, and bring me a 6-pack when you come home." I wasn't disappointed. I knew I needed to go to this place, to see these people, my people still unrevealed to me. I remember walking into the Parliament House dance hall after the drag show ended. There were hundreds of folks, it seemed, women dancing with women, men dancing with men. For the very first time in my life, I felt like I was someplace where I belonged, though I didn't know a soul. I didn't talk with anyone, just watched, just allowed myself to be present in this space that I knew was mine. My coming out had begun.

My heart was very full that evening and I knew I needed to talk with another woman, another lesbian. I just had no idea where to begin to look for support or friendship. No rush though. I'd waited this long and I needed time to think about a game plan.

I got home from the Parliament that night around 2 A.M. I didn't get Jake's beer because it was late, but really, I just forgot. I'm not a drinker myself, and I had so much on my mind that didn't include him. Jake was waiting up for me. Though he had been in a fairly cheery mood earlier in the evening when he called me at work, he was furious now.

"Where the hell have you been?" he screamed.

"Shhh...you'll wake the kids."

"The hell with the kids. It's 2 A.M. Where's my beer? What've you been doing all night with those faggots?"

"Jake, what's your problem? Are you angry that I went without you? What?"

"I'm angry alright! Hell, I'm pissed! Faggots! If my son ever comes home and tells me he's a faggot, I'll get a gun and kill him!"

*What????* I felt both shock and terror, and deeply intense anger. Jake was a musician and had lots of gay friends. Some people even thought Jake himself was gay! And maybe that was the real issue but we, of course, didn't go there. But kill his own child if he were gay? This guy was losing it, and I was frightened. What will he do when he learns about me?

"Jake," my words were deliberate and measured so that I wouldn't explode. "How can you be so emotional, so angry, about something that may never happen, when you didn't give a shit when your daughter was sexually molested? What the hell is *wrong* with you?"

I turned on my heels and walked away, not needing an answer to either of my questions. I don't remember nor cared if or what his response might have been. My fear disengaged my brain.

I barely recall having another conversation with him for months, until I nearly filed for divorce, just after our anniversary that November of 1978.

## 11.

# *Coming Out*

---

### 1979

U.S. President: Jimmy Carter

Best film: Kramer vs. Kramer; All That Jazz; Norma Rae; Apocalypse Now

Best actors: Dustin Hoffman, Sally Field

Best TV shows: The Dukes of Hazzard; Angie; Hart to Hart; Nightline; Knots Landing; Antiques Roadshow; This Old House

Best songs: Le Freak, My Sharona, Da Ya Think I'm Sexy?, YMCA, Ring My Bell, Bad Girls, Reunited, I will Survive, Good Times, Hot Stuff, Don't Stop Til You Get Enough

Civics: Margaret Thatcher becomes British Prime Minister; Iranian militants seize U.S. embassy in Teheran: Kent State University massacre in Ohio; Nuclear power plant accident at Three Mile Island, PA; CAT scan developed.

Popular Culture: *The Dead Zone* by Stephen King, *The Executioner's Song* by Norman Mailer, and *Sophie's Choice* by William Styron published.

Deaths: Arthur Feidler, John Wayne, Nelson Rockefeller, Charles Mingus

---

*J*ake and the children and I went to Los Angeles to see my family during the winter school break of December, 1978. I tried to file for divorce a month earlier but didn't have the courage to go through with it. Jake found the papers and demanded an explanation.

"Why are you doing this?" he screamed through clenched teeth. It was Sunday of Thanksgiving weekend, our seventh anniversary. (Funny, neither Jake nor I could ever remember the exact date of our anniversary from year to year. I finally mounted our wedding invitation on the wall of our bedroom just so it looked like we cared.)

"Are you leaving me?" His anger escalated quickly.

"We fight so much, Jake. It's so hard on the kids, on me. We've had serious issues arise and we've not dealt with them. I just can't do this any more." These were real reasons. I just couldn't tell Jake the truth. I was afraid of his recurring rage so I let him believe it was because I was unhappy. He singularly decided that if he found a job in Los Angeles, I would be near my family and everything would be okay.

I secretly thought if I could get the kids and myself to L.A. without Jake, we'd be in the arms of my loving family and I could somehow pursue my coming out as a lesbian in a safe environment. With this plan, we'd all go to Los Angeles though he'd be there, too. Jake managed to get a courtesy interview as a band director at a school in Westwood near UCLA, but the Los Angeles Unified School District was eliminating its art and music programs at the time, so the job search was unsuccessful. Was there a Plan B for me?

While Jake was in that interview, I spent the time by walking with the children along Westwood Boulevard, looking in the windows of the little shops that dotted the street. Suddenly, from one of the windows the word lesbian popped out at me. *Lesbian*? Did I really just see that? I stopped, backed up, and looked again. There! On a poster! *Lesbian*. There it was! The first time I ever saw it in writing beyond that old 1962 *Encyclopedia Britannica* entry! *Lesbian*...me. I turned the stroller around and pushed my two small children into the Sisterhood Bookstore on the corner of Westwood and Rochester. It was early January, 1979.

The bookstore was small but the isles were wide enough for the stroller. Books were piled high all over the tiny store, on shelves, on counters, next to magazines, posters, buttons, and coffee mugs.

"Kids books section?" I inquired at the counter, trying not to look like I needed the Lesbian section which is what I really wanted to see. I just couldn't say the word.

"Sure, back there. Holler if you need some help." The young woman pointed to the back right corner of the store, next to the books about goddesses, just past the herbal healing section. Of course.

*Lesbian.* The word kept catching my eye, all around me, everywhere. It was, after all, the reason I went into the store. I saw the

59

word in writing only once before and now it was surrounding me, like an old friend, or maybe a new lover or an exciting new adventure. There was both comfort and intrigue in that word, and yet the fear of it made me shudder. I never acted on my feelings, never kissed a woman, never embraced my sexual identity. But there was no doubt in my mind that the word described me. I took my children to the kids' section and found something Berit could read to Erik. I began to explore.

*Lesbian.* Everywhere.

"I'm sorry," I said to the young woman at the counter. "Tell me about this place. I'm visiting from Florida. Great kids' section."

"Thanks. We're a feminist bookstore, " she said. "Simone Wallace owns it. She has a daughter who is probably about the same age as yours." She looked over towards my children. "How long are you here for?"

"Just a short time. My husband is interviewing at a school nearby for a band director position."

"You know, the school district just cut many of their arts and music classes, so don't be disappointed if he doesn't get it. It's pretty sad when the good courses get slashed," she told me. "What brought you into Sisterhood?"

"I was just walking by and, uh, something in the window caught my eye," I said cautiously. " I think I really need to be in here."

"Why?" she asked very gently, coming out from around the counter. I saw she was probably about my age but seemed younger. Hipper clothes, I think. Maybe it's the "L.A." look as opposed to the central Florida no-I'm-not-a-redneck-but-have-no-fashion-sense look.

"I need to talk with someone but we live near Orlando, not a very forward-thinking place."

"How about calling Orlando NOW?" she suggested.

"Orlando what?" I didn't know what she meant. The women's movement had been marching right past me for years, without my participation, understanding, or even notice.

"NOW. The National Organization for Women. There's a chapter in Orlando. Let me see if I can find a phone number for you." She looked through some newsletters. "Yep! Here it is." She wrote it on a slip of paper and handed to me. I tucked it away in Erik's diaper bag.

Sisterhood Bookstore on Westwood Boulevard near UCLA in Los Angeles. 1979. Ironically, eighteen years in the future, I would be working at UCLA and sending students to Sisterhood to buy their books. Sadly, Sisterhood closed in 1999, not long after the giant Borders Book Store opened across the street from it. But I do believe that my finding Sisterhood that January of 1979 saved my life. Nothing happens by accident. Another survivor moment...


The day after we returned to Florida that January of 1979, I called the Orlando NOW number, often. I called, and hung up every time someone answered. For weeks! Finally, in early February, I mustered up the courage to speak.

"Orlando NOW. This is Patsy. May I help you?"

"Uh, hi, yes...uh, I think I'm a lesbian and I'm, uh, married with two small children," I stumbled over my words but it was time to come out. The colitis was raging again and I could no longer live a false life. In my fantasy, or rather, my stupidity, I figured I would eventually tell Jake I was a lesbian, take the children and move to Los Angeles to be with my family, figure out who I was, and raise my children in the company of those who loved me.

"I was married and I also have two children, sons. You called the right place." Patsy told me about Orlando NOW. "We have a meeting this Thursday at 7 PM. I'm happy to meet you there and introduce you to others like us."

I showed up. I was scared, excited, curious, and felt painfully shy. Patsy met me. "Ronni?" I nodded as she took my hand. "Come on in." She introduced me to Debbie and Cheri and Randy and others who soon became my family of choice for the next several years. They helped me move when I separated from Jake a month later, and they included the children in our daytime activities on my visitation days. On holidays and birthdays, my friends showered the children with gifts and were especially kind and generous during the times when I had no money. That summer, Debbie, though much younger than I, became my first official girlfriend.

It was March, 1979, two weeks before my 32 birthday. I had to tell Jake. It was time.

"Jake, I just can't do this anymore. We're both miserable and so are the children. It's time for me to be honest with you." I started to cry because I was so incredibly frightened. I know my voice was shaking but my heart felt strong. The Holly Near song *The Woman in Your Life is You* was playing loudly in my head. Yes, I was leaving Jake for a woman. That woman was me. Jake was silent, staring out the window of our dining room, not looking at me. We were sitting at the table.

"Jake, we have lots of problems but the biggest issue, the one we cannot overcome, is that I'm a lesbian." There. I said it. I was perspiring profusely. Ironically, though, my tears had stopped. Jake said nothing. And then he slowly turned his head towards me as if the words were finally sinking in.

"What???" His voice was quiet, in disbelief. "What?" he repeated, trying to comprehend what I had said.

"I'm a lesbian, Jake, and I can't keep living a lie. It's not fair to either of us."

"Just what am I supposed to tell my parents?"

"How about the truth, Jake."

"What do you plan to do?" He was still in shock.

"I think I'd like to go to Los Angeles and live with my folks."

"What about the kids?"

"They'll come with me. They'll be safe and happy with my family, and you can see them often."

"What???" Louder. Oh-oh…he finally heard me. "You're taking the kids???" His voice rose.

"Of course. You've not been an involved father so I didn't think there'd be a problem."

"Can't you wait a while? Can you wait a while so we can figure this out?"

"Sure, Jake, I can wait awhile. Let's figure out what we need to do and then we can decide."

"Are you leaving me because I'm not a good husband? Do women do it better?" His voice was still soft but his anger was palpable. Though quiet, his face was blazing red.

"Jake, I've not been with a woman. I just know who I am. I cannot continue to live this lie. I'm sorry...." He glared at me then stormed out the door.

I wrote to my family before I told Jake. I knew I would need the support from the people who I believed loved me unconditionally. I was afraid to call them, afraid to hear their responses, but I needed to tell them. I wrote the first letter to my youngest sister, Bebe, the psychology major, as I took the first early baby steps of this new journey.

*January 26, 1979*
*Dear Bebe,*

*Hi, kid. I hope things are well with you. I've got to tell you something. I should have told you while I was there. You may be shocked and confused by this but I've got to start somewhere in the family. Being a psych major and hopefully the most open-minded in the family, you become the first to know. This requires no comment, no suggestions, no advice—only your love and support.*

*I'm gay. Two words and everything is blown to pieces. I'll say it again. I'm gay. It's something I've known and battled for 20 years. I can no longer fight it. As I grow older I become more and more compelled to live my life in honesty and mental peace. I've known about me at least since I've been 11 years old but I knew it was "bad." Well, you can't like yourself feeling like you're bad or sick, therefore you can't be a contributing productive member of society.*

*I feel good about me, Be. For the FIRST time in my life I like me. I've stopped running. The door is open and sunshine is barreling through. I've finally accepted myself. As I emerge from my dark well-padded closet, I find I have some self-respect. Years ago Aunt Fran told me, "Bullshit everyone else but to thine own self be true." Well, I finally am, Be.*

*Ultimately, I wish to see gay people accepted in our society—without guilt or shame on the part of the gay person and their family. If society were more open, I would never have married. But the best reasons for my having been married are Berit and Erik. They are my heartbeats and my life-blood. They are the future and they are being taught love and open-mindedness.*

*You may be wondering if I have a lover. No, I don't because it would be unfair to involve yet another person in this tangle.*

*I won't tell the rest of the family until I'm free or if there is a court fight which would be blown up in the news. They probably can't handle it, but I feel strong enough for all of us. I'll never disown my family whether they disown me or not.*

*I'm sorry to lay all of this on you, Be, but please don't be sad. Be happy that I've found the strength to be myself.*

*I love you,*
*Ron*


Bebe responded within a couple of weeks:


*Dear Ron,*

*What do I say except for the fact that you're my sister and you're no different than you ever have been, and I love you! I have never had any negative feelings towards gay people in general, but I have never known any women who I knew were gay. What difference does it make as far as who you are as a person? To each her own. I am surprised by the news, but for some reason which I can't pinpoint, I'm not 100% surprised. Maybe it was just some intuition or perception. I never really wondered about it, though. I knew when you were here that you had something heavy on your mind. I feel sadness for you and for gay people in general only because of the way so many people in our society feel threatened by it. I hope you have surrounded yourself with other people with whom you are comfortable and free to be yourself. It must have been so difficult all these years. I'm sure that you will still have the love of all of us. Our family is not the kind to disown any of its members for anything. I think everybody will try to understand but we'll need your help.*

*I love you,*

*Bebe*

My sister Sherry and brother Len wrote similarly loving letters. I didn't tell my parents until after Jake and I separated. My mother wrote:

*Dear Ronni,*
    *I don't know what to say except please give us time to think about all of this. You just didn't sound like the fun-loving Ronni we know. Now I'm really confused. Your marriage to Jake was my first shock, the divorce an even greater one, but I don't know just how to accept the new situation. Or that I will be able to understand it. How do you bring children into a world like that? How can they understand? We'll write or call soon. Please give us time.*

*All our love,*
*Mom and Dad*

    As time passed, each of them, including my parents, became strong and affirming, and never tried to force me back into the closet. Years later my parents joined Ventura PFLAG—Parents and Friends of Lesbians and Gays (www.pflag.org)—and they never missed a UCLA Lavender Graduation, the commencement ceremony I created where we honor the lives and achievements of lesbian, gay, bisexual, and transgender graduating college students.
    I sometimes think about those 20 years, from ages 11 to 31, in which I was so afraid to tell my truth to my family. My fearful self-talk words were *if they know the truth, they'll lock me up and throw away the key*. With all the love that's always been the foundation of my family, I can't imagine now why I didn't trust them all those years ago. When it was time for me to come out, they were the first people I told. I instinctively knew they'd be there for me even though they needed time to marinate in their own coming out process about having a lesbian daughter and sister.

I wanted to tell Mitra, my old roommate and beloved friend. I was still in love with her despite the years that had passed. She was married now and had two children of her own, but maybe.... That summer of 1979, after coming out to my family, I went to Los Angeles to visit them, and to see Mitra. Our getting together again was as if the years apart had never happened. We immediately and easily fell back into our old patterns of chatter. I told her that Jake and I were divorcing.

"Mitra, I need to tell you something about myself. I divorced Jake because I'm a lesbian, and I've loved you for 15 years." There! It was finally out. I felt a sudden and immense sense of relief.

"Ronni, I love you, too," she said without hesitation, "but not like that." There was such kindness in her voice as she put her arms around me. "I love you as the best friend I've ever had, and I'm flattered that you feel this way about me. I'm just happy that you've discovered who you truly are. Now you need to figure out how to be in the world."

## 12.

## *August 20, 1979*

*J*ake and I separated when the children were six and three. I moved into an apartment very close to the house. Jake and I devised our own joint custody arrangements. We each had the children on different days during the week and we alternated weekends. Though it was prior to the joint custody laws in Florida, we created a plan that worked for us, and our intentions were to continue the plan indefinitely.

On the days I didn't have the kids, I used my alone time to try to figure out who I was and how I was supposed to be in the world. I saw a therapist and developed a friendship network of lesbians in the Orlando area through NOW, but I struggled with my feelings and my actions. I felt like a fool, really. My thoughts overpowered me. *What kind of woman does this to her children?* I beat myself up daily, hourly, so confused, about whether or not this was the right thing to do. As a lesbian I couldn't stay married to a man. As a mother, how could I stay away from my children? My heart ached constantly, so I learned—once again—not to feel my feelings.

My true feelings—what were they? Did I even know? I stuffed them down when I was a kid, knowing I was so different from family and friends because of my sexual orientation and because of the colitis. I stuffed down grief when beloved grandparents died, though I think the "happy, happy" culture of my family sometimes actually served me well on some level. If everything was happy, then nothing was sad, so when my grandmother Frances died I didn't know how to feel my sadness. Years later, I couldn't share my true feelings with and for Mitra when she and I lived together, and certainly not my feelings about getting married. The only depth of feeling I allowed myself was my infinite love for my children. So what did I do? I left them! But I couldn't stay! I would have died. No drama here, just truth. I was physically and emotionally ill. I would have died if I stayed, and THAT kind of leaving would have been final. I wasn't ready to do that now.

The sharing of the children worked for Jake and me, but I felt so incredibly sad when I had to take the kids back to him. I cried every night, wondering if they were crying, too. Did they miss their mom? Did they need my hugs and kisses as much as I needed theirs? Both Berit and Erik were such loving children, always touching me, always wanting my arms around them. They loved their mom, I had no doubt, and I loved them—still love them—so deeply.

Today, as I understand the struggle to avoid my feelings back then, I miss what I missed, and I know I can never regain those years.

August 20, 1979. The day our divorce was final. Jake and I worked out the details over the months as we practiced our joint custody set-up. But when we went to court to finalize our divorce—on August 20, 1979—the show belonged to Jake's mother Cynda.

August 20, 1979. The day I lost custody of my children. Jake's parents provided him with the best lawyer in our county. I had Legal Aid. The courtroom was in a stately old Southern-style building in the heart of an old Southern-style town with old Southern-style attitudes. The judge, a long-time crony of Jake's parents, peered down at me with the most condescending glare I'd ever experienced. His voice was deep and booming and deliberate and scary. It made me shudder.

"I award full custody of the two children in question to their father. Young lady, if you have any intentions whatsoever of ever seeing your children again, do not fight this. Considering your, uh, situation and your, uh, lifestyle, you have no rights under the law in this state to have children. You will have the right to visitation two days every other week if you don't fight this. The children's father will select the two days, neither of which is to be on a Sunday because the children will be in church with their grandparents."

What???? That's not how Jake and I worked it out! We shared weekly duties and we alternated full weekends with the children. That's how it was supposed to be! Not this! I seethed! We were supposed to have the children equally!

"I'm so sorry, Ronni. It wasn't supposed to happen this way." My lawyer seemed as shocked as I. "They pulled a fast one. They can do that."

"Do WHAT? What just happened here?" My panic was visible in

the courtroom. My attorney was nearly crying.

"It's the law. No kids. No joint custody."

"Young lady," the judge said again in an exasperated and still condescending tone. He looked like a missing-link mammal. "I'm sure you know the law regarding..." he looked disgusted in his Southern hesitation and then enunciated every syllable, "hom-a-sek-sha-al-a-teh."

I looked at Jake, his head hanging low on his chest. His mother sat next to him, beaming, looking every bit as wicked as I knew her to be. I knew in an instant who was behind this.

This day was the nightmare of my life. For 20 years I hid my truth because I was afraid I would lose the people I love. And now—damn it!—I told the truth about myself and my deepest fears were validated. That day, that August 20, 1979, I lost custody of my children because I told the truth, because I'm a lesbian. I died a death that day, and unknowingly, I was also reborn.

Several months later I lost my job at Burdines Department Store because of my sexual orientation. Fuck the state of Florida and its hateful law

# 13.
## Out On My Own

1980

U.S. President: Jimmy Carter
Best film: Ordinary People; Raging Bull, The Elephant Man, Coal Miner's Daughter
Best actors: Robert De Niro, Sissy Spacek
Best TV shows: Lou Dobbs Tonight; Bosom Buddies; Magnum P.I.
Best songs: Another One Bites the Dust, Upside Down, Lady, It's Still Rock and Roll To Me, Woman in Love, Funkytown, The Rose, Ride Like the Wind, Lost in Love, Do That To Me One More Time
Civics: Iraqi war begins; U.S. Supreme Court upholds limits on aid for abortion
Popular Culture: John Lennon killed; Ted Turner launches CNN.
Deaths: Erich Fromm, Alfred Hitchcock, John Lennon, Jesse Owens, Jean Piaget, Jean-Paul Satre, Mae West

*As* I was learning to live on my own, I desperately needed information about what it meant to be a lesbian. While I was a lesbian in my head for 20 years, I had no idea how to court another woman or what to do when a woman was interested in me, and I sure didn't know how to be sexual with a woman. I needed instructions. Patsy and her girlfriend Dawn gave me a book called *The Joy of Lesbian Sex*. They said I should call them if I had questions. I called constantly!

I started the dating process very slowly. Debbie, my first girlfriend, was an outdoorsy young woman and invited me to go boating with her. I wasn't sure but I thought it might be an actual date, my first woman-date. It was. She brought sandwiches, sodas, and fishing gear. Her small motor boat was in tow behind her 1975 Ford pick-up. We put the boat into the water at Sanford Harbor and motored up the St. Johns River, stopping in

70

the area of Blue Springs near Deland for a picnic. As Debbie handed a sandwich to me, she leaned over and kissed me. I held my breath, my eyes wide open. OOooooo....my first real-woman kiss! So gentle, so sweet, so soft. In the daylight of the warm Florida sun, she put her arm around my waist and kissed me again. My heart pounded. So this is what it was like! I liked it! It was everything I knew it would be. We kissed again. Nothing else, just sweet kisses. It was all I needed, and really, the thought of anything more scared me and my inexperienced self! Young Debbie was the perfect gentlewoman. We continued boating, marveling at the flora and fauna of the river, and at the beauty of the day.

I read *The Joy of Lesbian Sex* with amazement! *We're supposed to do THAT!??! How on earth...????* After about the 20th call to Patsy and Dawn, they suggested that I needed to meet with a pro. A pro what?

"You just need a good teacher, Ronni, and we know the best." They set up a sex lesson for me with Eileen, a woman 25 years my senior but with the reputation of being THE best lover, bar none. I dressed in my tightest tank top and shortest shorts and showed up at Eileen's house at the appointed time. I couldn't wait to begin, to learn, to eventually have the same reputation as Eileen! Illusions of lesbian grandeur!

As Eileen began to work on me, I quickly realized that she was about to do things that seemed awfully risqué, and risky! I don't think I'd gotten to *that* chapter in *The Joy of Lesbian Sex*! Some of her, uh, techniques just did not seem joyful to me at all! I did the only thing that made sense to me. I left! Actually, I ran out of Eileen's house, carrying more of my clothes than what I was wearing, and high-tailed it right back to my apartment. So much for my sex lessons. I was left to my own devices and novice explorations, illusions of lesbian sexual grandeur shot to hell.

Another time, several months later, after Patsy and Dawn broke up, and during a time when I had a whopping case of laryngitis, Patsy called me. Patsy was the lesbian extraordinaire of Orlando back then. Everybody wanted to date her, but she selected her escorts, dates, and lovers judiciously. Her method of operation was to ask one woman to take her to the dance club, then go home with someone else, all the while dancing with many others in between. Everyone knew that was how Patsy worked, and apparently no one cared. I figured she'd never be attracted to me since she could have anyone she wanted, so I didn't play those games with her. As a result, we had an easy friendship. During this bout of laryngitis, Patsy called me for something, but she was apparently attracted to the deep raspy sound of my voice. She asked me to take her to the club that night. Me! I had not intended to go out because I was so sick, but this was Patsy! And I was the one she asked! YES! My turn! Laryngitis be damned!

I arrived at Patsy's condo at the appointed time and knocked. She opened the door and kissed me lightly. She took my hand and led me to her living room. I'd heard about her set-up but could never have anticipated this. The living room walls were floor-to-ceiling mirrors, with candles strategically placed around the room, glowing softly. Patsy sat me down on the white leather couch, no words spoken. On the coffee table were two glasses of wine and two marijuana joints. Patsy leaned over to kiss me. I quickly surveyed the situation: *I'm sitting on a white leather couch with Patsy who already scares me. The reflecting candlelight made it all look surreal. I was sick as a dog. I don't smoke pot!* I panicked! I slugged down the wine and bolted for the door! I could hear Patsy cackle as I ran out, back to my apartment and the safety of my bed, snuggly under the covers. I saw Patsy often after that episode. She graciously never mentioned it to me or to anyone, her trademark.

Shortly after the non-evening with Patsy, someone loaned a book to me, not about sexual training but a book of lesbian poetry. I don't remember the book's name, but there was a poem in it called *How to Make Love to a Woman if You're a Woman*. The poem said something like, "Know what you like, then do that." I didn't know what I liked. I got a copy of JoAnn Loulan's *Lesbian Passion: Loving Ourselves and Each Other*. That did it! Maybe I wasn't as proficient as Eileen, but I developed enough of a fun technique that women seemed to enjoy.

If Patsy was the woman most desired among Orlando lesbians, Cheri Goyette was the lesbian ring leader. Her house was home-base for many lesbians in the Orlando area, it seemed, and Cheri often provided me and many others a place to stay when we needed it. She was incredibly opinionated and highly animated but amazingly generous. She had a gruff demeanor and was strong as a friggin' ox.

I remember the second time I saw Cheri, the first being at that NOW meeting. It was at the Parliament House club in Orlando. She always had an entourage, and walked with a swagger that made John Wayne look like a drag queen. I watched Cheri saunter into the Parliament that night, moving slowing, deliberately, with a group of women behind her. Without even looking—I swear!—Cheri tossed a giant wad of keys over her shoulder. They landed on a table that was already occupied by several women. Without hesitation, the women deferred to Cheri and vacated the table. That's how she worked. She was tough, she owned the place, and everyone knew it. Yet she had a heart that was huge and open. Years later I helped her get a job in the AIDS Surveillance office with the Florida Health Department in Orlando. Cheri Goyette died a few of years ago but her swagger lives on, in my memory and now in my writing.

I had no money because I had no job. I kept getting fired for being a lesbian. Therefore, I had no transportation. When Jake and I separated, I got our old orange MG Midget which was already on its last wheel. I traded it for a little blue Datsun pickup truck. I had an orange stripe and University of Florida insignia painted on either side. But lack of employment and funds forced me to trade my truck for a beat-up old car that didn't work very well. Then no car. Jake's father occasionally loaned his old car to me on the days I had the children, which I'm sure chapped Cynda's ass.

I needed reliable, regular transportation so I bought a motorcycle, a light blue Kawasaki 250. I hated it from the day I got it but it was all I could afford, and didn't "dykes ride bikes" anyway? I remember one day when I was trying to impress a potential girlfriend, I was at a dead stop in her driveway. The engine wasn't even on. I will never understand how I fell over sideways. I felt like Arte Johnson, the little guy who always fell over sideways on his tricycle on the *Rowan and Martin's Laugh In* television show in the late 1960s. I was so happy to get rid of that thing. I just wasn't *that* kind of dyke!

Researcher Vivienne Cass created a model of sexual identity development in 1979. She theorized that there are six stages through which each lesbian or gay person must go before they are fully synergistically integrated into their sexual orientation. Stage One happens when one realizes she or he is different but unwilling to deal with it. For twenty years I was in the Cass Stage One in which I remained silent, closeted, unwilling to acknowledge my sexual orientation to anyone. Stage Two occurred when I accidentally found relevant information at the Sisterhood Bookstore. I realized I wasn't the only one and finally told another person about myself. Stage Three was about becoming comfortable in my identity as a lesbian. Stage Four happened when I found the lesbians of Orlando and became part of a community. Stage Five is leadership, and Stage Six is full integration of my sexual orientation with all my other identities—as a woman, a Jewish person, a white person. That had not happened yet back then, but I was on my way...

# 14.

# *Finding Voice*

---

## 1982

<u>U.S. President</u>: Ronald Reagan

<u>Best film</u>: Gandhi; Tootsie, E. T. Extra-Terrestrial, The Verdict

<u>Best actors</u>: Ben Kingsley, Meryl Streep

<u>Best TV shows</u>: Late Night with David Letterman; Cagney & Lacey; The $25,000 Pyramid; Family Ties; Silver Spoons; Cheers; St. Elsewhere; Newhart

<u>Best songs</u>: Eye of the Tiger, I Love Rock N Roll, Truly, Up Where We Belong, Chariots of Fire, The Girl is Mine, Hold Me

<u>Civics</u>: Equal Rights Amendment fails ratification; John Hinckley Jr. found not guilty in shooting of President Reagan by reason of insanity: MRI machines introduced;

<u>Popular Culture</u>: Michael Jackson releases Thriller; Cats opens on Broadway; permanent artificial heart is implanted in a human; *Schindler's List* by Thomas Keneally and *The Color Purple* by Alice Walker published; Parents & Friends of Lesbians & Gays (PFLAG) founded; Wisconsin first state to enact gay civil rights legislation

<u>Deaths</u>: John Belushi, Ingrid Bergman, Grace Kelly, Satchel Paige

---

After Jake and I divorced in 1979, I rented a two-bedroom apartment near the kids' house. It was in a large family-type complex so that Berit and Erik could have their own room, a playground, and other children nearby when they were with me.

I worked at Burdines Department Store but got fired—for the first time but not the last in my work history—when the store manager learned I was a lesbian. He told me I just needed a good stiff dick—his, to be exact. Since I didn't agree with him, I lost my job. (This was years prior to the Anita Hill-Clarence Thomas case so sexual harassment was not yet in the law books.)

I was also fired from the gas station where I pumped gas, the wholesale sporting goods store where I stocked fishing lures, and the T-shirt company where I silk-screened Panama Jack shirts on the night shift. Being an open lesbian and staying employed appeared to be a diametrically oppositional proposition.


After I lost custody of my children—which was shortly after I came out—I vowed never to return to the isolation of the closet I had inhabited for the previous 20 years of my life. I lost the most precious things in my life, my kids. There was nothing more to lose. The fear was gone. The pain, however, coupled with an intensely burning anger often overpowered me. I knew the risks of being so open, so vocal, or at least I learned the risks over time. I found my voice and started speaking truth to power. From the various NOW chapters with which I was involved (I co-founded the Sanford and Daytona chapters) to the Orlando Gay and Lesbian Community Services to the Florida Task Force, I became a loud, proud gay activist, a "militant homosexual," my former mother-in-law often said. I was the first woman to direct (as a volunteer) the Orlando Gay Community Services. My first action was to add the word *Lesbian* to their name: Orlando Gay and Lesbian Community Services. I spoke on radio and at other public venues about the discrimination lesbian and gay people faced in Florida. That's how I lost my jobs. My respective bosses heard me or heard about me. Fired. Back then—and still today—it's not illegal in Florida to fire people because of their sexual orientation. I lost my jobs and had no recourse.

After being fired from Burdines, I needed to find a (much) less expensive place to live, the first of many moves over the next five years. I found a one-room shack in an African American neighborhood in Winter Park, near Orlando. I never felt unsafe there—white Jewish single woman that I was—just impoverished. When the children visited, I got food stamps so we could eat. I hated getting food stamps. I—and everyone else on food stamps, I observed—was treated like dirt by the food stamp workers who sat behind those barred windows. (Years later, as an employee of the Florida Health Department, I understood. Food stamp workers were very often treated disrespectfully by their supervisors, and many were on food stamps themselves because of their low wages.)

For Thanksgiving that year—it was 1980—I arranged my few still-unpacked boxes and draped them with a sheet. Voila! A multi-tiered table on the floor (I had no furniture other than my bed) beautifully set with my wedding silver, just for my children and me in my little Winter Park shack. My wedding silver—a full set of service for twelve by the International Silver Company—was beautiful and expensive, given to me by my mother when I got married. "Every woman needs her silver, just in case," she said. It was one of the very few items I took from my house when Jake and I divorced. Afraid it would be stolen, I kept it underneath my waterbed mattress, under hundreds of gallons of water. Safe for sure! But before I stowed it there that year, I kept it out for Thanksgiving with my children.

That silver saved me more than once. With a bachelors degree in music and little experience beyond some retail, and probably in a precarious though undiagnosed mental state, I began to sell pieces of my silver, one piece at a time and very judiciously, to keep myself afloat. I remember weighing each piece, learning from my pawn shop forays, deciding which piece would yield the most money depending on my needs that day. I could eat all day for a pawned teaspoon. A salad fork could fetch enough for a cup of coffee and a burger at McDonald's and maybe a bottle of aspirin for my nasty migraines. Back then, in the early 1980s, silver was fairly high in value and the cost of quick-serve meals was low. I would be okay as long as my silver was sold or pawned carefully.

My family, 3,000 miles away in Los Angeles, was unaware of my dire financial and mental situation as well as any number of other issues in my life. I shared nothing with them. I could have gone to Los Angeles in my desperate times but I was just too embarrassed, too ashamed, and I felt I needed to stay in Florida to be near my children even though I saw them only intermittently. The power of my survival instinct continued to guide me though I was still unaware of it.

By early 1980 I had job-hopped and moved several times, trying to keep my head above water in a time of personal instability. I had heard about the Florida Task Force, Florida's lesbian and gay civil rights organization in Tallahassee, Florida's capitol. It was a new organization, the only state-wide gay-related lobbying group in the country with a full-time paid lobbyist. Patrick Land was its first executive director/lobbyist. I became the second. I was hired by the Florida Task Force in 1981. My qualifications? I was a jobless, fearless, penniless, angry lesbian. The Task Force gave me a job, a small salary, a car, and a target on which to focus my anger. Perfect!

Florida is notorious for its anti-gay laws, its Deep South mint-julep mentality, the 1970s serial killer Ted Bundy, hanging chads, and darned near every other stupid thing that ever happens in the news. Frankly, Floridians are just plain screwed by Florida government, which makes sense if you've seen the capitol complex. Picture this: both legislative houses—the Senate and the House of Representatives—are short squatty buildings with round-domed roofs. The capitol building itself is a very tall pointy structure situated right smack in-between the two smaller domed buildings. Balls and a dick. See for yourself: http://www.leg.state.fl.us/Kids/tour/index.html

I moved to Tallahassee in 1981 and began my work as the executive director and lobbyist of the Florida Task Force. Having no money to start, and being paid very little—though the job came with a car which I needed—I moved in with Karen who was an assistant superintendent of schools for Leon County and a semi-closeted lesbian. I met Karen through the outgoing Task Force director Patrick Land who knew Karen had an extra bedroom in her house. Her donation to the Task Force was to provide that space to me without charge. I was deeply appreciative though I felt like an itinerate activist.

The work of the Task Force was both important and powerful to me. The Task Force—well, I, really—was the voice of the lesbian and gay community in Florida government. I spent a great deal of time working with staffers of senators and representatives in Florida's legislature, and often invited other lesbians and gay men to join me in the lobbying process though few ever did. It was a frightening proposition to be openly gay in Florida. I felt very alone in the spectrum of the work. Interestingly, though, lesbian and gay people around the state seemed to want my attention, so when the legislature was not in session, I went on the road like the elected folks, mostly to raise enough money to pay for my salary and the small office the Task Force occupied near the capitol. Despite the low pay, I loved the work. It was hard at times, and often lonely because few people wanted to be seen with an open lesbian, too afraid of "guilt by association." But I was driven to right wrongs—to prevent others from losing their children—and I saw myself as a lone crusader of sorts. I often felt spread too thin between the work in Tallahassee, the fundraising in every major city in Florida, and my egotistical desire to be desired.

In between all of this work, or perhaps in spite of it, I made sure that I saw my children regularly, even if only for a few hours. I was wearing myself ragged with no personal time to just rest and reflect, which served me well as I kept my feelings buried. If I didn't feel, there was little pain. If I didn't feel, I could move through the world at break-neck speed. People could—and did—come and go in my life. It was okay with me. I had neither time nor energy for relationships. It was all I could do to keep myself together enough to do my work and be with my children.

There was one critical piece of work during my time in Tallahassee, the Equal Rights Amendment notwithstanding. In 1981 the Florida Legislature passed a law—a line item in the budget, to be accurate—stating that any university which recognized or provided meeting space to groups advocating a "homosexual way of life or sexual relations between unmarried persons" would lose all state funding, including precious football money. The purpose of the law, of course, was to prohibit recognition of lesbian and gay students, faculty, and staff. The Florida Task Force joined with other organizations to fight this new law in the Florida Supreme Court. The Supremes unanimously declared the law unconstitutional and removed it. The Florida Task Force then filed suit against the two makers of the law, Tom Bush—no relation to the Bush dynasty—of Ft. Lauderdale, and Alan Trask of Winter Haven, for violating their oaths of office by deliberately creating unconstitutional legislation. We won. Trask resigned his seat, the first Florida Senator ever to do so, and Bush was not re-elected. This was a tremendous victory for the Florida Task Force and for lesbian and gay people in Florida. I was elated, and felt as if I had finally done something worthwhile to help create change in my home state.

79

In June of 1981 I was the keynote speaker at the Ft. Lauderdale gay pride celebration. As I spoke, I used the words *lesbian and gay* which was new to the ears of many people in the community. The word *lesbian* was just beginning to be included in our language and still sounded awkward to folks, including lesbians. After my speech a couple of gay men approached me.

"You're just going to divide the community if you keep using the words gay AND lesbian. We should have just one word for all of us," one of the men demanded.

"Great idea!" I said enthusiastically. "Let's all be lesbians!" The collective groan could be heard throughout South Florida! Apparently, that wasn't the word they had in mind.

Tallahassee is about a five-hour drive from Orlando. I had visitation with my children every other weekend—Friday after school to Saturday night, no Sundays—so I drove to Orlando on Friday, picked up the kids, and drove back to Tallahassee, then did it again the next night to take them home. On some weekends I just rented a cheap motel in Orlando so I wouldn't have to subject the children or myself to so many hours in the car.

I stayed with the Task Force for about two and a half years, loving the work but always struggling with my salary, or rather, the lack of it. The Board of Directors, made up mostly of white wealthy gay men, was charged with raising money to support the Task Force and my $12,000 a year salary. There were months when I didn't get paid. My self-esteem was sinking lower and lower. By the end of 1982, not only had I not been paid for several months and therefore had no money to my name, I was expected to squire the executive director of the National Gay Task Force, Virginia Appuzzo, around the state. It was embarrassing and demoralizing. I quit the Task Force in January of 1983 but was asked to stay until March. I did.

During my time with the Florida Task Force I dated many women around the state, nearly all of whom were interested in going out with Ronni-Sanlo-the-Florida-Task-Force-executive-director, not Ronni Sanlo, the person. I didn't care most of the time. One evening while in Orlando, at the Southern Nights bar, I met Susan. She was politically clueless, had no idea who I was, and knew nothing about the Task Force.

Refreshing! We began dating.

In the meantime, a woman named Helen Schwartz—who became my mentor and is now my very dear friend, but who I didn't know at the time—owned the Spindrift Motel on Simonton Street in Key West. Helen sent a letter to me in Tallahassee, thanking me for the work I was doing on behalf of the Florida lesbian and gay community, and invited myself and a guest to stay at her motel. I didn't need much prompting. Susan and I headed for the Keys. When we arrived at the Spindrift, we found gift certificates to numerous restaurants in town along with a welcome note from Helen. I tried to thank Helen in person but she was nowhere to be found. It was a couple of years later before we finally met.

I'd been to Key West many times prior to that particular visit, and had a deep fascination for the island. Whenever I was there, I felt as if my feet, my heart, and my soul were connected to the combined land and sea. I knew I would return.


Susan and I dated, then lived together, for about eight months. When I left the Task Force in March of 1983, I had nowhere to go so I moved in with her in her mobile home on five acres of land in an isolated area near the St. John's River, just west of Daytona Beach. Susan and I were both unemployed. I was receiving unemployment checks. Susan said her father was supporting her, guilt money for years of abuse as a child. I believed her. Soon, though, I learned that Susan was actually a cocaine-using high-priced call girl, seeing clients at lunch time when she went into Daytona "on business." When I said I needed to leave, that I couldn't be lovers with a druggie and a hooker, especially since AIDS was becoming more prevalent in Florida, Susan kicked me out before I had time to figure out a plan.

"You're leaving me? You must be nuts! You have no money and nowhere to go! You have to stay here. I demand you stay!" Her small size was overshadowed by her large raspy voice. She was enraged at my desire to leave, never mind that I had no place and no plan in that moment. I just knew I had to go. It seemed reasonable to me to get the hell out of that strange situation.

"I'm the best thing that's ever happened to you. My business is

81

keeping you fed!" She was screaming, pacing like a madwoman, shaking her tiny fist, then flailing her arms. Even her dog, a Doberman Pinscher named Bunny, was cowering!

"Susan, I'm sorry. I just can't do this anymore." In reality, I don't know if it was her "business," her drug use, or me just being over another crappy (and creepy) relationship. I didn't know. I didn't care. I just needed to get out.

Susan went ballistic! She gathered my few things like a tornado, tossed everything into our truck, and with a 22 caliber gun in her hand—*Crap! Where did THAT come from????*—she yelled, "Get into the truck. NOW!" I foolishly thought she was going to give me the truck since she drove an anniversary-edition Corvette, a gift from one of her "clients."

"Get IN!" She screamed at me. "Not THAT side! I'm driving. Just shut up and get in." I did. She drove me to Orlando and left me downtown near Eola Park. I was once again in a precarious emotional state, this time finding myself homeless and on the streets in Orlando. Waving the gun, her last words to me were, "Get OUT! Get your shit and get OUT." She peeled away. I was scared but at least I didn't get shot.

The good news was that horrible relationship with a crazy drug-using hooker was over. The bad news was I was homeless. But I still had some silver left, tucked away in my clothing. I also still had my beloved Selmer Mark VI alto saxophone, that beautiful instrument my father bought for me while I was in high school and on which I majored in college. While it hurt my heart to part with my saxophone, the money I got for it and the remaining pieces of silver kept me from hooking or getting involved with drugs for street survival. Because of my love for the Keys and my feeling of belonging there, I bought a bus ticket and left Orlando for the place where I had found solace several times in the past—Key West.

Like many Bohemians (better word than *homeless*, I thought), I "lived" on Bahia Honda Key. Once voted the best beach in the U.S., it's at the western end of the 7-Mile bridge. It's fairly remote, and to this day, is still a haven for Bohemian types. Henry Flagler's railroad bridge, built right through the island, was destroyed by a hurricane in 1935. The remains of that bridge, my temporary home, still provides shelter for folks like myself who needed a place to stay for a while. (Ironically, years later, my own son, as a young adult who needed to find himself, did his self-searching under that same bridge, not knowing that the mother from whom he was estranged had been there a decade earlier.)

I still had not hit bottom, though I suspected I was getting close. I was so ashamed of my poverty, my homelessness, not having my children, who, by now, I suspected, were better off where they were. I was ashamed about being a lesbian, though I knew so clearly that it wasn't something I chose. I was a loser, unlike anyone else in my family, and I couldn't—didn't dare—tell any of them what I was experiencing. When I spoke with them or wrote to them, I acted as if everything was fine, just fine. I was an expert liar, desperately trying not to feel any of this. To feel it would bring me down, would take me to a place of utter despair from which I might not survive. The big question for me, I realized, was this: *why on earth do I want or need to survive?* Life was shit, and I could see nothing of any kind of future. But for some absolutely unknown reason, I still felt that I had not hit bottom. Bottom must be really, really low, I figured.

In late 1983 during one of my forays into Key West from Bahia Honda, I ran into a couple of women who had supported my work with the Task Force. I returned to Orlando with them. They made arrangements for me to stay with a friend of theirs named Rhea who had a spare bedroom. Rhea was very active in her church so I spent much of December of 1983 there as she practiced with the choir for their Christmas program, begging God to let me know all would be well. I sat there, either on a wooden pew or out in the church garden, reflecting on the past and the future. Both scared me.


After being fired from so many piddly jobs, being on unemployment, being homeless, living on food stamps and the cash I got from selling my silver piece by piece, I was ready to do something—anything—else. I knew I could and should do better. My life certainly wasn't over and, really, I deserved more than this, I decided. I needed to figure out how to move forward.

I talked my way into a job as a receptionist with Snelling & Snelling, an employment agency in Orlando. While helping others find jobs, I found a great job for Rhea. Her areas of expertise were religion and technology, so her new job was as an audio/visual sales rep where she would sell equipment to churches, utilizing both of her skill sets. Though Snelling employees were not supposed to search for jobs for themselves, I saw a job as a social worker of sorts, with International Rehabilitation Associates, or IRA, a subsidiary of CIGNA. The position seemed interesting, certainly within my abilities, and came with a decent starting salary and a car. I applied and was hired. Things were beginning to improve. It was early 1984.

My former girlfriend, Susan the hooker, learned of my new job and called my boss, one of the biggest fears for gay and lesbian people who have extricated themselves from failed relationships with crazy people. She proceeded to list my character defects to my brand new boss and also told her that I was a lesbian. Though I wasn't closeted at all, I just hadn't mentioned it yet. My boss, a woman, told me about the phone call. "Ronni, you were hired because you are qualified for this job. I'm glad you're here. She can't hurt you." I breathed a giant sigh of relief.

I enjoyed the work at IRA which was to assist people who had been injured on the job and were receiving workers' compensation. The real purpose of the work, of course, was to eliminate CIGNA's financial exposure by finding appropriate work for clients which would get them back on someone's payroll in jobs they could physically do. Sometimes that meant getting clients into re-training programs at community colleges; sometimes it was re-engineering the seats of their vehicles so they could drive. I enjoyed the career counseling part of this work, and I especially enjoyed the creativity of helping people improve their lives. I also learned to read medical records which I found fascinating and which would serve me well later.

Rhea's company transferred her from Orlando to Jacksonville so I requested a transfer, too, which was granted. In Jacksonville my boss, the regional vice president, was an openly gay man. I felt I had finally found a safe employment environment. As long as I did my work well, I would not be fired because of my sexual orientation. With that barrier removed, I felt free to explore my capabilities.

I rose quickly in the company and was soon a regional supervisor for the Northeast Florida area. I became known as the one who made sure clients were treated fairly and satisfactorily while still effectively protecting company assets. I loved the work and hoped to continue moving up the administrative food chain with IRA.

Rhea and I became lovers though she insisted on maintaining a relationship with her long-time "straight" woman friend from her church. Rhea had a temper that frightened me, and she treated my children disrespectfully when they were with us. After one particularly disturbing episode with Rhea, I put the kids in my car and headed for the beach (remnants of my own childhood when my mother took us kids to the beach when the neighbors fought). Berit, my eight year-old daughter, sitting behind me in the car, patted my shoulder and said, "It's okay, Mom. People who don't have kids don't understand about people who do." Out of the mouths of babes...

While I felt very successful with my work, my relationship with Rhea dissipated rapidly and we separated in early 1985. I moved aboard my houseboat, the *Curious Wine*.

# 15.
## The Curious Wine

---

### 1985

<u>U.S. President</u>: Ronald Reagan

<u>Best film</u>: Out of Africa; Kiss of the Spider Woman, The Color Purple, Witness

<u>Best actors</u>: William Hurt, Geraldine Page

<u>Best TV shows</u>: Mr. Belvedere; National Geographic Explorer; Larry King Live; The Golden Girls

<u>Best songs</u>: We are the World, The Power of Love, Careless Whisper, St. Elmo's Fire, Crazy for You, One More Night

<u>Civics</u>: Gorbachev becomes Soviet leader; first report of an enormous hole in the earth's ozone layer over Antarctica

<u>Popular Culture</u>: Rock Hudson dies of AIDS; Madonna launches Virgin Tour.

<u>Deaths</u>: Rock Hudson, Marc Chagall, Kousie Brooks, Frank Oppenheimer

---

*I had been hungry all the years,*
*My noon had come to dine,*
*I trembling drew the table near,*
*And touched the curious wine.*

*Emily Dickinson*


When I was young my parents would often take us kids to two places that thrilled me: the Bayfront Park docks in downtown Miami to buy freshly caught fish from the incoming boats, and the Dinner Key Auditorium in Coral Gables for the annual Miami Boat Show. I loved

86

boats. The promise of great adventure on the high seas touched the heart of this young Pisces.

When Jake and I married we bought a small Sunfish sailboat. It was fun but awfully tiny and could be sailed safely only in the lakes near our Central Florida neighborhood. After we divorced I often went to the many marinas along the St. John's River, checking out houseboats from Sanford to Jacksonville. I wanted to live on the water, in my floating home, a full-fledged laid-back Bohemian type, the vision I held of myself.

I wasn't much of a Bohemian at all when I was finally able to buy my boat. I was an upwardly mobile corporate type. But my desire to live on the water never waned. When Rhea and I separated, I headed straight for the Lighthouse Marina in Jacksonville and bought the brand new houseboat of my dreams. I named her *Curious Wine.*

After years of cruising the cruisers at boat shows or dealerships, I knew exactly what I wanted. She was a 43-foot Aqua Cruiser—with three bedrooms, a bathroom, kitchen, living room, and front and rear covered porches. A ladder on the back wall led up to the roof which had outdoor carpeting and railing around the top. The boat itself was constructed of two 43' fiberglass pontoons. A much shorter center pontoon at the rear of the boat held the single 115 horse power Mercury engine, too small for such a big boat, but what did I know? She had an engine. She would go.

The cabin was a long rectangular box, much like a mobile home. An aluminum railing wrapped around the entire deck, surrounding the boat to prevent anyone from falling off, which was usually—though not always—effective. A much smaller 12-foot by 4-foot rectangular box across the back deck housed the gas tanks, battery bank, and generator. The *Curious Wine* was 14-feet wide, white with blue stripes and blue outdoor carpeting on the decks and roof. She was brand new and she was mine!

One weekend while the *Curious Wine* was still in the boatyard being prepped for placement into the water, my children were with me. I couldn't wait to show them our new home! I picked them up in Orlando and drove directly to the marina in Jacksonville. We climbed aboard the dry-docked boat. I wanted the kids to see the inside, especially their bedroom with the neat bunk beds. We walked around the outside deck then went into each of the rooms. I was very excited but I noticed that the children were rather subdued.

We left the marina and went to the Waffle House. As we sat down, Erik said, "If I go to the hospital, I'll die." Die? Hospital? What was he talking about?

"What do you mean, son?" I asked, trying to be calm, never knowing what to expect.

"Well, if people touch people who are sick then they get sick, too, and they go to the hospital and die. I don't want to die." Die? Where did this come from?

"Berit?" I asked. "What's he talking about?"

"Mom, you're gay. Granny says all gay people have AIDS. Do you have AIDS?"

*What????* I was shocked! "Of course I don't have AIDS! Why would you think that?"

"Granny said you do. She said if we touch you or hug you, we'll get sick and go to the hospital and die."

"Oh, Berit, that's just not true! First, I don't have AIDS. Second, you can't get it from touching someone with AIDS. I can't believe Granny told you that!" Yes, I could. The witch was going in for the kill. I could feel it. Berit was 12, the age of consent in Florida back then. She could make a decision to live with me if she wanted to, although that conversation never came up between us. I had no doubt it was grand chatter in Jake's parents' house.

"I believe her," said nine year old Erik so innocently, "and I want to go home now."

"Home, like back to Orlando, home?"

"Yes."

"Berit?"

"Me, too, Mom. We don't want to be here. We'll get sick."

I was dumb-founded! Truly, I was beyond understanding what was happening. We drove the two-and-a-half hours back to their house in Orlando. So many things raced through my brain. What were they hearing from their father and his crazy mother? What do they know and not know? I tried to talk with them as I drove but there were no words back from them. Just silence. It was all I could do to not cry as I drove.

When we got to their house, the children quickly jumped out of my car. As they walked towards the door to their house Berit stopped and turned around to look at me. She said, "Mom, don't call us anymore" and ran into her house. Erik also stopped and looked back at me. He said nothing, then ran into the house behind his sister. The door shut. The battle was over. I lost.

I drove around the block, stopped the car, and cried harder than I can ever remember in my life. The end. My body ached. I drove back to Jacksonville, up the coast on A1A, my favorite road. I stopped at the beach to breathe the healing salt air and to watch the waves. I was exhausted from the years of anger, of fighting these hateful people for my children's love. The ebb and flow of the water calmed me a bit as I tried to figure out what had just taken place. Stuffing it all down inside of myself, I knew I could at least go back to the safety of my home, my boat. I suspected in that moment that I wouldn't see my children again for a long time.


I named my boat the *Curious Wine* for the Emily Dickinson poem, a fitting name for a dream come true in the midst of the nightmare of rejection by my children. I held my breath as I watched her be lowered into the water, the big arms of the boat lift hoisting her gently from yard to river. Slowly the water parted and soon she was bobbing gently on her own. She came fully furnished in every room. All I added were the outdoor chairs and tables and flower pots, and the barbeque grill on which I cooked nearly every day. Beautiful red portulaca plants hung all around the front and back patio roof.

I moved aboard the day she went into the water. The Lighthouse Marina was situated on the Ortega River in Jacksonville, in the redneck-laden west side of town, although the marina itself was a little bit of yuppie heaven. I could barely breathe, knowing that I finally owned my own home, my beloved *Curious Wine*. Jeff, the owner of Lighthouse Marina, told me to spend a couple of days getting used to her and then we'd take the first cruise down the Ortega. That day I moved my clothes and kitchen items aboard, and stocked the fridge and pantry. I sat in each room, looking at the floors, the walls, the ceiling, feeling the essence of myself in the moment on my very own boat. That first evening, after dinner and alone by choice, I sat on the front deck, opened a bottle of wine, and toasted my good fortune in the midst of my heartache. I went to bed and slept peacefully on the water.

I awoke at sunrise as I always do. The circadian rhythm of my body is tied to daylight—up when the sun rises, down when it's dark. I poured a cup of coffee, my first on board. In my sweatpants and work shirt and with my coffee mug in hand, I went out onto the deck to greet my first boat-morning. Whooop!!! I landed hard on my butt, coffee flying! I slipped on something that looked like raisins, hundreds of them, all over the deck.

"What ARE all these little black things?" I asked the guy who lived on the boat next to me, and who jumped aboard my boat to help when I went down with a giant thud and a yell.

"River rats, " he said evenly. "Welcome to the Lighthouse Marina."

"S'cuze me?" Did I hear him correctly?

"River rats. They live all around here but we don't hardly ever see 'em." He had a drawl. "Just the gifts they leave behind for us."

"Shit!" Literally! I was dumbfounded and not at all happy. I did NOT want river rats—or their gifts—on my boat.

"What should I do?" Incredulously, I was feeling violated by those rodents.

"Cat."

"What?"

"Get a cat. That's the only thing I can think of that might work," he suggested, half smiling.

I am not a cat person. I've had dogs my whole life, except not right now. I know nothing about cats nor about being a cat owner, but I was willing to do whatever it took.

It was Saturday. No work today. I showered and dressed and took myself to the Jacksonville County Pound out on Beach Boulevard.

"Hi," I walked into the reception room. "I need a cat."

"Perfect timing," said the young woman as she got up from her desk. "We had a momma and eight kittens dropped off just yesterday. The kittens are adorable and old enough to be adopted out."

"I don't know. I never had a cat. I think I need an adult." I explained about the river rats.

"Let's walk through the shelter and see if any of the cats catch your attention."

So many cats. I stood before every cage, seriously considering each one. Orange cats, white cats, noisy cats, sleepy cats, and one obnoxious black cat who seemed perfectly aloof. Black with white paws. He watched me with one eye, ignored me with the other. I stopped at his cage. I'm sure his face said, "Big friggin' deal, lady." I moved on, then came back, moved on, came back. He hated me.

"Okay, pal, " I said right in his face. "I need a working cat. I'll provide room and board, no questions asked. All you have to do is keep the river rats off my boat." I swear I saw his eyes twinkle for a split second when I mentioned river rats.

"I'll take this big boy."

"Great!" The woman suddenly seemed a bit too cheerful. "His name is Farley."

Farley came home with me. He took to the boat like a true pirate. In fact, I was convinced he must have been a boat cat in one of his previous lives because he knew exactly what needed to be done and I never had raisins on my deck again. Farley and I kept our agreement with one another as we adjusted to life on the *Curious Wine*.


Farley hated it when the engine cranked. He'd jump off the boat and make a bee-line for some derelict vessel in the marina. I discovered that I needed to toss him into a bedroom prior to turning the ignition key. Once away from the dock, I could let Farley out. He never attempted to jump to shore. Ever. He hated the water more than he hated the sound of the engine.

The first ride was the shakedown, the inaugural cruise of the *Curious Wine*. Jeff, the Marina owner, started the engine. My friend Miley was with us. Farley was safely in a bedroom, hollering at the top of his furry little lungs. Jeff moved us slowly away from the dock then guided us down the Ortega and into the St. Johns.

The Ortega River is narrow, maybe two miles long, lined with statuesque antebellum homes on either side. One of the oldest draw bridges in the U.S. still crosses the river at about mid-way. The St. John's River opens up dramatically around the last bend in the Ortega. The Jacksonville skyline and bridges are easily visible to the left, to port, while the long Buckman Bridge and the Naval Air Station (NAS), loom large to the right, to starboard. At the point where the Ortega flows into the St. Johns, the St. Johns is very wide, several miles perhaps, and often has small waves and whitecaps when the wind blows. Today, though, the water was smooth as glass.

Jeff had me practice piloting my boat. It was a bit tricky because the drive station was inside the cabin, with visibility severely limited on either side and non-existent to the rear. The long flat 43-foot sides of the boat acted almost like sails when the wind picked up . The 115 horse-power Mercury engine was just way too small for efficient maneuvering. She was slow as molasses and awkward to maneuver. Top speed was about 7 knots, or 8 mph, if we were lucky enough to have a tail-wind. The boat sometimes moved on an angle—crabbing is what airplane pilots call it—but I didn't care. The joy of the boat for me was simply being on it. I didn't need to go anywhere to enjoy my life on the *Curious Wine*.

As we returned to the dock from the shake down cruise, Jeff had me practice parking, or rather, docking the thing. It was much easier, I decided, to simply throw a line to someone standing on the dock and have them pull me in rather than to try to actually maneuver such a big boat with such a small single engine. I quickly became an accurate line-tosser.

I read an article about how glorious night boating could be, so the next trip after the shakedown was an evening cruise to downtown Jacksonville for dinner at the Charthouse. I invited Miley and several of our friends to come along. The weather was perfect, the moon was full, and there was little other boat traffic on the water. Even the docking was easy both at the Charthouse Restaurant and back at the Lighthouse Marina. A perfect evening which served to bolster my confidence about my skills as a skipper.

Several weeks later Miley, now my girlfriend, moved aboard the *Curious Wine* with me. She was about 12 years younger than I, spunky as all get-out, and just plain fun. She had a variety of jobs during the time we were together—an apprentice in a printing company, a director of sorts for a satellite Planned Parenthood clinic, an exterminator, a time-share hawker, a pizza delivery person. Through it all, she was also first mate on my boat, which meant that when the engine blades got tied up in crab trap lines, Miley was the one who jumped into the water, knife in mouth Errol Flynn style, and cut the line to free us. Such a gallante swashbuckling little dyke!

For as outrageous as Miley was at times, her mother was truly wacky. Miley's mother had a desire to make more money than she was paid in her various places of employment, usually dentists' offices, so she helped herself to some of the dentists' insurance money on a fairly regular basis. Of course she got caught—repeatedly, and sent to Lowell, Florida's women's prison near Ocala. Each time she went "up the river" we ended up with her poodle, Fluffy.


Feeling confident of my new skippering skills, Miley and I went onto the St. Johns River for a long weekend cruise. Out of the Ortega, we turned right on the St. Johns and headed south towards the Buckman Bridge. Just after going under the Buckman I accidently ran over a Styrofoam ball. The ball, it turned out, was attached to a crab trap that sat on the river floor and captured unsuspecting crabs who entered the trap for the dead chicken bait. Yuck! The rope that tethered the crab trap to that particular Styrofoam ball was tightly wrapped around my engine's propeller. Since I was the skipper and Miley was the mate, she jumped into the river with the knife to free the propeller. We learned later that messing with someone's crab trap even in dire straits was illegal.

Once free from the crab trap rope, we continued on down the river which was absolutely glorious. Everything was perfect. Through Orange Park, past Green Cove Springs, we approached Palatka late in the day. The water was like glass as the sun set. We found a spot in the river, near where the cranes and egrets were searching the tall river grasses for food. We threw the anchor and settled in for a lovely evening and night. The sounds, the full moon, and the very gentle rocking of the water made for a setting truly created only by God.

Just as the sun was rising the next morning, we were abruptly awakened by a loud horn and a megaphone. "Hey! Ahoy! You on the houseboat!"

*What????* Holy crap! A barge was coming around the bend to the north of us! Coming right at us! I scrambled to get the engine started as Miley pulled the anchor. We had to get out of the way of that floating flatbed fast! Whew! Made it just in time! As they passed us, the captain from the tug hollered into his bullhorn.

"Hey! Are you crazy? You're anchored in the Florida Barge Canal! You could have been rammed!" The Florida Barge Canal? Who knew? "We tried to hail you on the radio. No response."

Huh? Radio? I didn't have a radio! Didn't know I needed one! I'd been taking classes for the Captain's exam but we apparently hadn't gotten to the chapters on barges and radios yet.

We were spared a horrible accident but I must have shocked the engine because it was now deader than a door-nail. There was a small fishing boat nearby so we hailed it for assistance. As it got closer we saw that it carried two young men who were seriously drunk. At 7:00 AM. They boarded my boat and tried to grab us. Miley shoved one of the guys overboard as I grabbed a kitchen knife and threatened the second guy. He jumped. Once they were back into their little boat, they left quickly. That was fine but we were still stalled. I threw anchor so that we didn't float back over into the barge canal. What a morning! Anything else?

Our engine was still dead. We could see another small boat off in the distance, a lone person checking crab traps. I waved the orange emergency flag in the boater's direction. It worked and soon a weather-beaten old woman with a dirty fishing vest and a frayed straw hat boarded the *Curious Wine*. She expertly assessed the situation. We were out of gas.

I made breakfast for the three of us while she told stories of her life as a crabber. That's when I learned about crab trap etiquette and the law. After breakfast she took Miley and a spare gas jug to the marina in Palatka which was visible from the *Curious Wine*. Not far at all. They returned quickly. Soon we hugged the old woman goodbye and headed back in the direction of Jacksonville.

We stopped at the marina in Green Cove Springs. Although it was early afternoon we decided to spend the night there and walk around the quaint little village that was Green Cove. We were going to go into town for dinner but it turned out that the dock master was a gay man who lived with his partner on a nearby boat. We stayed on the dock and visited with them, sharing dinner and a bottle of wine in the clear night sky. We left early the next morning, heading for home.

As we travelled north on the St. Johns, we again went under the Buckman Bridge. We could see a sailboat regatta up ahead, just past the Naval Air Station. I was driving the boat while Miley was upstairs on the carpeted roof, working on her tan. Soon, I noticed that the planes from the NAS were flying awfully low over the *Curious Wine*. They were doing touch-and-go's at the Naval Air Station nearby, then circling back around, flying too low over my boat, again and again. And then I noticed that we were fully engulfed by forty-some small boats from the regatta. *What was going on?* I felt like a target from both air and sea.

"Hey, Miley! " I hollered out the window, up to the roof. "What's going on out there? I feel like we're in a war zone or something, between the planes and the sailboats. Can you tell what's happening?"

Miley leaned over the top front edge of the boat's roof to respond to me, her head and upper body hanging upside down. Her ample breasts were nearly covering her face as she tried to speak. My dear Miley, it turns out, was working on her tan, stark naked, all the time waving friendly hellos to pilots and boaters alike. Mystery solved.

95

# 16.
# *Farley's Revenge*

*I* invited my boss to hold our company's monthly regional meeting aboard the *Curious Wine*. The *Curious Wine* had a large front deck with multiple chairs, tables, and a decent barbeque grill like those in one's back yard, not the tinny little grills attached to the railing of those fancy-pants yachts. The galley was a full kitchen complete with every appliance to accommodate preparations for any meal, but I had the good sense to have our meeting catered. While I prided myself on my well-appointed kitchen, I simply am not a chef. Hell, I'm not even a cook! But it was a great place for a gathering.

People arrived around noon and boarded the boat which was fully gassed and ready for what I hoped would be an easy and impressive departure, not like the one a few days earlier when I slammed the bow of the boat into the pilings of the slip in front of my dock. So embarrassing, but luckily there were no witnesses or damage.

I rounded up Farley and tossed him into my bedroom. He whined for a while then settled in for the trauma of that horrible sound: the engine, as if it were much larger than the single 115 horsepower Mercury. In reality, the engine purred quietly, unlike Farley who was making a terrible racket. But he would get quiet, as he always did, as soon as the boat was underway and moving smoothly down the narrow Ortega River.

Guests and crew—the crew consisting of my girlfriend Miley who gladly took the day off from her exterminator job, and myself—were aboard and making way down the Ortega towards the St. Johns on which we would cruise south to the Buckman. The day was absolutely perfect. There was a light chop—okay, maybe a medium chop—that was causing only one person, Richard, the vice president and head of the office, to feel a bit queasy. He stationed his deck chair at the portside rail of the boat, just in case. He looked like he was hoping his cookies remained exactly where they were, intact inside his getting-greener guts.

Apparently it's difficult to preside over a meeting when one's entire bowel structure is rumbling to greet the light of day, so Richard suspended the formalities. All of us aboard the *Curious Wine* were thrilled. Some folks went above decks to work on their tans and enjoy the scenery while others stood at the fore or aft rails and waived to boaters who cruised by. We were even greeted by a family of manatees who must have come inland from the Atlantic, navigating their way south to spend the winter in Blue Springs near Deland.

About an hour into the ride, when I went to use the head, I heard Farley scratching around in my stateroom. I'd forgotten all about him! Once under way and away from the dock, Farley was always released from captivity to walk around the boat as he wished. He hated water more that he hated the sound of the engine, so he never attempted to mutiny overboard once we were away from the dock.

As I opened the bedroom door, Farley looked up at me with what could only be described as intense disdain. He stared, really, with something that now looked like a smirk. I had no doubt he was thinking, "Just wait, Pal." I said to him, "You're a cat, you mean little beast. Just try it," not knowing what the "it" might be.

Farley slowly, deliberately, schemingly made his way to the forward deck of the boat where Richard was trying very hard to keep his nauseated self together in the presence of his regional staff. Farley walked over to Richard and planted himself squarely between Richard's legs. In the next moment—if I hadn't seen it with my own eyes I wouldn't believe it—here's what happened: Farley, staring right up into Richard's face, barfed. Richard, looking fully miserable and now surprised, lost it. He dove for the side rail and spread his intestinal wealth all over the St. Johns River. And I swear, Farley, that mean cat, was laughing as he casually walked away.

Farley's version of the events:


*I hate her today. She threw me into that room again, cranked that hateful engine, and then made me stay there for hours. My stomach hurt, my brain hurt, and frankly, I was seriously pissed off. When she finally remembered to let me out of that damned little room, I was neither thankful nor amused. I couldn't let this pass. No way. I had to take revenge. I wasn't sure what it would be until I saw that jerk sitting on the deck, clearly moments away from barfing his brains out. I decided to help him out of his misery by showing him what to do. The end. Do NOT put me in that fucking room again. I mean it.*

# 17.

## *Aground with Mom and Dad*

*My* parents often helped their children move, whether we needed assistance or not. It was one of the sweet ways they showed they loved us. My move from one marina to another was no exception for them. Actually, I invited my folks to come to Jacksonville from Los Angeles to cruise with me as I moved from the Lighthouse Marina on the west side of Jacksonville to the Jacksonville Beach Marina on the Intracoastal Waterway near the ocean. They had not yet seen my boat and I thought they'd enjoy the experience. They did, of course, and like most of my cruises, it wasn't without incident.

My parents loved my boat. More important, they loved the fact that I finally had a home of my own. "Maybe now you'll stop moving so often," they said at least a hundred times. I lived in far too many places over the years. My addresses and phone numbers were written in pencil in their address book. They wanted ink.

My parents arrived in Jacksonville the day before we were to embark on the moving process. The next morning was filled with excitement. There was no furniture to lift or clothes to pack, just lines to throw and an engine to start (after I put Farley in my bedroom, of course). We unplugged the phone and electrical lines, unscrewed the water hose, and untied the four dock lines. With a fresh pot of coffee and a day's supply of bagels, lox, and cream cheese, we were ready to go. Miley stayed on land and drove my car over to the new marina. She'd meet us there when we arrive later in the day.

My parents took seats on the front deck of the boat as we slowly made our way down the Ortega River to the St. John's and towards downtown Jacksonville. The I-95 bridge, the Main Street bridge, the Matthews bridge, all color coded, the local lore goes, so the Mayor can find his way home. The ride through downtown was perfect.

The St. Johns river gently curves to the northeast and then east to the Dames Point Bridge as it meanders through downtown Jacksonville and makes its way out to the Atlantic. The Port of Jacksonville, with its huge cargo ships and multi-color boxes and cranes, was on our left. Directly in front of us but to the right of the main channel was a small island in the river. To the right of that island was a narrow waterway. I chose to bear to the right of the island for two reasons: first to keep us out of the way of the shipping lanes and those humongous ships, and second, because my boat needed only 18 inches of water to remain afloat despite her size. I thought for sure there was at least 18 inches of water on the right side of that island. I was wrong.

The pontoons at the front of my boat hit sand. "Holy shit!," I exclaimed, embarrassed that I had just cursed in front of my parents. My engine conked out as I tried to maneuver around the sand bar. I was aground and stuck in some really shallow muck. While the back of the boat was still afloat, it was too shallow to start the engine. My father, who had never piloted a boat a day in his life, figured out what to do. There was a giant cargo ship in the St. Johns River not far from where we were aground. We were safe from it because we were in that protected waterway and it was in the shipping channel, heading away from us.

"Okay," Dad theorized out loud. "That cargo ship makes a decent wake. See?" He was right. It did.

"When the wake gets to us, Mom and I will jump up and down on the back deck while you push us backwards with your pole in the muck. As soon as you're free, gun the engine backwards." It could work. My "pole" was a 12-foot long, six-inch round dowel, the biggest Home Depot sells. I used it as a tool to measure water depth. No radio, no depth sounder, just a pole. I was an electronic ditz!

The wake hit. My parents jumped. I put the pole into the muck and pushed. Damn if it didn't work! It sure did and we were floating in deep enough water to start the engine. I backed us up and moved into the deeper water of the shipping channel but kept to the far right side. We safely continued on our way toward the Intracoastal Waterway. We turned starboard (that would be to the right) at the Intracoastal, then headed south to marker 34 and the Jacksonville Beach Marina.

As we cruised down the river, I wondered how my parents were coping with my situation, or lack thereof, with the kids. By now, of course, they were fully aware of what had happened over time and that the children were no longer visiting me. I suspect their hearts were as broken as mine though we never talked about it. Probably too emotional for any of us to deal with. Not a happy situation at all, and we had no history of dealing with issues as difficult as these. But I knew my loss was also their loss. They loved their grandchildren as deeply as I loved them. During the children's early years, Berit and Erik spent a month each summer with my parents, the only positive condition of the custody decree. Once the kids said they no longer wanted to see me, they also stopped seeing my parents. Cynda, Jake's mother, did her best to effectively cut the children off from my side of the family.

My parents were as affected as I by the loss, but I didn't know how they felt, how they coped. I know that I struggled, every single day. I called the children, sent them cards and gifts, with no response at all. One day, shortly after Christmas in 1985, I called to see if they received the gifts I sent. Erik answered the phone.

"Quit calling here, Mom, and don't send me any more presents." The meanness of Cynda was channeling through my precious baby boy. I stopped calling. There was a tremendous hole in my heart that I tried to fill with people, with relationships, but really, the hole was filled with nothingness.

Miley and the dock master were waiting for us when we arrived at the Jacksonville Beach Marina. Dad accurately threw the ropes to them and they pulled us into my new slip. To this day, Dad tells the story of how he saved my boat. For me, it was the first time my parents ever heard me curse.

# 18.
## *Cruising to Key West*

---

1986

U.S. President: Ronald Reagan

Best film: Platoon; Hannah and her Sisters, Children of a Lesser God, Room with a View

Best actors: Paul Newman, Marlee Matlin

Best TV shows: The Oprah Winfrey Show; Matlock; Designing Women

Best songs: Higher Love, On My Own, Greatest Love of All, Kyrie, Glory of Love, That's What Friends are For

Civics: Nuclear accident at Soviet Union's Chernobyl plant; Space shuttle Challenger explodes after launch at Cape Canaveral; U.S. Supreme Court upholds sodomy law, *Bowers v Hardwick*; New York passes anti-discrimination law.

Popular Culture: The Oprah Winfrey Show debuts on television; Nintendo video games introduced in U.S.

Deaths: Georgia O'Keefe, Harold Macmillan, Duchess of Windsor; Terry Dolan

---

*D*amn! I hit a boat! I hate it when I do that! I had just pulled out of the slip, didn't even make it into the channel, and ran into that giant sailboat with its big butt sticking out. The day was a tad windy so my 43' houseboat—with the long sides that sometimes act as non-maneuverable sails—was difficult to handle in that narrow space. The ladder of the swim platform on the back of the sailboat cut into one of my fiberglass pontoons. The sailboat wasn't disturbed or scratched at all and no one was aboard. But I now had a puncture in my pontoon, only three minutes into the 10-day cruise to Key West. Swell. Luckily the pontoon was chambered. If water did get into it, it had no place to go. The trip continued as planned.

I requested this move to Key West from my company. Several of

102

the people in the office where I worked in Jacksonville used cocaine. It felt too risky for me to stay there. I was never a drug user, had never even seen cocaine, and didn't want to be around people who were using it, especially when it put my livelihood in jeopardy. My company had recently hosted a retreat in Key West which rekindled my desire to live there. We had clients there but no office or staff, so I requested the transfer which was granted. (Tough work but somebody had to do it!) My houseboat would serve as the company base of operation.

I was excited about moving to Key West. I loved that island, the one place where I felt whole, felt connected to my self and my space. And I was as excited about the trip itself as I was about the prospect of being in the Keys. Mmmmmm....I could taste the key lime pie every time I thought of this adventure. I couldn't wait to get started.

My boat wasn't exactly outfitted for a trip of this length. I had no radio, no depth sounder, no anchor for the grassy bottom of the Keys. I didn't know these were important items—yet. I had passed the Coast Guard captain's license course, received a license to pilot a 50 ton vessel (how big is *THAT???*), and was now a commercial captain who was totally, thoroughly inept. Miley and I stocked the *Curious Wine* with what we thought were the essentials, a case of Captain Morgan spiced rum and a case of merlot. We had plenty of food, a full tank of drinkable water, an empty holding tank for the toilet, and several reserve tanks of gas.

We also had a couple of four-legged pirates aboard. Farley, of course, was the resident working cat. And Fluffy Miley's mother's dog. We had custody of Fluffy because Miley's mom was once again vacationing in Florida's Lowell Prison for Women due to her ongoing problem with embezzlement. Fluffy, we were assured, was trained to do his business on paper. He wasn't, which was a big logistical problem as we slowly made our way south down the Intracoastal Waterway, the ICW.

We left Jacksonville Beach Marina at 7 A.M. on a Monday and pulled into the St. Augustine Marina around 4 P.M. that afternoon. The ICW is very narrow between Jacksonville and St. Augustine, almost wild and pristine. There weren't many houses built up to the waterfront just quaint old-timers fishing off rickety docks, waving their weather-beaten hats in our direction as we passed by. It was a perfect day—well, except for the sailboat incident that morning. Our first night out was spent docked at the municipal marina in the Old Town area of St. Augustine, just under the Bridge of Lions.

We might have been able to get farther down the ICW than St. Augustine that first day but we had to stop to walk Fluffy—on dry land—twice! Fluffy, as it turns out, had absolutely no interest in pooping or peeing on paper. Walking Fluffy meant we had to find an island in the ICW or dock at a public marina, then walk Fluffy until his job was finished. Docking and going ashore was easy. Finding an island proved more challenging because we had to throw anchor, inflate the 12' dingy, and row to Fluffy's personal potty stop. Every day, all the way down the ICW to Key West. Ten days. Damn picky dog!

The ICW is a protected waterway with a 12-foot ditch in its center, dug out by the U.S. Corp of Engineers to accommodate large private yachts that traveled up and down the eastern seaboard of the U.S. The mainland is on the western side of the ICW while Florida's barrier islands—Jacksonville Beach, St. Augustine Beach, Daytona Beach, West Palm Beach, Miami Beach, and other "beaches" in-between—line the ICW on the eastern side. There are only a few areas along the ICW where open ocean is visible. We didn't go there.

Our second night out was spent in the Daytona municipal marina. Again, another lovely day on the ICW with nothing more serious than trying not to kill the dog that kept needing to pee. On day three we found ourselves in the widest part of the ICW, the Cocoa Beach and Cape Kennedy/Canaveral area. We could see the launch pads of the Cape, disappointed that there were no rockets attached at that time. A pod of dolphins swam along side the *Curious Wine*, almost as an escort through the wide, somewhat choppy Indian River which is the name of the ICW at that particular point. By mid-afternoon we entered Sebastian Inlet and down a very narrow jungly waterway that reminded us of The African Queen adventure with Bogey and Bacall. I was Bogey. Miley was Bacall.

"Hey! Ol' cap'n drivin' this bath tub. I'm crazy 'bout ya." Miley was not much of a Bacall but I appreciated her efforts.

"Here's lookin' at you, kid." I raised my glass to her, never mind that it was from an entirely different film.

We docked at Vero Beach Marina for the night. It was that evening that our small Honda generator quit. I don't know why. It just died. Its death was unfortunate because it kept the refrigerator, coffee pot, and other kitchen appliances working while we were under way or anchored out at night. (In marinas, though, we simply plugged into the dockside electricity.) Luckily, we still had plenty of Captain Morgan and wine which needed no refrigeration.

We had turned off the clocks and removed our watches before we left Jacksonville, deciding to eat, sleep, and wake whenever we felt like it, when our bodies said it was time, and not by clocks that guided our work-a-day lives. Miley continued her nudie tanning atop the boat as she had that day on the St. Johns River when we were buzzed by Navy jets and 12-year old boys in a sailboat regatta. It was an effective method of getting the draw bridges to rise—erections, if you will—without ever needing to radio, which was validation that a radio, or rather, the expense of a radio, just wasn't necessary.

Smacking into a couple of boats notwithstanding, I had one serious near-miss on the way to Key West and one actual accident while in Key West. The near-miss happened as we were cruising through West Palm Beach. The ICW is narrow there with multi-million dollar homes on either side of the waterway. Each home has a cement seawall at the base of the property. A very large and sleek deep-sea fishing yacht, maybe 60' in length, whizzed past us, illegal in that low-wake zone. Jumbo jack-ass was going way too fast, his wake bouncing off the cement walls and coming back into the waterway, tossing my pontoon houseboat around like a cow in a tornado! Things went flying. Dishes broke. Fluffy pooped—finally—on the paper (and the carpet). There was no name on that boat and no state-required license numbers so I figured it for a drug runner. Welcome to South Florida. Luckily, except for a few tossed items and some shot nerves, we were okay.

We had left Jacksonville on a Monday morning. It was now Friday afternoon as we cruised into the Miami section of the ICW—Biscayne Bay. I knew I didn't want to be out on Miami's main channels on the weekend—too many boats—so we spent the weekend at the Miami Beach Marina.

I remember Miami Beach Marina from my childhood. My

grandparents lived just blocks from it on Bay Road, just off Alton in South Beach. I'd often walk down to the Marina and marvel at all the boats back then. Big ones, little ones, sail boats, power boats. The Port of Miami is there as well, just inside the channel to the Atlantic Ocean, called Government Cut. The north side of the Cut is the southern-most tip of Miami Beach where Joe's Stone Crab restaurant still operates. That area is all condos now but back in my childhood it was the famous Miami Beach Race Track where my Dad bet on the horses that, he says, put me through college. The south side of Government Cut is the elite Fisher Island. I loved to watch the big cruise ships and the small private boats move to and from the ocean as I sat on the docks in the marina as a kid—and now here I was, on my own boat in that same fascinating place.

We pulled into the Miami Beach Marina late in the afternoon. An adorable young Caribbean guy named Billy helped us at the dock. After trying to maneuver into the designated slip, and after smacking into yet another big-ass sailboat, I finally parked the boat for the weekend. Once settled, I collected the materials I needed to do fiberglass repair and fix the two holes in my pontoon. (I could have used a book entitled *Fiberglass Work for Dummies* but this was years before the Dummies series.)

Billy, it seemed, was smitten with Miley. She was an attractive sailor with a hearty cleavage, a great smile, and a deep all-over tan on her small body. By dinner time, a dozen roses had been delivered to the *Curious Wine* for Miley from Billy. She invited Billy aboard the boat to explain the, uh, situation.

"Billy," she started slowly. "The flowers are beautiful and you're so sweet, but, uh, Ronni and I are together."

"Isn't she your mother?" Billy innocently asked. Miley's words had not registered, but Billy's did. I could have killed him!

"Oh no, my mother's in prison. Ronni's my lover."

"Oh... OH! Oh shit! I feel so stupid." Even with his beautiful mocha skin, we could see him blush.

"On, no, Billy, it's okay. Stay for dinner!"

"Stay for dinner? Is it, uh, okay with Ronni?" *Sure, why not? I thought. I can poison you.*

He stayed. He even helped me with the fiberglass repair work. We actually had a lovely evening as the sun set over the skyline of downtown Miami. Billy regaled us with stories of his adventures in the Caribbean, and we told him what it was like to be a couple of lesbians on the water.

We continued on our way on Monday morning, actually getting out of the marina without mishap. We cruised south on Biscayne Bay, past Bayfront Park where I used to watch the fishing boats, past downtown Miami, and past the fabulous Viscaya residence of American industrialist James Deering who lived there in the early 1900s. We stayed to the right of the channel where the water was rather shallow, making it easy to see the flora and fauna swimming beside us as we made our way past Homestead and into Card Sound.

Unlike Biscayne Bay, the ICW in Key Largo is very narrow. The houses on either side of the channel are quaint, seafaring-looking, almost like a colorful tropical fishing village. It was nearly dark when we got to Tavernier Key so we decided to throw anchor in the Tavernier hurricane hole for the night. Hurricane holes are generally places near land surrounded by mangroves or other trees where boaters could anchor or tie up and be safe from big storms. Anchor space surrounded by mangrove trees, as this spot was, worked well in the Keys. I threw anchor and we settled in for the evening, toasted our good fortune, then went to bed.

In the middle of the night, as we slept soundly, there was a jolt and a loud CRASH! Something banged against the side of the boat! We jumped up from bed, hearts in our throats, trying to figure out what in hell was going on! Fluffy barked like crazy. Farley flew under the couch.

The moon was full so it was easy to see what had happened. Our anchor hadn't held so we crashed into a stand of mangroves. I used the wrong anchor! It couldn't bite into the sand as it was designed to do because the sand was completely covered in long grasses. I needed a different type of grass-holding anchor. I didn't have one. Who knew?

There were at least twenty wrecks in that hurricane hole, according to the nautical charts. We were incredibly lucky that we didn't get our anchor hooked on one of those old wrecks, that we didn't float out into the open waterway, that there was no damage to anything but our nerves. After we surveyed the incident, I started the engine and drove us to a nearby condominium. It had a dock with a sign that read *Private! No trespassing! No docking unless you live here!* I docked anyway. We slept outdoors on the roof of the boat, taking watch turns, just in case someone called the police. As soon as the first ray of light was visible, we were out of there!

From Tavernier, the ICW opens up, with U.S. 1 and the Atlantic Ocean to the left as we headed toward Big Pine Key and ultimately Key West. The expanse of water to our right—Florida Bay—was as far as the eye could see and as turquoise, almost white, as you can imagine. We saw pods of dolphin along the way and even schools of flying fish.

"Miley! Look! Over there! Flying fish!" They weren't actually flying. They looked more like they were scurrying on top of the water for maybe 50 yards before diving back down into the waves which were really just ripples.

"Ronni, I think it finally happened. Sun stroke. You need a rest. I better drive for a while. You take a nap. Get out of the sun." I wasn't IN the sun! I was inside the boat where the pilot station was situated.

"No! Really! Watch! Flying fish!"

"Yeah, yeah, yeah....Wait! Hey! You're right!"

Later that day, a good distance from land, we threw anchor, took off all our clothes—what little we were wearing—and went swimming in the warm tropical salt water of the Keys.

Farley was doing pretty well on the trip. He had his litter box and his food so he was content. Luckily for Fluffy, there were many mangrove islands along the way where we could tie up and walk him on the sand. He didn't like it much but he did his business on cue. As we continued toward Key West on our second day out from Miami, Fluffy let us know he needed to go. The only place in sight was a small island next to U.S. 1—Ohio Key. It was too shallow to pull the *Curious Wine* up to the shore, and there were way too many jellyfish to try to safely walk to shore (which we usually did in the Keys), so we inflated the dinghy as we'd done all the way down the ICW from Jacksonville to Miami. Miley and I carefully got into the dinghy, Miley holding a squirming Fluffy while I tried to keep us balanced. Neither Miley nor I relished the idea of coming into contact with all those jellyfish. Fluffy, however, must have thought they were pretty interesting because he stood on the very edge of the dinghy, barking resoundingly into the water. Visibility of the hundreds of jellyfish surrounding us was easy in the crystal-clear water, which brought back memories of when I was stung by a man-o-war in Miami Beach when I was very young. No thanks! We finally got to shore. Fluffy did his thing, then back into the dinghy we went, back to the boat that was being protected by Farley the watch cat. We survived the Day of the Jellyfish!

That day was truly glorious as we cruised and swam and enjoyed the warmth of the clear water and the blue Florida sky with the white puff clouds. By late in the day we could see Big Pine Key and knew that we had only 30 miles to go to Key West. We docked at a fish camp and had dinner in their marina. There were folks, fishermen, divers, some touristy campers, but mostly old salts who just wanted to chat with the two bikini-clad women who had arrived on a 43' houseboat. We swapped stories with them, enjoying their tales of adventures on the high seas, as if Florida actually had high seas anywhere!

The next morning we set off toward Big Pine Key. The Corps of Engineers charted the ICW all the way to Key West but, for some unknown reason, they stopped digging the ditch at Big Pine. We had a choice: run the risk of cruising in extremely shallow waters to the north, behind the islands that lay in front of us, or take what I thought would be the better route, under the bridge at Big Pine and out into the Atlantic Ocean. My pontoon houseboat was definitely not built for ocean travel but the water was very calm due to the reef out to the southeast of us and as long as we stayed close to land. I chose the ocean route. The only real concern was the rocks in the water, but they were large and visible. There was no wind and the water was glassy so maneuvering between the rocks wasn't much of a problem. We made it to Stock Island Marina around noon without issue.

I had made permanent docking arrangements at the Harbor Lights Motel and Marina in Key West before we ever left Jacksonville, so I knew where we were going. Stock Island is the island adjacent to our destination. We docked there, hopped on the motor scooters we kept on the boat, and rode over to the Harbor Lights Motel in Garrison Bight, next to U.S. 1, the main road in and out of Key West.

We finalized the arrangements to permanently dock at Harbor

Lights then went back to the *Curious Wine* on Stock Island. Stock Island is surrounded in myth about its purpose and use in the early days of Key West. Supposedly, it was the island on which the residents of Key West kept their large work animals. To me, Stock Island looked like Key West-adjacent slums, with dirty marinas and rowdy bars. Today Stock Island is a rather upscale place to dock and to live.

We cranked the engine of the *Curious Wine* and headed out towards the southern-most part of Key West, past Smathers Beach and Flagler's Casa Marina Hotel to Zachary Taylor State Park where we would make the big right turn towards Truman Annex, Mallory Dock, then Key West Harbor. What I didn't know was that at the turn, the place where Florida Bay meet the Atlantic—the Southwest Channel as it's called—is almost always very rough with significant wave action. The *Curious Wine* was not built for rough water nor for waves of any height.

I could see the rough water ahead but I had no choice. I could either go forward and into Key West or turn around and go back to Jacksonville. We chose to tough it out, donned our life jackets, and moved forward. The first wave hit us broadside. The boat rocked hard to the right. I straightened her up as quickly as I could, getting us perpendicular to the crests so that the waves hit us from the rear. The waves were so large that as the boat was lifted, the engine propeller came out of the water, spinning way too fast in thin air. That's bad for the engine. I decided that the only chance we had to keep the boat in a forward-moving direction was to pretend we were surfing. I watched the waves and gunned the engine as soon as the propeller was back in the water, before the face of the next wave hit us. We gained enough speed to get up on the wave and literally ride it into the calmer waters in front of Truman Annex. Thank God I was a surfer as a kid!

As the water quickly calmed, we regained composure and moved forward, past Mallory Dock, past Key West Harbor, and past Trumbo Point and the Coast Guard station. We made the right turn at the Coast Guard Station into Fleming Channel. Garrison Bight was on our right. As we entered Garrison Bight, we could see the Harbor Lights Motel just ahead. For me, this was the great escape from the real-life pain of the loss of my children to a make-believe fantasy where life is perfect—and happy, happy, happy.

# 19.
## Life as a Conch

Residents of the Keys are known as Conchs. In 1982 the citizens of the Keys declared themselves a country, the Conch Republic. They attempted to secede from the Union in protest of a pot-related U.S. Border Patrol roadblock and checkpoint near Key Largo. The roadblock apparently inhibited tourism tremendously as well as inconvenienced the residents of the Keys. I couldn't wait to become one of them!

Living in Key West was great fun most of the time and terribly challenging some of the time. It was very expensive to live there even in the mid-1980s. Many folks worked two or three jobs. I was no exception. I had my regular job with the International Rehabilitation Associates. I also delivered pizzas in the evening on my motor scooter, did some housekeeping at the Harbor Lights Motel where I was docked, and I hosted a bed and breakfast on my boat.

With three bedrooms on the *Curious Wine*, there was room for several guests. I served fresh baked goods from the local bakery each morning along with coffee and juice, then shuttled my guests in my 15-foot motorized dinghy out to Waxing Moon, a 30-foot catamaran, where Captain Kathy took them on all-day sails and dolphin watches. I went back to the *Curious Wine*, did my work for IRA, retrieved my guests late in the afternoon, then went to my second job as a pizza delivery person on my motor scooter. It was what I needed to do to make ends meet. I was an extraordinarily busy dyke-about-town, and I loved it! I also thoroughly enjoyed meeting women from all over the world.

Lobster season is at the end of July each year, during late summer when few folks visit Key West for anything other than tasty crustaceans. I often worked as a dock hand for guests at the Harbor Lights Motel who came to Key West to catch lobsters. They trailered their fishing boats behind their trucks to the Harbor Lights then docked them at our little marina. At the end of each day they returned with their boats nearly overflowing with snapping lobsters. I helped them unload their catch and got paid in lobsters. My pal the Key Lime Pie Man brought his daily

111

leftovers to us each evening and I brought home pizza "mistakes." We ate well! Frankly, between the lobsters, the key lime pies, the pizza "mistakes," and the margaritas, I gained twenty pounds in Key West!

One day Miley and I were fishing in our dinghy just off the west side of Fleming Key. Fleming Key is across the narrow channel from the Coast Guard station at Trumbo Point. High cement walls surround the Point because the Coast Guard base sits up on a land-fill. We noticed a storm brewing to the west, not unusual for the Keys, so we started back to Garrison Bight, traveling slowly next to the wall of the Coast Guard base. At the same time, a large fishing vessel came zooming through that narrow waterway, sending its wake into the cement wall, which came back at us. The wake from the big boat itself made a direct hit on the dinghy, pushing the front of the it downward into the channel while the wake off the cement wall lifted the rear of the dinghy up in the air. The dinghy rolled over on an angle, landing upside-down in the water. Miley and our fishing gear were thrown out of the boat. I stayed with the dinghy, rolling with it as it overturned, ending up on the flipped-over bottom, the 25-horsepower engine sitting upside-down under warm salt water.

I was wearing a two-piece bathing suit, lots of exposed skin, much of which was slashed and bleeding from head to toe from the sharp barnacles that covered the bottom of the dinghy. Because the accident occurred near the Coast Guard Base—and perhaps because of our skimpy bathing suits—the Coast Guard guys got to us quickly in their rescue boat. They scooped Miley up out of the water then pulled my bloody self off of the dinghy and onto their vessel. They were able to right the dinghy with ropes and tow it back with us to the *Curious Wine*. Our fishing gear was lost.

Barnacles, I learned the hard way, have bacteria in them. The only thing that kills barnacle bacteria is ammonia. Yikes! Once back on the *Curious Wine*, Miley got the ammonia bottle. It took four Coasties to hold me down while Miley poured the ammonia all over me. I screamed! It hurt like hell! But it worked. I healed quickly and was bacteria-free. The dinghy engine, though, was toast. Nothing destroys an engine like salt water.

Because of the beating the *Curious Wine* took from those big waves when we arrived in Key West, the center pontoon on which the engine was attached began to dislodge. I had the engine removed so the pontoon could be repaired. Captain Kathy of the *Waxing Moon* knew how to do boat work, and the man on the boat next to me at Harbor Lights was a retired engineer. The three of us designed how the repair would take place. We maneuvered underneath the pontooned *Curious Wine* in my inflatable dinghy and made the repair. Good as new. The engine was reattached.

My IRA clients in Key West were as colorful as the flowers that bloomed all over the island. Perhaps the most entrepreneurial was Jose who had an accident at a local grocery store where he was a produce worker. He had injured his back somehow and now had a ten-pound lift restriction. He wanted to continue receiving workers' compensation while establishing a "business" selling stolen jewelry out of suitcases he carried to street corners. Irrespectful of the illegality of it all, the thing that really screwed him was that each suitcase weighed about 25 pounds. He was videotaped, busted, and arrested.

Miley's mom was released from prison again. She drove down to Key West to visit, attempting to regale us with stories of her prison adventures. We weren't interested. We learned from her previous incarceration that any positive attention she received about her prison life served only to encourage it. I think she actually liked being in prison. It was a safe place for her. She was a social misfit who couldn't stop embezzling, and, in fact, was back in prison shortly after her visit with us. But she took Fluffy with her, for which we were grateful. He was a cute pup but he was just too much for Farley, and for us.

In the mid 1980s, the "in" thing to do among the few lesbians who lived in Key West was to shave one's head, so I did. I buzzed my head. It was awful! I looked like my brother when he was 12! It was cute on him, not so much on me.

I was surprised that there wasn't much of a women's community in Key West. There was only one lesbian guest house, Ellie's Nest, and it left much to be desired compared to the many quaint and beautiful gay men's guesthouses. The men's places were tropically sublime and stylish. Ellie's Nest was a three-bedroom cement block box with—as the rumor goes—hidden cameras in each room. Nothing charming about it at all. There was one small lesbian bar in town, hidden away on Appleruth Street. There were very few reasons for lesbians to come to Key West; it was entirely a gay male mecca. A small lesbian artists and writers colony was up on Sugarloaf Key but those women rarely came the 25 miles or so into Key West.

Miley and I were from Jacksonville which had a vibrant lesbian community, focused primarily around a monthly pot-luck gathering that exists to this day. With the help of my friend Helen Schwartz who owned the Spindrift Motel in Key West and her then-partner Charlotte, we hosted a women's pot luck on my boat in September of 1986. Helen and Charlotte knew all the lesbians in the lower Keys and invited them. Even the Sugarloaf women joined us. We had a large crowd with tropical foods and a lively discussion of how we might get women to come to Key West. We decided that there needed to be an annual women's event, held during the off-season so that it would be affordable. The result was the birth of the now-popular WomenFest Week in Key West that takes place every September.

International Rehabilitation Associates promoted me to regional supervisor so I was transferred to the Miami office. It was time to leave my beloved Key West. One thing was for sure: we were NOT going to go out of Key West the same way we came in! I refused to attempt those waves again. I got maps and charts and talked with some of the folks who knew the waters behind the Keys, the waters that were charted by the Corps of Engineers but never dug. I discovered that at high tide, the water was deeper than the 18" it took to keep the *Curious Wine* afloat so we figured out the best time to leave Key West based on the tides. As high tide approached, we left Garrison Bight.

The backwaters were more beautiful and pristine than I could possibly imagine. There were stands of red mangroves everywhere, destined to become new islands in some future century. The water was so clear that anything swimming or growing was easily visible, and the sky was that breathtaking Florida blue, reflected in the turquoise liquid all around us. We did run aground a few times, but it was easy to push back with the pole and go a different way.

There was a big unexpected problem, though, in going this route. Mosquitoes! The size of horses! In all my years of living in South Florida, I'd never seen such large hungry mosquitoes before! We kept ourselves covered from head to toe in Skin-So-Soft, the oily Avon product known for being an excellent bug repellent. Even Farley the cat was doused in the stuff. I swear, the mosquitoes could have flown away with him!

We spent the first night anchored out in the water, thankfully not needing to dinghy the dog to an island to pee. We no longer had the dog nor the dinghy so it worked out well. The second night was spent at a dock in Old Jewfish Creek in Key Largo. We woke up the next morning, had breakfast in the restaurant adjacent to the dock, then attempted to resume our trip to Miami. There was a slight problem, however, with the Old Jewfish Creek drawbridge on U.S. 1. I still didn't have a radio nor a horn (I knew I should have bought a horn in Key West!), so we had no way to notify the bridge-tender to open the drawbridge for us. The *Curious Wine* was too tall to make it safely under the bridge due to the high tide. I re-docked the boat and Miley hopped off. She walked up the hill to the bridge-tender shack and knocked on the window. The old man who was supposed to be tending the bridge was asleep. He apologized profusely, embarrassed about getting caught sleeping on the job. As he started the mechanism that lifted the bridge, Miley ran back to the *Curious Wine* and hopped aboard. We were on our way once more, through Card Sound and up into Biscayne Bay.

As we approached the Coral Gables area on Biscayne Bay, a huge quick-moving storm blew in. Although the water was shallow, the boat was tossed around like a toy. I was so frightened that for the second time—the first time being our entrance into Key West—we donned our life vests. I threw anchor to keep us from being blown out into the open expanse of Biscayne Bay because it's several miles wide at that point. The anchor helped but it was a rough ride until the storm blew over. The day cleared quickly as it does in the tropics. Miley and Farley and I collected our scattered nerves and continued north until we reached the Venetian Causeway, one of the many bridges that connects Miami with Miami Beach. We headed east, just north of the Venetian Causeway, making our way over to the Flamingo Marina at the 79th Street Causeway, docking at our new home in Miami.

## 20.

# *Home Sweet Miami Home*

---

### 1987

<u>U.S. President</u>: Ronald Reagan

<u>Best film</u>: The Last Emperor; Moonstruck, Fatal Attraction, Broadcast News

<u>Best actors</u>: Michael Douglas, Cher

<u>Best TV shows</u>: Unsolved Mysteries; The Bold and the Beautiful; Married…With Children; 21 Jump Street; Matlock; A Different World; Thirty something

<u>Best songs</u>: I Wanna Dance with Somebody, Nothing's Gonna Stop Us Now, La Bamba, Open Your Heart, You Keep Me Hangin' On

<u>Civics</u>: U.S. Supreme Court rules Rotary Clubs must admit women: Oliver North, Casper Weinberger, and George Schultz tell Congress of deception and intrigue regarding Iran Contra Affair

<u>Popular Culture</u>: Prozac released for use in U.S.; AZT wins FDA approval for use in treatment of AIDS; Beloved by Toni Morrison published; ACT UP is formed to help fight AIDS; second national LGBT March on Washington on October 11<sup>th</sup> and first display of the NAMES Quilt.

<u>Deaths</u>: William Casey, Andy Warhol, Rudolph Hess, John Huston, James Baldwin, Bayard Rustin

---

*I* went to work at my IRA office in Miami by bus and MetroRail. Miley rode the motor scooter to her new job as the assistant dock master at Miami Beach Marina. We'd meet on the *Curious Wine* at the end of each day and walk across the street to Benihanas where we ate free hors d'oeuvres, had a cocktail, then returned home to enjoy the Miami evenings on the docks. My friend Barbara, from the Jacksonville Beach Marina, was docked next to us at Flamingo in her 45-foot Gibson houseboat. She was a colorful itinerate type, in her late 40s, who slept with nearly every sailor who docked at the marina as long as the sailor had a big, uh, boat.

In December of 1986 unrelenting winter storms raged in South Florida. For almost a week, from Christmas to New Year's, seven-foot swells pummeled Biscayne Bay. Boats in every marina came loose from their moorings and slammed into each other causing tremendous damage. We who lived on our boats at Flamingo spent almost the entire time running up and down the docks, tying, untying, and retying other people's boats. We were happy to help save the boats in the marina, but we were really just protecting our own. It was a 24-hour watch. We—Barbara, Miley, two guys who lived in the marina, and I—took turns around the clock, keeping watchful eyes on the neighboring vessels. We were all exhausted from both fear and lack of sleep. By New Year's Eve, I had had it. It was time to smoke the long-forgotten joint that had been in my freezer.

I happened to have this joint thanks to a former girlfriend's ex-brother-in-law. Rhea, with whom I lived in Jacksonville just before I bought my boat, had a sister who was in the midst of a nasty divorce. The soon-to-be-ex husband and I became friends because he owned a battery company and I needed more than just the one battery that came with my boat. Bob installed the bank of batteries that, he assured me, would take care of all my electrical needs. We bonded by sharing our versions of the wicked sisters. When he finished the battery work and we finished complaining about our exes, he took out two joints. We smoked one on my boat after which he left and I promptly fell asleep. For twelve hours! I put the second joint in a baggie in my freezer and forgot about it. Now, several years later, voila!

I'm not a druggie nor much of a drinker. I don't know what most drugs look like and I'm under the table after only two drinks of anything. A lightweight and a cheap date, which is why I completely forgot about the pot in the freezer until Barbara said, "Wish we had a joint!" We did. We had one joint, to be shared by the five of us who were saving boats. For me it was enough to finally put me to sleep for a full night. Such a party girl. I've not smoked since.

Then there was the day I found "cocaine." Most boaters are

transients in that they come to a marina for a day or two then leave for points elsewhere. A few weeks after the storms, a sailboat with some rather laid-back types docked a few slips away from us. In the Flamingo Marina, as is typical in most marinas, there are dock boxes at each slip. When transients leave, we live-aboards check the dock boxes to see if they left any goodies behind. The transient sailboat left so I dutifully checked the dock box. There it was: a bag of white powder. White powder! It MUST be cocaine! After all, this IS Miami! I wondered: *What's its value? How much could I get for it? To whom would I sell it? Crap! I'd probably just get busted!* I decided to do the right thing. I called Miami Vice. The police officers came to the dock and looked in the bag. They each put a finger into the white powder then touched it to their tongues. When they finished spitting and laughing, one of the officers looked at me and said one word: *Tide*. It was laundry detergent! I felt so stupid.

Meanwhile, Farley enjoyed the numerous derelict boats in the marina. The junkier the boats, the more he was drawn to them. Luckily for Farley, Flamingo Marina was home to one of the most derelict boats I ever saw—a 1926 Trumpy called the *Sunset*. She must have been very regal in a long-gone era, and, in fact, she was the sister-ship to the Presidential yacht *Sequoia*, also a 1926 Trumpy. There was a third sister ship as well, the *Lady Mary*, that I'd seen in Ft. Lauderdale a while back. Like the *Sequoia* and the *Lady Mary*, the *Sunset* was 109 feet long with her original wood and ceramics and sterling intact. She just looked like hell from neglect and disrepair. Originally she was christened *Freedom*. I don't know when her name was changed to *Sunset*, but her owner at the time bought her at a sale of impounded boats, all of which had been used in the 1980 Mariel Boat Lift. The Mariel Boat Lift was a mass movement of people who escaped from Cuba at Mariel Harbor, seeking refuge in Miami or the Keys. Many U.S. vessels of all shapes and sizes participated in the illegal operation. Many were caught and impounded. The *Sunset* was one of them. Now she was docked at Flamingo, a total wreck but, incredibly, still afloat. (As of this writing, a new owner is restoring her back to her original condition and name.) The *Sunset* was Farley's favorite. He boarded her every day, doing and chasing who-knows-what below her decks.

119

Farley was a strange cat. He did his job well of keeping river rats and other unwanted critters off the *Curious Wine*. He was medium in size but, for some strange reason, his poops were gigantic! From the start of our relationship, I was astounded that such a small creature could make such big poops. One morning I was awakened by the sound of a man having a hissy-fit on the 36-foot Grand Banks trawler across the dock from me. Trawlers have high sides so they're difficult to board without a stairway. When the owner of the stair-less trawler found giant poops on his deck and screamed that some dog had somehow gotten onto his boat, I knew it was Farley. No dog could jump that high, and I'd seen Farley sail through the air from boat to boat when he was chasing seagulls. Farley pooped on this guy's deck, I was sure of it. I didn't confess. Thank goodness the guy was a transient and gone before sundown.

Life at the Flamingo Marina would have been fun had I not become so depressed. I was fired from International Rehabilitation Associates. What little was left of my self-esteem was shattered. The company was fairly gay-friendly yet I was fired because of sexual harassment from my female heterosexual supervisor. She had hosted a staff meeting at her house one evening. Eight of us enjoyed a collegial barbeque and a soak in her Jacuzzi in the balminess of the Miami moonlight among the Florida-gorgeous plants and trees in her back yard. Her horticulturalist husband was with us, answering our questions about his green-thumb talents. After the meeting, as I prepared to leave, my boss came on to me.

"Ronni, " she said as she came closer, her voice lowered. She reached for my hand. "I think you're really attractive. I never thought about this before."

I instantly felt creepy. "Thought about what?" I asked, not wanting to hear her response. She was my boss!

"This." She leaned over to kiss me. I did the only thing I could think to do on short notice. I ducked!

"Whoa!" I jumped back. "Sorry, but I don't mess around with straight women or women with whom I work. You're both! And—jeez! Your husband!" I felt panicky! "He's in the next room. And you're my boss!" I was shouting but in a whisper. "This is nuts!" I said as I practically ran out of her house. I dreaded seeing her at work the next day.

Around 2:00 PM that next day, a Friday, she summoned me to her office. We managed to avoid one another to that point. With an exaggerated business-like voice she said, "While your work is fine, you are being let go because you're insubordinate. Clean out your desk now. You're fired." Just like that.

"I'm WHAT????" I wanted to vomit.

"You're fired. Leave." She was so sickeningly calm.

"Is this about last night?" I was incredulous.

"There's nothing about last night. Get OUT." She was emphatic.

Fuck! Fired again! I couldn't believe it! What is wrong with me?


How could she do that? Once again, I was a victim of sexual harassment, but, as before, this occurred prior to the 1991 Anita Hill/Clarence Thomas case. I did nothing wrong, and, in fact, ethically, I did everything right. But back then in Florida, as now, it's not illegal to fire someone based solely on their sexual orientation, although, ironically, that wasn't the stated reason for letting me go. I fought the insubordination accusation and won which entitled me to unemployment compensation, but really, I just wanted my job back. I didn't get it. I had to job-search while again receiving unemployment checks, but because my work was so specialized, nothing was available. I had lots of time on my hands to think—but I refused to feel. Another fucking loss. Another piece of my life and my self-esteem gone. Another piece of my heart torn away. Feelings? No, thanks!

Losing that job frightened and emotionally immobilized me. Finding other gainful employment just didn't happen. I didn't believe or trust anyone. I dove into a deep depression and even deeper silence. I had been fired a number of times in the past for being a lesbian. I thought I was beyond that now, that I was moving up the corporate ladder in a gay-friendly company despite Florida's seemingly ongoing commitment to anti-gay laws.

I had lived from paycheck to paycheck and had no money saved. Between my unemployment compensation and Miley's small salary from

121

the Miami Beach Marina, we were okay, barely, but my self-esteem was shot. I got an under-the-table job working on a 62-foot sailboat, preparing her for sale in the 1987 Miami Boat Show. What I appreciated about that work of polishing teak decks and shining silver stanchions was that I didn't have to think about much of anything. When that job was over it was because the boat was ready, not because I was fired. When I was busy, I didn't think much about the desire to die. Now, I did. I wanted to die.

I kept losing—people, jobs, self-esteem. There was so little left of me. So much of myself was simply gone. I cried when I could, but mostly, the pain felt so overwhelming that I was immobilized. I had just enough of myself left to know I couldn't take any more. *Enough! Enough already! What on God's green earth does it take to be okay?* I was so lost.

Once again, I felt like I had tried so hard to be normal, whatever that means, and once again I was an outcast. I decided that as soon as the Boat Show was over, I would jump into the warm waters of Biscayne Bay with a cement block around my feet. I had the block, I had the rope, and I had the drama. Sarah Heartburn, my grandma Frances used to call me.

The day came. I remember standing on the edge of the dock at Flamingo where the water was the deepest, the point that looked out into the Bay, towards 79th Street, only blocks from where my grandparents used to live when they first moved to Miami Beach in the early 1950s. I felt nothing, no sadness, no sense of anything. I left no note, no message to loved ones, no need to explain this action that made perfect sense to me. I was childless, jobless, penniless, worthless. Society hated who and what I was enough to take my children away, and I was legally powerless to stop my company from taking away my livelihood. The battles had become too much. I couldn't, wouldn't do it anymore. The warm water called to me as it always did—the water was where I went as a teen for solace and acceptance. The waters of the Keys calmed my head and my heart when I needed to escape. The water was where I sought comfort. The water was where I lived and it would be where I would die.

The sun was just setting and the Marina was deserted as I knew it would be. I sat on the end of the dock, the block tied to my feet but still in place on the dock next to me. I stared out at the water, no thoughts or feelings in the way. I looked across the water along the 79th Street causeway in the direction of where my grandma Frances once lived and wondered if I would be with her soon. I wanted to be with her.

Suddenly, arms grabbed me, surrounded me, pulled me away from the edge. Hands untied the rope around my legs. Miley and Barbara had seen me, horrified at what I was about to do. They ran to me, pulled me back, held me, rocked me all through the night. The tears, the sobs, the pain of all the things I refused to allow myself to feel came pouring out of my heart and my body. I shook with the intensity of my sobs, shook with the realization of what I almost did, stunned that I had even gotten to that place of self-destruction. They were still holding me as the sun came up the next morning. They held me as I cried and poured my guts and soul out into the universe. They held me as I grasped the magnitude of my depressed self. And they held me as I began to calm, began to understand, ever so slightly, what I almost did. I went over the edge. I have an edge and I chose to cross it. The next day, still in the arms of two women who cared about me, I made a promise to myself that I would always remember that edge, always remember where it resides, and never, ever, ever go there again. Be vigilant for the edge, and stay away.

Several weeks later, as I was still processing and recovering, my friend David Jones from Jacksonville came to Miami for a visit. He told me about a job in the AIDS office in what was then the Florida Health and Rehabilitative Services, or HRS—the Health Department. David had AIDS and described himself as a "short-timer." (Sadly, back then, in 1987, almost everyone with AIDS was a short-timer.) The job was as an AIDS Surveillance Officer, an epidemiologist who focuses on how HIV moves through a community.

"We have this position open. We advertised it twice but not one person applied for it. Everybody's afraid of people with AIDS but I know you're not. Ronni, the Health Department needs you and you need a job. You're smart and you know how to read medical records. You're as qualified as anyone. Come back to Jacksonville and do this work. What do you think?"

What did I think? How about: *how on earth does a person with an 18-year old bachelors degree in music get this kind of gig?* But David was right. I could read medical records, thanks to IRA, and because I had so many friends with AIDS, I was never afraid. I applied for the job, got hired, and began working for the Health Department in May of 1987. Suddenly, I was the highest ranking open lesbian in Florida government.

My dear friend David Jones died of AIDS later that year.

## 21.

# *Finding Sarah*

*M*ay 1987. I sold my boat in Miami and moved back to Jacksonville to become an AIDS surveillance officer, a one-disease epidemiologist. The State of Florida sent me to the Centers for Disease Control and Prevention in Atlanta to learn how to pronounce *epidemiologist* and how to do the work.

Miley and I rented an old Victorian house in the Springfield area just north of downtown Jacksonville, within walking distance to my office in the Health Department. Most of the houses in Springfield were built between 1885 and 1930 There were bungalows, Revivals, Queen Annes, and the stately Victorians. Springfield saw many communities of people come and go over the decades. By the 1980s the area was overrun with crack houses, drugs, and prostitutes of every gender variation. A few homes were being renovated, but full-tilt gentrification had not yet begun. It was a difficult area, perfect for the location of the Health department.

I went home for lunch one day, a Thursday, to find that someone had broken into our back yard and stole our matching motor scooters— the last remaining vestiges from the *Curious Wine*—as well as our barbeque grill and lawn mower. I called the police.

"They'll be back. This was too easy. Go to the pound NOW and get a couple of big dogs." Not very encouraging. That night we were too scared to sleep. We stayed awake as long as we could but by 1 A.M. we couldn't keep our eyes open. When we awoke at 7 A.M. and went downstairs to the kitchen, to our horror, we saw that most of our belongings were gone. We moved out of there that afternoon and into an apartment complex on the St. Johns River.

Shortly after we moved, Miley, who now worked for Planned Parenthood, was given a tiny gray Himalayan kitten named Sarah by a patient who couldn't otherwise pay for services. I've never been a cat person. Farley was an anomaly for me. We had an understanding: he was a working partner. There was no emotion in it for either of us. Sarah,

125

though, grabbed my heart.

She was still a very young kitten when she went missing for over twelve hours. While she often went outdoors, she rarely left the small area around our apartment patio. I searched for her, first outside and then inside the apartment. Suddenly I heard the teeniest, tiniest sound in the guest bedroom that doubled as my office. I searched, trying to hear the sound again. There! There it was, coming from behind my large teak desk. There was little Sarah, unable to move. I could tell there was something seriously wrong with her legs. I was afraid to move her so I called a veterinarian, a long-time friend, who came right over. In the meantime, I laid on my stomach on the floor, my fingers from one hand resting lightly on Sarah's front paws while fingers from my other hand fed her. Our eyes locked. There was trust in her eyes, and love, as she kept her gaze on my face. I felt my heart melt into a thousand pools for this little being. I understood that she was in pain, and she understood that I was there to help. The vet arrived. She gently pulled Sarah up from behind the desk as I carefully moved the desk away. Sarah had apparently eaten some poison outdoors that caused her legs to become paralyzed. After a few days of tender loving care, she was fine. She and I knew without a doubt that we were bonded for life, a family, and that we would be there for each other no matter what, for the rest of our lives. I was blessed to have Sarah for another 13 years.

Farley left. He preferred to spend most of his time outdoors and our apartment was only blocks from the river. When Farley didn't come home one day, I just knew he had headed back to the water in search of his favorite thing—some old derelict boat. That pirate cat was back in business, I truly believed.

Though Miley and I had not been lovers for the last year of our time together, we had a wonderful friendship. She found a new girlfriend with an apartment on the beach and moved in with her, which was fine with me. I understood that it was the boat and the water that kept the three of us—Miley, Farley, and me—together. With that liquid glue gone, so were they. Miley and I remained friends for many years. Farley is probably on some derelict vessel in the sky after all these years. And my

126

beloved Sarah, whose ashes are in a beautiful little flowered box, sits on the window sill at my house in Palm Desert where there is an abundance of hummingbirds and doves. She would have loved that.

# 22.
# *AIDS*

U.S. President: George H. W. Bush

Best film: Driving Miss Daisy; Born on the Fourth of July, Field of Dreams, Dead Poets Society

Best actors: Daniel Day-Lewis, Jessica Tandy

Best TV shows: The Arsenio Hall Show; Coach; COPS; Quantum Leap; Rescue 911; The New Mickey Mouse Club; Tales from the Crypt; Seinfeld; Doogie Howser, MD; Baywatch; Family Matters; The Simpsons

Best songs: Like a Prayer, Don't Wanna Lose You, Straight Up, The Living Years, Real Love, Forever Your Girl

Civics: Beijing's Tiananmen Square riots; Berlin Wall comes down; Exxon Valdez oil spill; Colin Powell named first Black Chair of Joint Chiefs of Staff; San Francisco 7.1 earthquake

Popular Culture: World Wide Web server and browser developed; *The Joy Luck Club* by Amy Tan published; Los Angeles, CA and state of Massachusetts prohibit LGBT discrimination; Columbus, Ohio adopts a hate crimes bill that includes sexual orientation.

Deaths: Jim Baccus, Lucille Ball, Salvador Dali, Bette Davis, Billy Martin, Laurence Olivier, Sugar Ray Robinson

*I.* Shira

Shira had AIDS. She was 12 years old. Her tiny body was covered with multiple bruises and sores and bandages, tubes protruding from her bloated abdomen. Her young life was coming to an end after nine painful years of suffering from the disease she contracted at the age of three from her mother's drug-using customers during one of the many times Shira was sexually assaulted.

Shira was dying that day. People from throughout the AIDS communities were in her room at Wolfson Children's Hospital in Jacksonville. Her foster parents, those two big-hearted people who considered Shira their own child for the past four years, gave Shira the best possible life under the worst possible circumstances. Shira's biological mother was in jail. Her biological father, unknown.

"Shira," her foster dad asked, "what's your best wish?"

In such a small, small voice, and without hesitation, Shira said, "To be your real child. I want you to be my real parents."

I heard the words. I choked down the lump in my throat and called my partner Paula.

"Paula, find Father Joe fast!" Father Joe was the minister in the Episcopal Church. Paula was a member of the church and close with Father Joe. "Get him over here to Wolfson NOW. Tell him it's urgent! It's Shira…" My voice trailed as the lump rose again.

"Ahm on it, and Ah'll be there soon mah-self," her soft Southern drawl even more pronounced whenever something emotional was happening. She dialed Father Joe's pager number. Father Joe was a wonderful man deeply loved by the gay and AIDS communities. He arrived within 30 minutes, Paula on his heels.

"We need an adoption ceremony quick, Joe. Will you do it?" I whispered as soon as he entered the room.

Without hesitation, Father Joe was at Shira's bedside. He kissed Shira and her foster parents, then took their hands together in his. We listened as Father Joe performed the adoption service from the Episcopal Prayer Book. He pronounced Shira and her foster parents a "real family," to the sound of our collective sobs, we who were so privileged to be in that place in that moment. We cried, for Shira, for her parents, for all the people we'd lost and were losing to this damned disease. My heart broke for these two parents who would not let go of Shira's tiny hands. With her deepest wish realized, we witnessed Shira gently slip away, away, silently away. Their beloved daughter was gone.


II. Keith

"Please don't take me to Jax General again. I want to die in a classy

129

place, like Baptist." Keith was so fragile but powerfully insistent about where his last bed must be located. He was terribly ill with multiple complications from AIDS and had spent a great deal of time in Jacksonville General, the hospital where indigents received minimal heath care back then, and where people with AIDS were considered pariahs. In the 1980s, AIDS patients' soiled gowns were not changed, their rooms not cleaned, their food trays left on the floor by their doors with Florida roaches as sentinels. It was up to us in the community to make sure our gay brothers received the care they needed and deserved. It was an incredible heartbreaking challenge back then in Northeast Florida.

Keith's time was running out. He was exhausted. Keith, who was only twenty-two, suffered from severe wasting, one of the many diseases that defined AIDS. Keith called me that day at the AIDS office in the Health Department as he had hundreds of times before, but this time he sounded so much weaker, so fragile.

"It's time, Ronni. Baptist, this time? Please?"

I grabbed my assistant, a big, almost burley, woman named Bonnie, who was six feet tall and built like a football player. She was wearing her best jeans and a polo shirt that day, a stark contrast to me in my skirted suit, stockings, and heels. We were a formidable team, Bonnie and I, and all of our AIDS patients knew it. We jumped into my car and drove the three blocks to Keith's rooming house.

Keith looked even worse than when I saw him last, just two weeks earlier, and that wasn't good. He was skinny, with Kaposi's sarcoma lesions all over his face and chest, and a raspy cough from the pneumonia. Though African American, his cocoa color skin was now very pale. His room was filthy. It stunk of body waste and decay. Roaches crawled all over the food remnants in the sink. Bonnie and I washed Keith then carried him to the car because he was depleted of anything resembling energy. We took him to the Baptist Medical Center emergency room, in agreement that Keith's last wish deserved to be granted.

We poured Keith's limp and nearly lifeless body into a wheel chair though he could barely sit up. The three of us managed to make it to the registration desk. The woman sitting at the desk looked up at Bonnie, then at me, then Keith, and back to Bonnie. I guess she deferred to Bonnie because Bonnie was big, perhaps male-like, so of course she must be in charge.

"Uh, are you related to the patient?" the woman asked Bonnie cautiously.

Bonnie looked back and forth several times, from Keith to me to Keith again. With her eyes fixed on Keith, and with so much love in a voice full of sadness, she said to the woman, "Yeah, we're his parents."

Keith was admitted into Baptist Medical Center. He died six hours later as Bonnie and I held his hands.


III. The Condom Commandos

Donna Zimmerman, my colleague and friend in the AIDS office, and I created what we called the Condom Commandos. Our after-hours volunteer job, we declared, was to protect as many young gay men as possible from contracting this killer disease. We spent many hours in the men's restrooms at truck stops on I-95 and I-10 where we knew guys met for sex. We stalked Jacksonville's parks, the ones we knew to be gay male cruise spots. We went to the gay beach and found guys together in the bushes. We didn't try to talk men out of having sex. We just gave them condoms and, well, instructed them—on the spot—about how to use condoms correctly.

"Here. Be sure you use this. Roll it all the way down to the base of your penis, and don't let your semen spill out of it onto the other guy when you're finished. Have fun now!"

Coming from a couple of middle-aged lesbians, the moment was probably killed for those guys but we believed we were doing a good thing. We gave away thousands of condoms during the couple of years as the Condom Commandos, and frankly, we had the time of our lives in the no-woman places like men's restrooms out on highways and sea-grape bushes at the beach.


IV. The Work

The first Northeast Florida AIDS services group began around the

131

dining room table in my Springfield home in Jacksonville in 1987. Several of us from the Health Department—Ken Hunt, David Jones, David Andress, myself—and folks from the gay community—Marc Oswald, Dick Neiman, Michael Piazza, Tony O'Connor—designed what we believed was needed to provide both emotional support and specific physical care for people with AIDS. (Frieda Saraga was about to initiate the first support group for gay men with AIDS which she still facilitates today.) That small meeting at my house, and future iterations, eventually led to the development of what is now the Northeast Florida AIDS Network.

As an aside, another group began around my dining room table— JASMYN, the Jacksonville Area Sexual Minority Youth Network. In 1993, the idea of a youth group was brought to some of us adult leaders in the community by a young man named Ernie Solario. Today, nearly 20 years later, JASMYN is the only organization in Northeast Florida that provides services for lesbian, gay, bisexual, and transgender youth.

My work as an AIDS epidemiologist was to track the disease to determine how people became infected with HIV. I started that work in May of 1987 with the first wave of AIDS Surveillance officers in the U.S. I had many friends with AIDS, all but one of whom are now gone. I met so many wonderful people, mostly young gay men, and their families. It was a privilege to be of service to them in any way I could, and I made sure there were Health Department resources even if the resources weren't necessarily earmarked for such assistance.

Strange cases were sometimes assigned to me. I recall the case of the man who went to a hospital in St. Augustine for gall bladder surgery. The surgery never took place because he was reported as having AIDS. I reviewed the medical record which actually read: *We must not operate on this man. He walks funny and therefore must be homosexual. He should be sent to Jacksonville General for his medical care.* It's the only time I saw a diagnosis based on the way a person walked!

There were Catholic priests, Baptists ministers, Jewish rabbis. There were no closet doors tight enough to exclude someone from this horrible disease. The most insidious case involved a very popular twenty year old white male, Jason, the darling of his Baptist church and the one who every parent there wanted their daughter to date. A young woman from a

132

nearby town filed murder charges against Jason, reporting that she had contracted AIDS from him. The accusation made the papers—*From Mr. Clean-Cut All-American Boy???*—complete with a photo of Jason. The Health Department issued a notice asking anyone who had been sexual with him to come to the AIDS office for HIV testing. Over 300 people showed up during a two-day period of time! Women and men of all ages, sizes and colors. Jason, it seemed, was indiscriminate regarding sex partners. He went to prison.

I remember Ron who was in the state mental health hospital but released as his disease progressed. He was sent to the hospice facility that was adjacent to the Health Department offices. His last wish was to "cruise the mall." He was incredibly weak but I took him anyway and pushed his wheel chair around the mall. He was wildly obscene with every man we passed, but his voice was so weak that I was the only one who could hear him. Regardless, he was thrilled.

The truly difficult part of this work for me and for so many was the inability to fully mourn the loss of one friend before another died. In honor of dear ones lost, I did a tremendous amount of public speaking about AIDS and taught classes at both the University of North Florida for counseling majors and at the Florida Community College for health care providers who needed continuing HIV education. Regardless, it was yet one more time in my life when I stuffed my sadness down inside, left to linger for years.


As a state employee, one of the many gifts I received from my AIDS work was a waiver of tuition to the University of North Florida, so I went back to school. I was hired by the Health Department with only a bachelors degree in music. I wanted a masters in counseling. In 1989, I graduated from the University of North Florida with a Masters of Education with a focus in counseling. By 1991, I was back in school as a doctoral student in educational leadership and organizational development, and graduated in 1996 with an Ed.D.—a doctorate in education. I was Dr. Sanlo.

It remains truly ironic to me that the state of Florida, which took my children away from me because I was a lesbian, hired me and provided the opportunity to obtain graduate degrees that advanced my career—at no cost. Go figure!

# 23.
# *The Dock*

---

## 1991

U.S. President: George H. W. Bush

Best film: Silence of the Lambs; JFK, Beauty and the Beast, The Prince of Tides

Best actors: Anthony Hopkins, Jodie Foster

Best TV shows: Blossom; Sisters; Rugrats; Home Improvement; The Jerry Springer Show

Best songs: Everything I do I do It For You, Rush Rush, Rhythm of My Heart, Every Heartbeat, Emotions

Civics: Persian Gulf War ends; Apartheid repealed in South Africa; Two Libyans indicted in 1988 bombing of Pan Am Flight 103 over Lockerbie, Scotland: Anita Hill accused Clarence Thomas of sexual harassment but U.S. Senate approves Thomas as U.S. Supreme Court Judge

Popular Culture: Fox Broadcasting permitted to advertise condoms on TV; Connecticut, Minnesota, and Hawaii ban sexual orientation discrimination.

Deaths: Miles Davis, Frank Capra, Leo Durocher

---

In 1991, five months before I was to begin my doctoral work at the University of North Florida, my partner Lea dumped me for a much younger woman. I was a mess. I was unexpectedly single again, and rebound-dating a beautiful but somewhat deranged woman. For the first time in years the colitis came back with a vengeance.

Several years earlier, before Lea and I became partners, we had been friends. I had attended her commitment ceremony with her partner Leslie at the Metropolitan Community Church. In the winter of 1989, Leslie had an affair with the new female lesbian minister in town and abruptly left Lea, who was devastated. Lea was active in the church and

135

now felt betrayed by the two most important people to her, her partner and her minister. Lea often told me that she wasn't really a lesbian, just a woman who happened to love another woman, namely Leslie. Leslie's leaving hurt Lea deeply.

To cheer her up—and to make sure no other local lesbian had an opportunity to date her—I took Lea hostage. Well, not really, but in the big emotional picture, yeah, I did. I deliberately occupied all of her time. If she decided she really was a lesbian, I wanted to be the one she chose. I took her for rides in my jeep, out to the dunes where the Atlantic Ocean meets the St. Johns River. She loved to do that, though two years later when she broke up with me, she told me she hated my jeep. It "lacked creature comforts," she said, like a roof. (I just never thought it needed one. When it rained, I simply raised my big blue-and-white-striped golf umbrella, rested it on the roll bar, and held it tightly in place until the rain stopped.) The lack of a roof didn't seem to work for Lea anymore. But early on, she loved it.

In the spring of 1989, before they broke up, Lea and Leslie had reservations for a Caribbean cruise. With their untimely and unexpected dissolution, Lea now had an extra cruise ticket, so I bought it and went with her. The crazy thing about that trip was that it was with a group of women from Overeaters Anonymous. A cruise is nothing if not a feeding frenzy, so I suspected there would be many on-board OA meetings. It was indeed a food fest but it was also great fun, and the women, including Lea, along with the scenery and the fresh tropical air, were terrific.

Lea and I became lovers. In my own raging co-dependent self-esteem-less self, I believed that if I didn't snatch Lea up—so to speak—she would start dating others and stop seeing me. I made myself completely indispensable. It worked, and we became a couple. With Lea, I felt like I had finally "made it" into Middle Class. I perceived myself to have been rather Bohemian for so many years, and now I had a partner who owned her own ranch-style home with a manicured yard, a big kitchen and comfy furniture. I finally looked like my siblings and their families—normal, whatever *that* means. Life with Lea was pleasant but very predictable. I was happy at first but a recurring thought took hold: I was bored. Was Lea also bored? We didn't do a good job of talking with one another beyond the daily niceties. I was used to drama and chaos, and really didn't know how to handle anything that smacked of *normal*. But I tried, retreating into my usual relational method of operation: silence.

During the winter of 1989 Kal came to live with us. Kal and his partner Bob had moved to Jacksonville from Oklahoma several months earlier when Bob was hired as a minister at a local church. Unfortunately, Bob was killed in an automobile accident on I-95 near St. Augustine shortly after their arrival. Kal was only 22 years old and knew very few people in town. Lea and I invited him to live with us. He was sweet and charming and goofy and fun. He was the son Lea never had and the one I never saw. He was a delight, worming his way into our hearts and our lives, fully with our permission.

Several months after Kal moved in with us, he became ill. He didn't know he had AIDS and it overtook him quickly, as it did so many people back then. After his death that next summer, Lea and I didn't speak about Kal nor about the circumstances of his death. Strangely, we simply acted as if he had never been there.

Being the HIV epidemiologist and dealing with the almost daily deaths of friends and clients of the Health Department, and living with the constant pain of the loss of custody of my children and their lack of contact with me, I once again became depressed. Kal's death added to my intense sadness. It seemed that my friends—Lea included—and I were living in a constant state of mourning, never able to emotionally resolve the death of one friend before another friend died. I retreated deeper and deeper into my silent world, becoming neither a good friend nor much of a good partner for Lea.

By February of 1991, Lea was spending more and more time at work, the night shift actually, which was strange because she was the executive director of a very large social services organization. The night shift? She said she was doing evaluations of the night shift staff. In March, almost two years to the day that we had become a couple, and a week before my 44th birthday, we broke up. Well, that's when she dumped me.

"We need to talk," Lea said that Monday afternoon after work. *Oh no*, I thought. *That's never a good way to begin a conversation.*

137

"I've fallen in love with Kit and she's moving in here on Saturday, so you need to get your things out by Friday." It was Monday. I had five days. Shit!

*What???* I was absolutely in shock! I hadn't seen this coming, had no indication that Lea was having an affair. My own obliviousness and silence, I realized later, prohibited me from noticing what everybody else already knew. To make it worse, Kit was 20 years my junior. I bet she got a damned fine evaluation that year! I took an emotional nose-dive into a dark empty pit.

I became even more depressed throughout that summer. Dating a lunatic didn't help. I was fascinated, in a strange way, about my condition. I wasn't suicidal. I just couldn't make a decision. Not about anything, like what to eat or what to wear. Friends came to my little rented house in the Riverside area of Jacksonville every day to select my food and clothing. I was a wreck. Making a decision about living or dying simply wasn't in my realm of capability.

I met Frieda Saraga prior to that summer but I honestly can't remember when. I feel like I've known her my whole life. Frieda is a straight woman, 15 years older than I, with five adult children, three of whom are gay or lesbian. She's active in the AIDS community, and surrogate mother to many of us although I occasionally hold impure thoughts of her (apologies to her sweet husband Len). Frieda founded both the gay men's AIDS support group and Northeast Florida PFLAG—Parents and Friends of Lesbians and Gays, both of which are still active. She saved my life, gave me life really, when I had no visible means of humanity or soul. For that and so much more, I love her deeply.

One day late in that summer of 1991 when I was exceptionally low, Frieda said to me, "You have so much personal power, Ronni, and you don't even know it. You have no idea." *Really???*

She was right; I had no idea. I felt worthless and drained, anything but powerful. I was completely defeated and numb, and slipping deeper and deeper into a black hole of emotionless existence. Frieda hand-carried my sad sorry self to LifeStream, a four-day personal growth program in which she and her family were involved. She made my reservation and paid for it, informed me that I was going, made sure I got there, and stayed with me for the four days of the program. Since I was

138

unable to decide what to do on any given day, and certainly had no emotional strength to resist, when Frieda came to pick me up, I went. I needed to be there, and Frieda was the one who knew it.

I experienced a number of things at LifeStream that, even in my impaired state, seemed odd. I must have dismissed them, though, because I can't remember at all what they were. However, there was one activity that stays with me to this day, and for which I am forever grateful.

The participants were told to build our personal safe spaces. We were instructed to sit on the floor, get comfortable, and then close our eyes. We were then told to envision tools in our hands. The assignment was to construct in our mind's eye whatever we wished, but specifically to create a place where we could go if we were in emotional distress. Already in distress, and being a good dyke who knew tools, I thought about my safe space possibilities. Without hesitation I began to build a cheekee hut. *What??? A cheekee hut?* How did I come up with that one? Nevertheless, I worked diligently to build my cheekee hut on a small unpopulated palm-tree-covered piece of land that jutted out peninsula-style into the Intracoastal Waterway up near Fernandina Beach, almost at the Florida-Georgia border.

I hammered four big imaginary pilings into the ground, one at each corner of a square cement floor. (I must have poured the floor first, or maybe it was already there. I couldn't remember.) Then I wove and attached a thatched roof of palm fronds, leaving all four sides of the cheekee completely open. Then, to my surprise, I found myself walking over to the water's edge where I built a beautiful wooden dock. It was a short dock made of the finest teak, smooth to the touch, warmed by the sunshine. The dock, as it turned out, and not the cheekee hut, was my safe place. The cheekee hut was there so I'd have someplace to put my stuff when I went to my dock. I felt myself lie down on that warm wooden dock, water lightly lapping against the pilings, the sun embracing my body. A feeling washed over me, caressed me, reassured me that whatever was wrong in my life was going to be okay.

I was about to begin a doctoral program at the university in a few weeks. It occurred to me as I laid on my imaginary dock in that big room with all those people that day, that worthless people don't get accepted into doctoral programs, therefore I might not really be as worthless as I believed. Like an injured phoenix on the mend, I slowly began to rise out of my ashes of despair.

Several days after that weekend, my therapist suggested I would benefit from a five-day in-house program at a mental hospital. I felt so ashamed at the startling realization that I was truly nuts though I'd had plenty of hints along the way. Embarrassed, I called my mother and asked for the money to pay for the hospitalization since my insurance didn't cover it. My mother—God bless her—put a check in the mail to me that day, no questions asked.

I went to the university to speak with the professor who had been assigned as my mentor, Dr. Pritchy Smith. I told Pritchy about my precarious emotional state and that I would miss the first week of classes because I had to go to a hospital. In the kindest voice and with such understanding, Pritchy asked me to look at things in a different way. He said to consider every single day a victory, that each class and each completed assignment was a goal accomplished, to be celebrated. He suggested I wait a couple of weeks before going away. "Stay here, Ronni, and just try this for a few weeks. Go for the little achievable goals," he advised. I did, and day by day, one little goal at a time, I began to come back to the land of the living. Between Pritchy, Frieda, and my mother, and their loving support, I canceled my reservation at the hospital and destroyed the check.

To this day, twenty years later, in times of stress or sadness or anger, I take myself to my little dock on the river and feel the warmth of the sunshine as I lie down. My heart fills with memory and respect for my own difficult journey, and with deep and abiding friendship for Frieda, my gratefulness to Pritchy, and, of course, with my love and respect for my mother.

As for Lea, it took many years but today we're close friends. When same sex couples could legally marry in California for a brief period in 2008, I had the honor of being the witness for Lea and her longtime partner at their wedding. That jeep? Gone for decades...no creature comforts.

# 24.
# *The Southern Belle*

---

## 1993

<u>U.S. President</u>: William J. Clinton

<u>Best film</u>: Schindler's List, The Piano, The Fugitive, Philadelphia

<u>Best actors</u>: Tom Hanks, Holly Hunter

<u>Best TV shows</u>: Dr. Quinn, Medicine Woman; Bevis & Butthead; Late Night with Conan O'Brien; Rikki Lake; Frasier; NYPD Blue; The Nanny

<u>Best songs</u>: Can't Help Falling In Love, I Will Always Love You, Don't Walk Away, Ordinary World, Love Is

<u>Civics</u>: Federal agents besiege Texas Branch Davidian religious cult; Rodney King beating; Ruth Bader Ginsburg appointed to U.S. Supreme Court

<u>Popular Culture</u>: Michael Jackson accused of child molestation; first humans cloned; *The Shipping News* by Annie Proulx published; President Clinton signs *Don't Ask, Don't Tell* military policy

<u>Deaths</u>: Don Ameche, Arthur Ashe, Frank Zappa, Dizzy Gillespie, Audrey Hepburn, Cesar Chavez

---

Paula was a Southern woman with a drawl thick as molasses. She was born and raised in Georgia, and actually had a mammy when she was a child. She had three brothers, an unusual mother who demanded to be called Lady Winston though there was absolutely no evidence of royalty in the family. Her father was some sort of secret operative who slaughtered wild African animals and hung their heads in his house. I suspect he also beat up little children but Paula never talked about that, saying only that she had no recollection of life before the age of eleven.

Paula and I had been together in Jacksonville for a year before I was offered a job at the University of Michigan. We'd met years earlier on a speakers' panel because we were two of the very few lesbians in

Northeast Florida who had children. Paula had custody and I did not, so we often shared the stage at speaking engagements. Paula was a very supportive friend whenever my relationships fell apart, which was often and inevitable. In fact, she once gave me a copy of the book *Surviving the Loss of Love*. Good ideas in that book, but it didn't stop the cycle for me.

I had many short-term relationships with women. It was a predictable process. I would meet someone, initiate an intense sexual relationship with her, then lose interest. That sounds so cold and probably exactly the way it was perceived by others, but it was how I protected myself. I was desperately afraid of real intimacy. Not in a sexual way but in the deep, heartfelt meaningful way in which two people truly connect. I functioned under the guise of the old adage I set for myself when I was young: *If you know my truth, you'll leave me.* If I'm sexual, I don't have to talk, don't have to share anything about myself. Once the sexual excitement calmed down and conversation set in, I reverted to the silence that guided my life. It happened over and over and over, regardless of other dynamics in the mix. Paula watched me do this for years with a certain amount of interest and curiosity.

Paula and I got together as my volatile rebound relationship with Linda fell apart. Linda was a handsome woman a few years younger than I, with long silver hair that flowed and glistened down her back. Linda and I had separated seven times in eighteen months. The relationship had zero chance of survival.

I remember the December we visited Linda's parents in Colorado. It was freezing cold, her folks were drunk, and Linda was as miserable as I'd ever seen her. On our last night there, she came to bed after yet another fight with her parents. I tried to sleep through the mayhem but she woke me up and growled with clenched teeth, "I wish I could hurt you!" She then rolled over and immediately fell asleep while I laid there with eyes wide open, petrified, for the remainder of the night, vigilant of the body next to me. As soon as we returned to Jacksonville, I left her. Paula was waiting in the wings.

Paula held her feelings as close to her chest as I, so we pretended to be in love. We weren't, but we were both so afraid to be alone. There were many wonderful things about Paula but there were several unusual things as well. Paula had rules about protocol, many of which were baffling—like we couldn't say the word *toilet* because she considered it offensive, or that she would absolutely not be seen without her makeup, strange for a lesbian back then. But Paula had two outstanding traits: she never forgot a name, and she knew how to be a gracious hostess.

The name thing amazed me because I always had difficulty remembering names. I had a band director in college, Richard W. Bowles, who could remember names of people he'd not seen in 20 years! Remarkable! When Paula and I attended social functions, she would whisper people's names in my ear so that I didn't appear socially inept.

Her hostess skills were legendary. When my doctoral cohort colleagues and I took our two-day comprehensive exams, Paula gathered partners and spouses and organized lunches and snacks for us each day, and then a champagne reception at the end of our exams. The *piece de resistance*, though, was the full-on buffet, complete with floral arrangements, that Paula prepared for my committee the day I defended my doctoral dissertation. They still talk about it at the university!


They also still talk about the issue I had with my dissertation and commencement. Most institutions print the title of doctoral students' dissertations in the commencement programs. There were two of us graduating with doctoral degrees in education that December of 1996. I was informed by the University that my title—*Unheard Voices: The Effects of Silence on Lesbian and Gay Educators in Northeast Florida*— would not be published in the commencement program. The reason, they said, was their fear that I would be booed by the audience, ruining the sanctity and pomp of the event. My response was simple: either print the title or I'll sue for discrimination. It was their choice. The title was printed, no one booed, and the commencement ceremony was lovely for all of the graduates and their families. It was especially sweet for me because when I was a brand new first-year student at the University of Florida in 1965, an academic counselor told me I wasn't college material, that I should quit now and not waste my parents' money. Thanks for your vote of confidence, buddy. I'm a doctor now! Ha!

Paula had four children, and prided herself on being a great mom. The two younger ones, James and Jonathan, lived with her, and then with us. Her oldest son, who we rarely saw, was away at college, and then there was Martha, two years younger than the oldest, who rose from the dead. Literally.

"Ah neva cry, " declared Paula in her thickest—and sexiest, I might add—Southern accent. Still getting to know one another early in our relationship and before we lived together, we were having a discussion about the demonstration—or, rather, lack of demonstration—of feelings. I suspect Paula had tremendous issues from childhood that prevented her from recognizing or dealing with her feelings. I could easily relate. Not 24 hours later she called me at my apartment, sobbing without control.

"A ter-ruh-ble thing has happened." She was crying so hard. "Please come over raht away." I got to her house quickly.

"What on earth...???" I asked to the air. Paula was home alone and nearly hysterical.

"Th-th-the phone," she tried to talk between sobs. "S-s-some young wo-wo-woman. She said, she said..." Paula blew her nose. "She said she's my daw-ta. How can that beeee??? —sob—I have no daw-tas, just that one who died at birth. Who is this mean—sob—woman? So, so—sob—so cruel. She's—sob—she's gonna call back. Please talk—sob—ta her, Ronnnnni." She couldn't stop crying and didn't try. The heaviness of the world was riding down her face on her streaked mascara.

The story, as it turned out, was that Paula's first and second children were fathered by Paula's drug-addict boyfriend in the early 1970s. During that time there were several active black-market Florida-to-New York baby rings. When Paula went to the hospital in Jacksonville to have her second baby, she was knocked out on drugs for several days. When she awoke, she was told that her baby had died. This apparently was a typical method for procuring babies to sell in other states. Paula believed that her baby was dead, as she was told. She felt tremendous pain at not having the chance to see her baby, to say goodbye, before she was buried. Later in life, Paula became a nurse and made a point of always showing baby bodies to the birth mother if the child died.

The baby girl died, Paula believed, and the drug-addict boyfriend

144

disappeared. Later, Paula married an upstanding man and had a third child, then divorced him and entered into a relationship with a woman just prior to the birth of her fourth child. Fast forward 24 years and the phone call. Turns out that the second child, Martha, was quite alive. She had been sold, by either the boyfriend or a nurse or both, to an agency in New York and adopted by a loving family. She always knew she was adopted and, at age 23, had her adoption papers unsealed. She found her birth certificate and managed to locate Paula. Paula was so shocked about having a child rise from the dead that she wanted no contact with her. I met Martha when she came to Florida. There was no doubt in my mind that she was Paula's child. She looked and sounded more like Paula than any of the other three children. However, no matter what we did, Paula refused to have contact with the young woman. In her own way, Paula was a wonderful mother and loved her children fiercely but she never spoke of Martha again, at least not while I was with her.

We lived together, Paula, the two younger boys and I, in a rented 1930s bungalow in Jacksonville. About a week after we moved in, there was a knock on the door. It was the people who had lived in the house just before us. They had cats, several of which had died in that house and were buried in the bushes in the back yard. Another of their cats had died that morning. They asked if they could bury the cat near its siblings in our back yard.

"Yes, of course," I said after conferring with Paula and the boys.

"Thank you so much," they said through their tears. "We'll come back this evening."

They returned just as the sun was setting and asked if they could just sit in the back yard for a while until the body was ready. Ready? It was already dead. Apparently, when the cat died that morning, they put it in a freezer. All four legs froze, going every which way. They needed to wait until the cat thawed enough to fold it up and get it into its burial box. While we wanted to be reverent for the loss of their pet, we found the situation terribly funny and muffled our laughter behind closed doors.

145

I was in my last semester of coursework for my doctoral program at the University of North Florida, in January of 1994, when Shirley Webb, the then-director of the UNF Women's Center, handed a paper to me that she'd just received on her fax. "Here's your next job, Ronni. Go for it."

It was the director position for the University of Michigan's Lesbian and Gay Programs Office. *Michigan???* I was a Florida girl, and besides, my kids were here. Though I hadn't seen my children in years, what if they needed me? But by then they were adults, 22 and 18. Was this the professional break I didn't know I needed? I became aggressive about the application process for this job. If my children needed me, they would find me since I always let them know how to contact me with every card I sent. I was hired by the University of Michigan and moved to Ann Arbor in May of 1994. I finished my doctoral dissertation while there.

Paula and the boys, both teenagers, moved to Ann Arbor with me. Paula had the option of staying in Jacksonville and maintaining a long distance relationship with me as many academics do. I especially did not want to upset the lives and lifestyles of the two children. Over the years everyone in their world knew their mother was a lesbian, so they didn't need to come out over and over in school and with friends. In a new town and a new situation, that's all they'd be doing.

"We'll go as a family, Ronni," Paula declared. That meant I would work while she played the self-identified role of trophy wife (her words, not mine). I'd pay for everything including the house we bought, Jonathan's braces and James's college. At least I didn't have to cook or clean which I detested. Paula eventually got a job, working in the health department in Detroit.

We lived in Ypsilanti—Ypsi, the locals call it—whose claim to fame is the water tower in the heart of town that looks exactly like a circumcised penis. We chose Ypsi rather than Ann Arbor because Ypsi was more dynamically multicultural, an environment we appreciated in Jacksonville and preferred in Michigan.

James was the oldest of the two boys who lived with us. He'd wanted a tattoo since he was fifteen. Paula repeatedly told him that he must wait until he turned eighteen. James designed his tattoo—a dragon—and waited. He was such an interesting boy who perceived

146

himself as unique and out of the mainstream. He wore outrageous unmatched clothes—striped knee socks, and unusual vests and shirts. He colored his hair purple and gold, his school colors, then wondered why other students harassed him. He said he didn't care that they did. He just felt it was their lack of creativity and not his unusual attire that motivated their cruelty. He wondered, much like I always did as a teen, why people would go out of their way to be mean to someone who was different. On his 18th birthday, James' first stop was a tattoo parlor to which he went without fanfare. That meant he didn't tell us. Several weeks later we were in the family van. Paula was driving and James was lying stretched out on the second row of seats, his shirt slightly raised. Paula apparently saw James' tummy—and tattoo—in the rear view mirror and slammed on the brakes.

In her deepest, most indignant drawl she hollered, "What is THAT on your stomach, young man?"

"My tattoo. You said I could get one when I turned 18. I'm 18. I got it on my birthday."

"I NEVUH said any such thing," hollered Paula, her best Southern twang at full tilt. Actually, we'd all heard her say exactly that many times over the years. Regardless, before the day was over, Paula had purchased a one-way ticket for James to fly to Florida to live with his father. That was Paula! James left the next day. Two weeks later, I flew to Florida to bring him back home to Michigan.


While driving to work in Ann Arbor one morning, I heard an NPR radio program in which a mother who had just lost her daughter in the crash of TWA flight 800 (July 2006) was talking. Through her tears she said she was often told by well-meaning people that for as painful as the loss of her daughter is, she'll eventually heal and get over it. Another mother called in. She had lost her daughter on the Pan Am Lockerbie flight crash (December 1988). She told the TWA mother that it's impossible to "get over" such a devastating loss. She said, "The only thing you can do is incorporate the loss into who you are. Make your daughter's memory a strength and move forward, with your heart full of love."

I heard her words. She was speaking to me, too! I felt so conflicted about my children not being in my life. I mourned their loss every day of my life but they weren't dead, just out of my view, out of my reach. It was difficult to explain to anyone. How could anyone understand why a mother would lose custody of her children short of being an ax murderer? I beat myself up over and over and friggin' over for years, trying to move on, because that's what people said I should do. And now here's a mother telling me via my car radio what I needed to hear! I had memories. Hell, that's all I had, memories and a heart full of love for my children who I hadn't seen or heard from in ten years, yet the pain was always present. With that mother's words—*the only thing you can do is incorporate the loss into who you are. Make your daughter's memory a strength and move forward, with your heart full of love*—a small bit of the pain with which I lived had begun to heal, though the guilt remained. I shared this with no one, especially not with Paula.

Paula hated Michigan from the day we arrived. Too cold. Too hot. Too dark. Too bright. Too isolated. And she hated me for taking her there, though the boys didn't seem to mind the place too much. Paula and I separated a couple of years later. Neither of us was in love with the other and both of us were miserable. During our separation, in hopes of getting back together, I bought a ring for her. The Hebrew inscription read: *This is My Beloved, This is My Friend.* I looked at that ring for weeks without giving it to her. I couldn't. My beloved? My friend? We still didn't even like each other! I realized that *I* was the one who needed to be my beloved and my friend. I put the ring on my own finger and wear it to this day, next to my *RSL* ring.

I was recruited by UCLA to direct their Lesbian Gay Bisexual Transgender Center and moved to Los Angeles six months after Paula and I permanently separated. Several months after my move west, Paula returned to Florida—for about six weeks. And then she did the strangest thing. She went back to Michigan, the place she detested.

The sad part for me, which I believe was retaliation pure and simple, was that Paula forbade her sons James and Jonathan to have contact with me, knowing the power of the pain of the loss of my own children. She said if I attempted to contact the boys, she would charge me with stalking. Swell. I remain hopeful that one day those two young men, now in their 30s, will return to my life as my own children did. There's always room for more, and they are always welcome.

# 25.
# *A New Identity: Grandma*

1994

U.S. President: Bill Clinton
Best film: Forrest Gump, Pulp Fiction, Shawshank Redemption
Best actors: Tom Hanks, Jessica Lange
Best TV shows: Ellen; My So Called Life; Party of Five; Friends; ER
Best songs: I'll Make Love to You, Can You Feel the Love Tonight, Without You, You Mean the World to Me, Hero, The Power of Love
Civics: Nelson Mandela elected president of South Africa
Popular Culture: Skater Nancy Kerrigan attacked; President Clinton accused of sexual harassment; O. J. Simpson arrested in the killing of his wife; Kurt Cobain commits suicide; American Medical Association opposes medical treatment to "cure" homosexuals; Sheila James Kuehl is the first openly gay or lesbian person elected to the California legislature.
Deaths: Richard Nixon, Cab Calloway, Burt Lancaster, John Candy, Jacqueline Kennedy Onassis, Jessica Tandy

She stood at my front door, hands on the waist of her five-foot frame, defiant and sturdy. She was a small woman on the large covered porch of my turn-of-the-century Sears & Roebuck Victorian. I was expecting her. She sent an email to me the day before, Christmas Day, 1994, and asked if we could meet. Her email began with "Hi, Mom." So simple, so casual, so complicated.

Now she was twenty-two years old, my beautiful daughter, my Berit. I'd not seen since she was twelve. Her father and his parents kept us separated by lies, by miles, by years. But here she was, an adult, living in Dayton, Ohio, 1,500 miles away from her father's family's influence, standing on my porch in Ypsilanti, Michigan, with her husband at her side.

150

Seven months earlier I had moved to Michigan from Jacksonville, Florida, when I accepted the position of director of the Lesbian and Gay Program Office at the University of Michigan. Berit was married to Bill whom she'd met when they both worked at Disney World in Orlando. His parents lived in Dayton, so Berit and Bill moved there, just three hours south of Ann Arbor and Ypsilanti.

Berit and Bill, both in their early twenties, were married in December of 1993, the same weekend as World AIDS Day that year. (My mother and sisters were invited to Berit's wedding but I was not, so they didn't go, in solidarity for me.) I learned later that I wasn't invited because Berit feared there might be a nasty confrontation between her father's mother, Cynda, and me at her wedding. She didn't want to risk it. There's no way she could have known, of course, that I would never engage in such behavior, but now it was moot. (However, as a result, I staunchly believe that regardless of feelings and interactions, family should always be invited—and should show up—to events. You don't have to talk to someone if they're there but you can never undo an absence.) My AIDS guys surrounded me that day, held me, cared for me throughout the day, just as I always did for them. They were my family of choice, these dear men, and they were comforting me on the day of my daughter's wedding.


I was twenty-six when Berit was born. I'd never really given much thought to having children. When I was young, I'd hear my friends fantasize about marriage and children but it just never entered my thought process. It's not that it was a bad idea; it just was a non-idea for me. Getting married was my way to legitimately remain in the closet, that secret place where I slowly disintegrated. It wasn't something I'd ever wished for, like most girls. But pregnancy helped me feel as if I were involved in something good, something larger than myself. If I had to be married, I may as well go the distance.

"Jake! It's time! Now! Let's go!" We rushed to the hospital, the same one in which both he and his mother were born. As we checked in, he forgot my name. Not a good sign. Another reminder that something was amiss—like my life.

Drugs knocked me out as 8-pound 11-ounce Berit entered the world. It was 1973, before the various birthing methods gained popularity. When I regained consciousness, Berit was brought to me so I could see my little daughter, count her fingers and toes, and nurse her. I nursed her for six months—to the horror of Jake's mother Cynda who thought nursing was disgusting and "just plain wrong." Frankly, I would have nursed her for much longer than the six months, as I did her brother later, but I needed to go back on prednisone and azulfidine—medicine I'd taken for years—because the colitis had once again grabbed my gut.

The beautiful big blonde baby in my arms mesmerized me. Me, somebody's mother. Berit looked directly into my eyes and touched my face when she nursed, always, until she fell asleep. I had not felt a deeper love for another human being. She looked up at me with her huge brown eyes and my tears would fall, feeling a private serenity I never knew before. No judgment from this little person, no condemnation for being different, nothing but mutual love, full and complete and unconditional.

Berit was three and a half when Erik was born. In unstated jealousy, Berit wet her bed for a few weeks but as I reinforced my love for her and she felt secure once again, she became a model big sister. The three of us—Berit, Erik, and I—were a team. Jake was peripheral, generally absent or simply disinterested.

When Erik and Berit were three and six years of age respectively, my career as a mother, at least as a legal title, came to an abrupt end when custody was taken away from me. Of all the losses in my life, this was the most devastating and despicable. I felt as if death would come from my broken heart. At the ages of nine and twelve, when my children said they wanted no more contact with me, despair planted itself into my soul.

Now, in December of 1994, on my porch in Ypsilanti, Michigan, I was looking into my daughter's big brown eyes, for the first time in ten years. I always knew in my heart-of-hearts that my children and I would reunite. I anticipated it happening much later, perhaps when they were in their 30s. But here was Berit, at age 22, standing before me. As I opened the door, she looked me right in the eye.

"I'm pregnant and I have strong feelings for my baby. I want to know if you had the same feelings for me when you were pregnant with me." She was defiant! It was the gutsiest thing I'd ever heard, and I had no doubt that she knew the answer long before she ever asked the question.

"Yes, I did, sweetheart," I answered quietly, slowly. Tears welled up in our eyes as she gently, lovingly came into my arms. I pulled my daughter, my baby girl, against my body, into my heart and soul.

"Berit, I love you so much, and I've missed you terribly. The hole in my heart has been so huge without you."

"I love you, too, Mom, and I've missed you, too." As we cried, the others with us, Berit's husband Bill and my partner Paula cried with us.

Berit and I spent most weekends together for the next five months, rebuilding a relationship from such a strong foundation during the first six years of her life. When Berit went into labor in May of 1995, she called me from Sloan Kettering Hospital in Dayton. I raced down I-75, arriving at Kettering in less than three hours.

I was in the birthing room with Berit as she pushed and panted and pushed again. I breathlessly watched in awe as my granddaughter's head became visible. Her face, her shoulders, then her whole little body slid into this world. The doctor handed the scissors to me. "Cut the cord, Grandma?" I did, and then I held my first grandchild in my arms while the nurses did their work with her. I held her because I'd heard that the first hour of a baby's life is "angel time." If you hold a child during angel time, she's yours forever. I could not, would not, lose another child from my life, so I held my granddaughter, my Ellie, during her angel time. To this day there is a special bond between us. We both feel it without a doubt. Berit and Bill and Ellie moved back to Florida the next year. I went to Florida often to see them, and in 1998 I arrived just minutes after the birth of my second granddaughter, Candace.

Berit graduated *cum laude* from the University of South Florida, after overcoming tremendous challenges such as two small children and no money. She was always an outstanding student as a child. Because education holds such value for her, she found a way to go to school part-time for eight years, and to graduate with honors. My parents, my sister Bebe, and my son Erik and I were there to celebrate with her. I hosted her graduation party at our hotel and invited her father and his family to join us. Jake and his parents chose not to attend his daughter's hard-earned graduation nor the celebration party because *I* was going to be there. Jake never resolved his anger towards me, though we hadn't had contact in over twenty-five years, and his hateful feelings prevented him from sharing in his daughter's accomplishments. What a shallow jerk!

Berit and Bill divorced several years later. Bill was intimidated by Berit's growing intellectual life and success at the university. They were unable to communicate any longer in any meaningful way. Berit needed to talk.

"Mom, when you come to Florida next week for Grandma Mae's 100th birthday, can we carve out a few hours of alone time?"

"Of course, Berit," was my immediate response. I wondered—no, I was intensely curious about—what was on her mind. I played guessing games with myself. My first thought: *did I screw up somehow as a mother or grandmother?* My second thought: *is she considering divorcing Bill? What about the children* (remnants of what my mother wrote to me when I was divorcing Jake). My third thought, good lesbian that I am, was: *is Berit coming out?* I suspected the second, hoped for the third, couldn't think about the first. It was the second, divorce.

Six months later Berit shared with me that she'd started seeing Matt, one of her undergraduate religious studies professors (she was in graduate school now). They married in a very private quiet ceremony the following year.

I was there to support my daughter, for the birth of her daughters, for her graduations with her bachelors and masters degrees, for her divorce, and for her second marriage. I am deeply proud of Berit and I love her beyond words. I suspect she has her own set of struggles around my having left her as a child but at least we remain close. The door is always open as we each need to talk. In the meantime, I visit Berit and Matt and my precious granddaughters often, and my granddaughters know without a doubt that their grandma loves them fiercely!

154

# 26.
# In Search of History

## 1995

<u>U.S. President</u>: Bill Clinton
<u>Best film</u>: Braveheart, Apollo 13, Babe, Sense and Sensibility, Dead Man Walking
<u>Best actors</u>: Nicolas Cage, Susan Sarandon
<u>Best TV shows</u>: Cybil; The Drew Carey Show; Caroline in the City; JAG
<u>Best songs</u>: Kiss from a Rose, Water Runs Dry, Runaway, Candy Rain, Only Want to Be with You, I Believe
<u>Civics</u>: Oklahoma City bombing; O. J. Simpson found not guilty of killing his wife
<u>Popular Culture</u>: Rock and Roll Hall of Fame opens in Cleveland; Steve Fossett makes first solo transpacific balloon flight; first cloned sheep; University of Michigan hosts first-ever Lavender Graduation; Canada ends sexual orientation discrimination; Florida Baptist Convention boycotts Disney for extending domestic partner benefits to same-sex partners
<u>Deaths</u>: Howard Cosell, Jerry Garcia, Rose Kennedy, Mickey Mantle, Ginger Rogers

*The Weekly News*, or *TWN* as it was called, was Florida's statewide gay and lesbian newspaper for decades. I remember looking forward to reading each issue those many years ago: the drama *du jour*, the politics, the AIDS epidemic, Jesse Montegudo's book reviews, Bill Watson's editorials, Bike Daddy's ranting, and my own pathetically sweet articles and antics from when I was the executive director and lobbyist with the Florida Task Force, Florida's lesbian and gay civil rights organization. There were the far-too-numerous obituaries of young men, including my old Burdines Department Store friends, Tony and Richard, both of whom

155

died before they were twenty-five years of age. For nearly 30 years the *TWN* faithfully documented Florida's lesbian and gay history.

My doctoral dissertation, *Unheard Voices: The Effects of Silence on Florida's Lesbian and Gay Teachers in the Public School System*, was going to be published by Greenwood Press but some pieces of Florida gay and lesbian history needed further documentation. I was especially interested in reviewing the Bush-Trask era of 1981-1982. I contacted long-time editor Bill Watson at the *TWN* in Miami.

Bill was gracious in opening the archives of the *TWN* to me, none of which was computerized. He located the volumes of old papers I needed, then left me to my own devices in a private room. I was searching for specific information for my book but I found so much more. My own history as a lesbian, as a budding leader, as a Floridian, danced on the yellowing brittle pages of old *TWN*s.

I saw names and faces of people I had adored, some who I idolized, others after whom I simply lusted those years ago. I saw photographs of myself—a newly-out angry lesbian who had lost custody of her children and who jumped smack into the political fray as a result. I read about my early role as a leader and realized with time-trained eyes what I could have done, should have done, differently. But back then, thirty years ago, I simply didn't know. Like so many of my contemporaries, I was thrust into politics by an intense anger, fueled by the loss of my children. Without training, without role models, I led by ego, as so many of us did. Passion, and a need to create change, were deeply ingrained in my soul but my ego was the driving force, and it was my ego that eventually caused me to burn out. I'm grateful that I learned to do it differently. Over the years I've learned to lead through service rather than by ego, a concept I teach and try to model for my students.

As I continued my review of the *TWN* that day, I saw *TWN*'s first article describing an "unusual pneumonia striking gay men in San Francisco and Los Angeles," quoting the Center for Disease Control's June 5, 1981 *Morbidity & Mortality Weekly Report*. Reading that article took me back to a meeting in 1981 in the Coral Gables home of Jack Campbell, the owner of the now-closed Club Bath Chain. Many of us who directed gay and lesbian organizations around the country gathered that day to strategize about how to deal with this frightening new health issue looming over our heads like an ominous thunder storm.

I also saw the photo of the handsome face of my friend, Dan Bradley, who had been the president of the National Legal Services Corporation and the highest-ranking federal official to come out as an openly gay man. He died of AIDS at the age of forty-seven. I saw the 1981 photograph of the obnoxious fraternity boys at the University of Florida, my alma mater, who showed their butts in a collective moon-shot towards members of the UF student group called UFLAGS: the University of Florida Lesbian and Gay Society. The photo captioned the group as UFAGS.

That photo, in turn, caused me to recall a meeting with a group of students at the University of North Florida in Jacksonville, my graduate alma mater, in about 1991. The students wanted to stage an action at UNF without regard to the history that had paved the way for them to gather there in the first place. They were unaware of the consequences of similar previous actions. As I discussed the issue with this group, one impatient young man said, "You're too old to tell us about this stuff. What do you know anyway?" His words struck me hard, like a baseball bat to my head. Those words drove my need to teach young people about our history and about the giants on whose shoulders they stand. It is both imperative and critical that our future leaders know our—their—history. There is much to be researched and much yet to be written. Lesbian and gay history isn't really hidden, as suggests the title of the book *Hidden from History* by Martin Duberman and Martha Vicinus; it's available for the searching, in archives like those of *TWN*, the Stonewall Archives in Ft. Lauderdale, the ONE National Archives, the June Mazer Archives in Los Angeles, and other similar places around the country.

When I said goodbye to Bill Watson and left the *TWN* office that day, I felt a deep sadness for the passing of people and of time, yet I felt warm with the nostalgia of seeing photos of beloved faces from a time long past. I drove over to Haulover Beach on Collins Avenue where many years earlier I could be found waxing my surfboard, waiting for Miami's most perfect, albeit small, waves. Haulover, to my surprise, had become a clothing-optional beach (try hard as we might to remove the clothing of our lust-mates those decades ago). I did the only thing that seemed appropriate in the moment: I removed my shirt and let the sun wash over this old body as I fondly recalled yet another time and place on this road to freedom, and made a promise to no one in particular to continue to honor those who came before me by keeping their memories alive.

## 27.
## *Stalked!*

*I*'ve been stalked twice. Not the run-of-the-mill call-me-a-dyke-on-the-phone-and-hang-up annoying kind of thing—though that happened in Jacksonville, just days before the cross was burned on my yard and my car spray-painted with D-I-K-E by an ignoramus who couldn't spell *dyke*—but by real live people, requiring police intervention. Astonishingly, both of my stalkers were gay. Go figure!

Michigan has tough stalking laws so I rarely heard about anyone actually being stalked. My first stalker was a "typical" stalker who was acting out of "love," even when making very serious threats. Stalker #1 was a 68-year old woman who I had met about a year after I started working at the University. She was employed by the University but I didn't know where.

She seemed enamored of me right from the start. I looked different back then. I wore dresses and heels and makeup and contact lenses. I was once told that I was the best dressed lesbian on campus. I probably was, thanks to my partner Paula's tasteful assistance. Today I'm the sensible lesbian: no heels for which my back and legs are thankful, no dresses, no stockings, no makeup, and no contact lenses. Just me in all my comfortable glory as nature intended! Ah, the privileges of getting old!

Anyway, Stalker #1 started off casually by visiting me at my office every now and then. Since she was older, worked at UM, and seemed to be lonely, I always welcomed her. We would chat for a few moments and then she'd go back to work. Her visits, though, were becoming more frequent and she started bringing gifts to me, none of which I accepted. I asked her to consider making a financial gift to the Lesbian and Gay Office rather than spend money on gifts for me.

One Saturday as Paula and I were digging up tulip bulbs in our yard in Ypsi, I saw Stalker #1 drive by. She circled the block several times then drove away without a wave or acknowledgement. That baffled me so I racked my brain for the Perfectly Logical Explanation, that PLE we talk about in our social justice classes. I could think of none.

On Wednesday of the next week I received a package from Stalker #1. It contained very expensive winter boating gear—she knew my love of boating from our conversations in my office. A letter accompanied the gear. It read, *I know you're going to return this to me. There's only one way to do it. You must bring it to my house on Saturday* (a map was included). *If you do it any other way, you're going to make me do something we both are going to be sorry for.*

I called the UM police. I had just completed a series of training programs for them about sexual orientation and many came to see the LGBT office in the Michigan Student Union. I wanted them to know where we were located in case of an emergency. An officer who was tall and authoritarian in appearance, with a resonating bass voice, and who I knew to be very kind, responded to my call. When I showed the letter to him, he said, "I believe there's another way to return this package." He took the box, went to my stalker's office, and explained Michigan's stalking laws which were considerable. For good measure, I was given a UM police escort to and from my car each day for a week or so, but I never saw Stalker #1 again. However, it wasn't the last time I needed a police escort.


Stalker #2 was the president of a local gay and lesbian association which awarded scholarships to outstanding lesbian, gay, bisexual, and transgender students. The scholarships were presented at an annual awards ceremony in the Michigan Union. The room that year was filled for this wonderful celebration. Students, their parents, university officials, faculty, staff, and alumni were present. I opened the event with a brief welcome after which I introduced Stalker #2 by name. His job was to welcome folks on behalf of his organization then present the awards.

Stalker #2's initial words were fine. It was what he said as he introduced the awards that created the problem. I had helped design the new award application because the old one asked irrelevant and probably illegal questions regarding identity, such as race, sex, and age of the applicants. The awards were based on achievement, not identity, so I removed the identity-based questions. The form was then approved by

160

his organization's board of directors.

Stalker #2 began his unscripted talk. "I hate these new application forms," he said. "You can't tell who's black or who's white, who's male or female, or who's a top or a bottom!"

*What????? Top or bottom??? Did he really just say that???* I froze. I don't remember another word or even the remainder of the event. I went to my office after the ceremony and sent an email to Stalker #2 and his organization's board, most of whom were in the audience that evening and heard the same words I heard. I wrote, "While I love working with your organization, [Stalker #2] will never again speak before any event I produce. I am appalled, embarrassed, and outraged at his fully inappropriate words."

Stalker #2 was removed from the organization's board the next day, and chose to quit the organization altogether the following day. He blamed me for his fall from gay leadership in Ann Arbor and began harassing me with emails and phone calls. I ignored him.

One day a few months later two parents came to my office in the Michigan Union. Their seventeen year old son was a swimming champion at a local high school and had just received a full scholarship to college. Their son's eighteen year old boyfriend was one of my students. Stalker #2, a man in his mid-forties, was apparently harassing the young swimmer so my student referred the family to me for help. The son had spurned the Stalker's attention, so during a recent swim meet, the Stalker placed fliers of a photo of the young man on all the cars in the parking lot, announcing the young man's homosexuality. I encouraged the parents to file charges against Stalker #2. Somehow he learned of my meetings with the parents and again blamed me for his fall from grace. He sent emails to me with threats of blowing up my house. He also slashed all four tires on my car. His harassment became so serious that I executed a court order for him to stay away from my home, my family, my car, my office, my staff, and myself. Hence, the police escort.

In the summer of 1997, I was recruited by and accepted a position at UCLA. My going-away party at UM was packed with folks from all over campus and Ann Arbor. An unfamiliar man entered the room and handed a paper to me, a subpoena. Stalker #2, that ass, had filed charges against me for discrimination based on sexual orientation! Since he was a gay

161

man, I, a lesbian, must not like him. He was right! I didn't like him but it had nothing to do with his sexual orientation or mine! I didn't discriminate against that sleaze bucket. I was merely appalled at his ongoing mean actions for which he would not own responsibility.

Luckily, the campus attorney was at my party. She said, "Don't worry about this, Ronni. We'll handle it. You go on to UCLA." The UM lawyers represented me in court. The judge threw the case out and fined Stalker #2 for filing a frivolous suit. Stalker #2 is now serving time in prison for child sexual abuse. He should only rot there.

The moral of the story is this: if you're feeling yucky because of someone else's behavior, trust your feelings. Don't look for the PLE, the Perfectly Logical Explanation. There is none. It's real! Seek assistance immediately! Trust your gut.

## 28.
# Go West, Old Woman

---

1997

U.S. President: Bill Clinton
Best film: Titanic, As Good As It Gets, The Fully Monty, Good Will Hunting
Best actors: Jack Nicholson, Helen Hunt
Best TV shows: King of the Hill; Just Shoot Me!; The Practice; Port Charles; South Park; Ally McBeal; Family Matters; Dharma & Greg
Best songs: Don't Cry For Me Argentina, Say You'll Be There, All By Myself, Unbreak My Heart, Men in Black, I believe I can Fly
Civics: U.S. shuttle joins Russian space station; U.S. Appeals Court upholds California ban on affirmative action; Timothy McVeigh sentenced to death for Oklahoma City bombing
Popular Culture: O. J. Simpson found liable on civil suit; Heaven's Gate cult members commit mass suicide in California; The Notebook by Nicholas Sparks published; National Consortium of LGBT Campus Resource Center Directors founded; Florida Constitution Review Committee rejects including sexual orientation for protection; Ellen Degeneres outs herself as a lesbian on her sitcom.
Deaths: Princess Diana, Jacques Cousteau, John Denver, Mother Theresa, James A. Michener, James Stewart, Gianni Versace

---

*I* enjoyed working at the University of Michigan. I was well connected to students and staff and to the community, and I loved living in the Ann Arbor area. I especially appreciated the change of seasons, something I never experienced in Florida. I remember when I first moved to Ann Arbor. It was May, 1994, springtime, and gloriously colorful with flowers I'd never seen before. A colleague told me, "There are no bad days. Just bad clothes. Go to Eddie Bauer now and get yourself a good winter coat while they're on sale." I did. The coat said it would keep me warm to thirty-below. I bought it, hoping with my Florida-self that it would never be that cold, but with the warmth of that coat, I thoroughly enjoyed the winters. The golf courses became cross-country ski courses, their bunkers became moguls. Reflections of sunshine in the snow during the days and the street lights at night provided hues I'd never seen. And for some strange reason, perhaps because of the cold on my skin, hot chocolate never tasted so yummy!

I would have stayed at UM, ensconced in Student Affairs and LGBT work, but I also wanted to teach. The UM School of Education wasn't crazy about having an open lesbian on it's faculty back then. UCLA recruited me to direct their LGBT Center, accompanied by a lecturer appointment in the Teacher Education Program. I would teach a course on social justice and cultural diversity in education. Perfect. I accepted the UCLA position.


I met Kim at a conference in Chicago in the spring of 1997, just after Paula and I separated for the last time. Kim's bright sea-blue eyes, thick mop of blonde hair, and quick hearty laugh caught my attention. We ran into one another several times on the day we met. That evening we went to the conference's social event and danced and talked and danced some more. She walked me back to my hotel room and stayed longer than either of us had expected, wrapped in each other's arms. She flew back to her home state the next morning. Our time together was way too brief, but we knew we'd see each other again.

Over the next few months we travelled back and forth to each others' homes in our somewhat neighboring states. I was in Michigan, Kim in Kentucky. When I accepted the job at UCLA, Kim made the drive across the country with us—my cat Sarah and me—in my lavender Chrysler LeBaron convertible.

We spent the last night in Ann Arbor at the Hamilton House Hotel, the place I stayed when I first moved to Ann Arbor three and a half years earlier. Kim and I were never particularly quiet in our nighttime activities. Because we were happy to see each other and excited about embarking on an adventurous road trip, that last night in Ann Arbor was no exception. In the morning there was a note under our door that read: *Sounds like you had a great time last night!* Yep! We sure did!

We said goodbye to Ann Arbor and headed out towards Indianapolis, acknowledging the hometown of *Rebel Without a Cause* star James Dean because we saw the sign that said so. We stopped in St. Louis and rode the tram to the top of the Arch, marveling at the expansive view of the Mississippi River from north to south, across the river to Illinois and over the city of St. Louis. We took a driving break in Abilene, Kansas, near fields of sunflowers taller than ourselves. We visited the Abilene Civic Center and ate cookies and drank lemonade made by three elderly women who chatted at the front desk. In eastern Colorado, we drove up to the top of Pike's Peak, over 10,000 feet in elevation, then back down to spend a day at the United States Olympic Training Center in Colorado Springs. We went white-water rafting down the Arkansas River in Canyon City, Colorado, to the breathtaking 1200-foot granite Royal Gorge crevasse. At a roadside café where we stopped for lunch, a deer put her head inside the car in search of snacks. My convertible was easy pickings for her.

We drove up the Rocky Mountains to Independence Pass at the Continental Divide which was already dusted with snow though it was only early September. The road down the other side took us into Aspen. Along the highway into Utah, we stopped at roadside tables where Native American women and children were selling trinkets. Red rocks and sculpted mountains provided backdrops for their small portable businesses. We hiked around Bryce National Park, took photos at the Fairyland Canyon sign, then drove across the plains of the Painted Desert to the north rim of the Grand Canyon.

My cat Sarah stayed in her crate on the floor of the back seat during the drive so she wouldn't blow out of the car since we never put the top up. The ride was just too beautiful, and it was much easier to take photos with the top down. We stayed in motels along the way each night, letting Sarah out of her crate, fixing her litter box and a meal service (as she saw it, I'm sure). She was quite the trooper, and, I say with great admiration, an awfully good sport.

We arrived at the north rim of the Grand Canyon the weekend before it was to close for the winter. We had no reservations for hotels anywhere across the country because we didn't know where we'd be on any given night. So far, a week out on the road, we had no trouble finding rooms. But on the last weekend of the season at the north rim of the Grand Canyon, nothing was available. The hotels were fully booked as was the campground. The manager of the campground told us about a clearing in the woods not far from the entrance to the Grand Canyon. There were no amenities at all but we could sleep in our car there without hassle.

The clearing was just off the main highway, very close to the entrance to the Grand Canyon park area. We weren't the first folks in there but we were able to find a spot that felt safe and unobtrusive. There was one—well, more than one but this was the first—problem. We were in a convertible, probably resembling Thelma and Louise more than we cared to. I put the top up for our camp-out and let Sarah out of her crate. She howled, scolding me, no doubt, for this imposition, used her litter box, ate some food, then howled some more. I put her back in the crate. She stopped the racket and settled down. The temperature began to drop. Into the 60s, now the 50s, approaching the 40s fast. We were wearing shorts. The trunk of the LeBaron was very small so we traveled with very few items. We gathered what clothing we had, got into our seats in the car, and covered ourselves with all of our belongings. We nestled in for the remainder of the cold night.

After a few moments of quiet, I heard a loud whisper, "Sanlo." Kim always calls me Sanlo. "Sanlo. I heard something." I didn't care. I felt perfectly safe because Kim was a large, strong, athletic woman. I thought if anything went wrong, she'd handle it. I never figured her for a chicken,

"Sanlo." She always says my name as if it were a full sentence by itself. With purpose. "Sanlo. I think there're bears out there." Bears? How did she know? Well, she's from rural Kentucky. Maybe they have bears there and she's familiar.

"Sanlo. The bears are gonna come through the convertible top. I just know it. We're screwed this time."

"Kim, why do bears want us?" I innocently asked in my regular, non-whispered though somewhat amused voice.

"Not us," she was agitated but still in a loud whisper. "Sarah. They can smell her. They want her." Bears want my cat? Oh no they don't! I

166

stayed awake all night long to make sure the bears didn't get into the car to get my beloved Sarah. Kim—damn it!—slept like a baby.

Because I didn't sleep, being awake for sunrise wasn't a problem. Just before daybreak, I drove us over to the park entrance. I woke Kim up and we walked out onto the rim with dozens of other watchers, cameras in hand. As the sun began to rise, so slowly, gently peaking over the hills on the east side, the west side of the Canyon began to glow. I was stunned! I meant to take lots of photos, but really, I just stood there in awe of the grandeur I was experiencing, of the golden light of day that was surrounding us, of the warmth of the sun that was quietly, quickly embracing us. I knew the trip was for this.

Once the sun was fully awake, so were we. We continued on our trek west toward Los Angeles. We drove through Zion National Park then onto Highway 15 that took us across the desert to Las Vegas. The desert was hot, really hot. Over 100 degrees. I was so tired from not sleeping the night before that I was groggy and possibly experiencing heat exhaustion. I thought I needed to drive faster, hurry up to Vegas and cool off in a hotel pool. It didn't occur to me to just pull over, drink some water, put the top up, and turn on the air conditioner. By the time we got to Las Vegas, Kim and I were collective wreaks, both overheated and completely sleep-deprived. Sarah desperately needed to exercise her legs. We pulled into the Flamingo Hotel around 2 P.M., got a room, catered to Sarah's needs, then went to sleep until the next day.

After a good night's sleep and a refreshing dunk in the pink pool at the Flamingo, we became shameless tourists. We ate everything in sight at one of those pig-out buffets, and had a fun time at the slot machines. The following day we headed out on the last leg of our trip, the five hour drive to Los Angeles. We arrived just in time to meet my parents and the moving van at my new apartment near UCLA.

Kim stayed for a couple of days, helping me get settled in Westwood. We spent hours walking around Westwood Village in search of celebrities. After several successful celebrity sightings and a good visit with my folks, Kim flew back to Kentucky. She talked about moving to Los Angeles to be with me. I loved her and missed her but I knew I would make her life a living hell if she moved out to LA. I can be terribly high maintenance, and Kim was too gentle a soul to have to deal with the likes of complicated drama-queen me. But to this day, Kim is one of my all-time best friends. I am so blessed to have this wonderful woman in my life and I'll road-trip with her any time, anywhere.

# 29.
# *Marathon!*

Six months after I had turned 50, I moved to Los Angeles to work at UCLA. As part of my seemingly on-going mid-life crisis, I decided to run a marathon. I'd not done that before, not that I ever really thought about it, but I had run a few 5Ks and once even came in second in my age group in a 10K in Jacksonville. After a few months of contemplating such a ridiculous feat, I went to a running store, The Starting Line in Marina del Ray. If I had any real intention of running a marathon, I'd need running shoes.

While in the store I noticed an advertisement for the National AIDS Marathon Training program. I had been away from AIDS work for four years and this seemed like a good way to do something for the HIV community while remembering those far-too-many dear friends I'd lost. The advertisement guaranteed that I'd be prepared to run the Marine Corp Marathon in Washington D.C. in six months. *Yeah? Prove it!* I signed up.

I did indeed run the Marine Corp Marathon six months later. What a great way to enjoy Washington D.C.! I saw every national monument in town because I peed behind each one on the route! I subsequently ran three Honolulu Marathons and the Los Angeles Marathon, plus four training marathons over the next eight years, all part of the National AIDS Marathon Training Program. People always asked about my time. How did I do? Frankly, I didn't care about my time. If I finished a 26.2 mile marathon on the same day I started, standing up, I won! And I did, every time!

I'm hyperactive, so I can—and did!—become bored during marathon training. Usually by about the twelfth mile tedium would set in, so I started running with a tape recorder in my hand and talked to myself as I trained. During my few years as a marathoner, I wrote one book and six articles, and then reminisced about my life, much of which was the material for this book. As I prepared to write my memoirs, I read the transcripts from those tapes and thought: *Really? Glad I remembered that one!*

I quit running marathons when my feet rebelled at the thought of one more event. I remember being at about mile 24 in the 2004 Honolulu Marathon, running back up the Diamond Head Road hill towards the finish line at Kapiolani Park, thinking, *I am NOT having fun, even in this beyond-gorgeous setting. This is it.*

In the spring of 2008, I began to review the transcripts of my tapes that I made while running. I sat at my desk with my left foot in a cast from the surgery to repair the nasty heel spur I acquired because of my marathonly accomplishments. As I wrote, I pondered this question: *why doesn't anyone ever tell you that marathons are 26.2 miles long because that's how far the first guy, Phedippides, ran from Marathon, Greece to Athens in 490 BC, before he dropped dead???* I think I'll stick with golf where I can ride in my purple golf cart and not hurt my feet any more.

# 30

# *Reunion: Perspectives of Mother and Son*

---

## 1998

<u>U.S. President</u>: Bill Clinton

<u>Best film</u>: Titanic; Shakespeare in Love; Elizabeth, Saving Private Ryan, Life is Beautiful

<u>Best actors</u>: Roberto Benigni, Gwyneth Paltrow

<u>Best TV shows</u>: Dawson's Creek; Sex and the City; The King of Queens; Will & Grace; Felicity; Becker

<u>Best songs</u>: My Heart Will Go On, Ray of Light, You're Still the One, Crush, The Boy is Mine

<u>Civics</u>: White House sex scandal between President Clinton and Monica Lewinsky; House impeaches President Clinton

<u>Popular Culture</u>: Titanic wins a record 11 Academy Awards; Citizen Kane tops the American Film Institute's list of 100 all-time top films; Viagra approved by FDA; last episode of Seinfeld; *The Hours* by Michael Cunningham published; Matthew Shepard, gay University of Wyoming student, killed.

<u>Deaths</u>: Gene Autry, Sonny Bono, Frank Sinatra

---

The letter began, *Dear Dr. Sanlo or Mom. I don't know what to call you, but in trying to find myself, I need to find you. I hope it's okay...* My son. My Erik. No contact for 13 years and now a letter. My heart beat hard and my hands trembled as I held the paper. My son, who I had not seen since he was nine years old. My son, now a 22 year old man, needed to find his mother. Me.

Erik was such a sweet little boy, tender, smart, quick to laugh, deep with feeling. He didn't cry when he was born. He just seemed happy to be where he was in that moment. I used the then-popular Leboyer method of childbirth which prohibited any forcing of the birthing process. We used minimal lighting while a Mozart violin concerto played softly in the background as Erik made his way into the world. At 9 pounds 11 ounces, Erik was a large baby, but ironically he, like his sister, was a small child, the smallest among his peers in those early years of school.

Erik was three years old when I lost custody of him and his sister. I saw my children intermittently until he was nine and his sister was twelve. While I maintained contact with both children with cards for every occasion, accompanied by checks that I knew were cashed, there was never a response from either of them. I knew, though, that it was not a response I needed from them so much as it was my desire to let them know they were in my heart. I always included my contact information so they could find me if they ever needed me. It worked. That's exactly how each found me years later.

I have wonderful little-Erik stories. He was a beautiful baby and I have the first-place ribbon he won at a Beautiful Baby contest when he was a year old to prove it! When Erik was nearly three, he modeled a little-boy Pierre Cardin tuxedo in the Burdines Department Store Easter show. How he loved that tuxedo! As his sister Berit modeled a pretty frilly pink dress which she detested, Erik knew he looked like a million bucks. He followed Berit up the stairs to the runway, strutting like a little pro, that is, until he saw the giant Easter bunny sitting at the far end of the runway. As Berit was trying to figure out a way to jump into the big bunny's arms, Erik was terrified of that giant furry bunny-monster! Erik froze at first, then screamed. He turned around, ran back down the runway as fast as he could, all the way to the dressing room. Ironically, though, for as upset as he was about that gargantuan bunny, he went ballistic when it was time to take off the tuxedo. He simply would not do it! He loved how he looked and felt in it. Fashion trauma in the toddler set! His sister, on the other hand, couldn't wait to get out of all that pink material and back into her play shorts!

I remember one day in the Downtown park of Disney World in Orlando. Erik was about five years old. He climbed a Jungle Jim apparatus in the children's arena there, slid down the pole, and ran to me in a grassy area from where I watched his acrobatics. He jumped on me, grabbed my ears, and kissed me all over my face, so happy to be with his Mom. Mothers nearby said they wished their sons were as demonstrative as mine. What they didn't know was that my son and I saw one another only periodically, so this day was special for us.

Erik loved Michael Jackson, the pop singer. In 1984, Michael Jackson performed in Jacksonville. I couldn't afford to take my children to the concert so eight-year old Erik asked if he could have something that at least looked like Michael Jackson. We went to the mall. Erik selected black nylon balloon-material pants, a tight black mesh tank top with silver thread running through it, silver socks, a spiffy black-and-silver belt, and the glove, the silver Michael Jackson glove. Erik was so proud! He loved that outfit and wore it the entire weekend, even when I returned him and his sister to their father's parents' house.

Two weeks later, because I had visitation every other weekend, I noticed that Erik was very sad. He told me that his grandmother Cynda made him take off his Michael Jackson clothes. then cut them up with scissors right in front of him. How cruel! I was so angry! Angry with Cynda, angry with myself for not being able to protect my children from her. I did the only thing I knew would get her attention: I charged her with abuse. I won the case but the battle was lost. The Southern-cracker legal system was securely in place, with cronies and office partners as lawyers and judges. It took only a few more months before the children told me they weren't going to see me anymore.


Fast forward thirteen years to Thanksgiving, 1998. The Los Angeles International Airport. My mind's eye saw a nine-year-old boy with a quick smile and a gentle spirit. I had no photos of Erik as an adult, no way of knowing who this young man was or how he looked beyond the fact that he was my son.

When I received Erik's initial letter several months earlier, I wrote back to him immediately. He had no email and he wasn't ready to talk with me on the phone, so we used the old-fashioned snail-mail method of writing letters for a couple of months. Finally, we spoke on the phone. His deep voice didn't match the nine year old boy in my heart's vision. I invited him to come to Los Angeles for Thanksgiving. He accepted. He had a large family in California—grandparents, aunts, uncles, a cousin, and a mom who remembered the wonderful little boy and who missed him beyond words. When he told his father's family that he would not be with them for Thanksgiving that year because he was coming to see me, his grandmother Cynda said, "I just don't understand why you want to go there. Your mother will just take you to West Hollywood and make you gay." Right. The magic wand with the lavender fairy dust.

It was 1998, before Homeland Security and heightened scrutiny at airports, when families and friends could still greet travelers at the gates of arriving planes. I was there, at the gate, looking for my nine-year-old boy, or at least a man who looked like the nine-year old who lived in my heart. I was excited and frightened and anxious, knowing that soon I would see my baby child, my precious son.

I recognized him immediately. He was still a small person, still had some of that nine year old impish gleam in his eyes. My beautiful son walked right into my arms, no words spoken. When Erik finally pulled his tear-streaked face from my neck, his first words were, "Every time I smelled that perfume, in the grocery store or the mall, I looked all around to see if you were there, Mom." My son, finally home in my arms…


*The Meeting: Erik's Story*
*(written by Erik)*


*The nervousness took hold once I boarded the plane. It was a flight I'd taken a dozen times before, long ago, when I was a small child. I knew everyone I was going to see there, but I didn't really know them, not after all these years.*

*Thirteen years since I last saw her. I found my seat on the plane. What do they think of me? I'm the one who rejected them for so many years. What was I about to walk into? Seriously, what could they possibly think of the son, the grandson, the nephew, the cousin who ignored them for thirteen years, and now it's Happy Thanksgiving, pass the yams? But it felt right, so here I am, on the plane, the flight. It all starts in five hours.*

*I was the one who took the first step. I had to be the one to do it.*

*There had been no contact between my mother and me since I was nine years old. Nine years old at the breaking point. Nine years old. Whom do I choose? Which parent do I pick? Do I choose my mother, who I barely knew and who moved so often from place to place? Or do I choose my father and stay in the house in which I grew up? After all, my mother lost all rights. You're out and you're proud, Mom. Congratu-fucking-lations.*

*During my teens years, all that I had of a relationship with my mother were the cards I'd receive on each birthday and holiday. Barely anything hand-written in them. I always figured that the real purpose for the cards was my mother's way of making sure I had her address. My grandmother was so paranoid that she made both my sister and me save every card as potential evidence, fearing some impending lawsuit to come. You know, the big one. That actually helped my mother's intentions because there was never a time when I did not know where to find her. Not that I would, though. Not for years to come.*

*Halfway through the flight I began to regret what I was wearing. It was the first time I would see my mother in over half of my lifetime, and I had on a ratty (but stylish) pair of twill jeans and a long-sleeve t-shirt. Heather grey.*

*In the letters I wrote to her, I tried to explain where I lived and what my situation was. I later learned that she had been using her connections through the university system to check up on me once she heard I had started at the University of Florida in Gainesville. Her own Alma Mater. I'm sure what she saw were poor grades, low attendance, and academic probation, until I flunked out completely. After that there was no way for her to find me.*

*I remained in Gainesville, near the university, after I bombed out. I was pretty heavy into the drug culture there, and I enjoyed it. I had always been such a good kid in high school but all that changed when I left home. I didn't care that I failed out of college. The only reason I even went to my classes most of the time was to deal. Now that I didn't have school to worry about, I was free to focus on my more lucrative endeavors. I lived in an apartment with three friends, Queen Diamond, Monique, and The K Fairy, each of us active in the business. In the life, really. It was a time of altered states with large quantities of drugs flowing in and out of our apartment. We each had our favorites. Mine*

175

*was ecstasy followed by a little GHB.*

*This lasted for about nine months, then things started to unravel.
One night, Queen Diamond was arrested for selling acid at a club. When
Monique, The K Fairy, and I found out about Queen Diamond, we
immediately cleaned house. We were hearing things about people we
knew, friends of ours, some who were busted, some under surveillance,
some who did business at my house. Buyers quit buying. Sellers feared
getting raided so they dosed their stock. People close to me were taken
from their houses, some in handcuffs, some on stretchers. My roommates
and I turned on each other. Queen Diamond made a deal with the cops.
A sting. In my apartment. I literally threw my things into my truck and
drove away in the middle of the night.*

*These are among the things my mother is about to find out about
me. I didn't plan to withhold any of it. Besides, I'm sure she suspects that
I got a little wild, but I think the reality will surprise her. But hey, this
trip is all about answers, as much for her as it is for me. For my whole
life, I had been well versed about my father's side of everything that
happened in our family. What I didn't know was my mother's side. What
I didn't know about my mother could fill a book. Mom, why did you move
so much? Why did you take us to rallies? Give me picket signs when I
was six years old that said ERA YES? So many questions I had for her. I
remember the visitations when I was young. Every other weekend. I
didn't know why she did some of the things I'd see her do. But the real
questions that I had were more about myself rather than about her.*

*Leaving Gainesville, I went to the only place where I felt safe—Key
West. I couldn't go home. The shame of what I had just been through was
too much for me to face my father and his new wife, stepson, and new
baby daughter. I went to Key West. I took enough pharmaceuticals and
barbiturates with me to end my life. Just in case. But soon after I got
there, I knew I wasn't going to commit suicide. I flung the drugs into the
sea.*

*During the next few months I lived on the streets in Key West. I
spent my days sitting along Duval Street, selling my hemp-weave jewelry
to the tourists. Some days I made enough money to sleep a night or two*

176

*in the youth hostel. When I didn't, I slept underneath the bridge at Bahia Honda. What I found there was clarity, peace, and a community of transients who showed me how to live out of the mainstream. I realized that what I'd been through made me strong. I found the courage to go home. While I loved being there in Key West, I knew it was not my place.*

*It had been a few years since I spent any time at my father's house—my house, the house in which I grew up. His wife had changed everything with which I was familiar. My father called it nesting, but I saw her for the insecure little girl she was. She systematically removed anything and everything in the house that could remotely be connected to when my mother lived there. I saw her fear about any idea that associated her husband with his ex-wife. There was only one thing left from my childhood, from my mother: the couch. And here I lay, sleeping on it, wondering what happened.*

*I was only somewhat prepared for the fallout. As far as my father was concerned, I had been missing for months though he hadn't tried to find me. And now here I was, asleep on the couch when he and his wife came home from a concert. Things were calm initially. Conversation was no more than "where've you been" and "what are your plans." The yelling came, but not from whom nor at whom I expected.*

*I heard my father's new wife yell at him in their bedroom at night. "Is he paying us rent to stay here?" "He's a loser. I don't want him around my baby." "You get him out of this house!" And he did. I had been there for two weeks when my father told me to leave. He spoke very mechanically. There was no disappointment in his voice when there should have been. I was confused. I distinctly remember countless times when he himself told me that this will always be my home, that I would always have a place here, no matter what. When one is told something repeatedly by someone he trusts, it's easy to believe it. Granted, it hadn't felt like my home since I got there, but now I knew it was not. In fact, this wasn't even my father. This is not the man that I grew up admiring. Respecting. Not anymore. No, that person was not in charge here. Fear rules this house. Her fear that I'll infect her family. His fear that he'll die alone if he doesn't placate her, even at the cost of his own son. My family was someone else's now.*

*Less than a month after coming home, I found myself back on the*

177

*street again, but it was okay. This was a much-needed confirmation for me. For the few years that I lived in Gainesville, away from my family, I suspected that I didn't belong any longer. I also realized that every event in my childhood was orchestrated, almost choreographed. I chose nothing. Hearing hateful things about my mother constantly for all of my childhood had great impact on my perception. All along, I believed my father was the victim of the worst theft and that I was the target of a predator. All I knew about my mother was exactly what my father wanted me to know. Now here I am, another one of his outcasts. Just like my mother. For the first time in my life I truly felt lost. Being homeless again didn't bother me. I just didn't know who I was anymore. So, in an attempt to find myself, I wrote a letter to my mother. I was twenty-two years old.*

*It was the week of Thanksgiving, 1998. As the plane pulled up to the gate, I knew she would be right there. My heart pounded as I walked up the gateway. I recognized her, could see her face in the expanding crowd. The uncertainty of how I would react was holding me until the last possible instant. I walked to her, tears welling in my eyes, feeling her arms surround me. I was suddenly struck by an unexpected familiarity—the gentle whiff of her perfume. I was a nine year old boy again, and safe in my mother's arms.*

# 31.
# Wearing My Genes

March, 2005. My son Erik, who lived in Orlando, visited me in my hotel room when I was at a conference in Tampa. It was two weeks before my birthday. Mom," he started, clear and confident. "There's something I need to tell you, kind of a birthday present to you. I'm gay." As he said this, he extended his arms to me and flicked both wrists. Classic!

"Oh my precious son, I know," I said with genuine gentleness.

"You do? How long have you known, Mom?"

"Years, honey. Since you were a year old and refused to wear your little plaid shorts with a striped shirt. And for sure when you were two years old and cried your heart out when you had to take off that adorable little Pierre Cardin tuxedo you were modeling for the Burdines Easter Pageant. A baby fashion queen!"

We hugged each other. "I love you, Mom."

"I love you, too, Erik, and I'm very proud of you."

A month later the phone in my office at UCLA rang. It was Erik. still in Orlando. "I want to tell Dad," he said. His apartment was only a few miles from his father who still lived in our original house, the house in which Erik was raised and from which he'd been kicked out a couple of years earlier.

"Erik, please, listen to me. Be careful. Call your dad or write a letter to him, but please don't tell him in person." Erik is a small man, about 5'8" and 130 pounds. His father is over 6 feet tall and 200 pounds. From somewhere in the cobwebs of my brain, I heard his father's words from years ago: *if my son tells me he's a faggot, I'll get a gun and kill him.* I was frightened for Erik.

Two days later Erik called me again, his voice small and shaking. "I told Dad, Mom. I called him on the phone and told him. He told me never to contact him again. Mom..."

Erik moved to Los Angeles two months later.

179

Berit divorced her first husband Bill and married her college professor, Matt, a few years prior to Erik's coming out. Strangely, her father Jake, had a giant emotional transference and fully identified in some sick way with Bill. As a result, Jake excluded Berit from his family. Berit told me, "Dad said I was just like you. He lost it when I said 'Thank you!'"

Today both Berit and Erik have lives that are good and healthy and full. They're successful in their very different ways, surrounded by family and friends who love them deeply. Too bad Jake and his parents and his young daughter, their half-sister, are missing out on these two truly wonderful people. Two children disowned. How stupid can one man be?


When Erik turned thirty-three, he said he wanted to write a letter to his father. "Mom, I want him to know how good my life is here in Los Angeles, how happy and successful I am. I'm just afraid he won't read it, that he'll throw it away unopened."

"He might, Erik, but you have no control over that. If you want to write to him, do it for yourself, then let the letter go with love. Write whatever you want to tell him. Write what your heart tells you to say. Write it for yourself, not for your dad. If it's time for him to read it, he will. Don't stop trying to communicate because of what you think your dad may or may not do." Erik hugged me.

"How can you be so open-minded about this, Mom? He was so mean about you, yet you always encourage Berit and me to not burn bridges. How do you do that?" I thought about Erik's question. How do I explain that it took years of therapy, commitment to a 12-step program, a deep and abiding belief in a loving God, and the ability to forgive myself and others? So I merely said, "I know what it feels like to be separated from you and your sister. The day may come when your dad wants to reconnect with you. Holding a grudge serves no purpose. That's all. You have no control over how your father feels and acts, but there may come a time for reconciliation, and you and Berit need to be open for it."

"You're amazing, Mom."

"Well, regardless, if you write the letter, be sure to include a photo of your new Mercedes." If Jake insists on being an ass, let him eat his heart out!


Here's an ironic thought: I believe Jake's mother Cynda is a lesbian and that's why she hates me so much. In fact, I wouldn't be surprised if Jake were also gay. I believe homosexuality is genetic and runs in Jake's mother's family.

Case in point: Two years after I had come out, I brought my girlfriend Karen with me from Tallahassee when I took the children home. It was the first time someone besides the children and I were in the car. Cynda walked out to the car to greet us in her syrupy-Southern phony way.

"Y'all brought the chil-run home rhat on time." And then Cynda stopped. She looked at Karen for a long minute, and then did something very strange. She invited us into the house! She *never* invited me in and, really, I never wanted to go in, but now curiosity got the better of me. We *had* to go in. What on earth was going on?

We followed Cynda into the house as she focused totally and completely on Karen. She invited us into her office where she dug deep into a drawer and removed a neatly wrapped stack of letters. Cynda handed the letters to Karen.

"I had a girlfriend once," she said with great calm. *What???* You could have knocked me right over. Did I just hear her say she had a *girlfriend*????

"She looked just like you," she said to Karen. *Holy COW!!!* Karen was trying to be polite. I was on the sidelines trying not to reveal my hissy-fit. This is the woman who has single-handedly made my life a living hell for years with no sign of a let-up. She had a *girlfriend*??? I was dumbfounded!

Cynda continued. "We were girlfriends before I married Big Jake. Her name was Maria. She moved to Daytona Beach right after high school. She wanted me to go live there with her. These are her letters from back then."

Okay, I had to try to breathe now. Cynda the Homophobic Witch had a lesbian lover? Karen was very polite. I was in shock and missed much of the conversation. Damn! Cynda a lesbian??? *Of COURSE, she was.* It all made sense to me know. She hated me because she hated herself! I was the embodiment of that which she detested in herself!

It was all very difficult to comprehend, but I had the woman's name. I did some research among my lesbian friends in Orlando and found Maria. She confirmed to me that she and Cynda were indeed lovers many years ago. When Cynda would not move to Daytona Beach to be with her, they broke up. For whatever reason, Cynda married Big Jake, the young town drunk, shortly thereafter. Wow!

Jake's possible gay history isn't as clear. In college I occasionally thought Jake might be gay. He often pretended to be a gay man, enacting all the "stereotype" behaviors with his jazz musician buddies. After we divorced, he apparently had a male friend for whom he bought a car, according to mutual acquaintances, and even his children were asked by classmates in school if their father, the school band director, was gay.

I do believe that the self-hatred that runs in that family translates into homo-hating rhetoric that has not released its hold on those people. Thank God my children escaped.

# 32.
# *I'm White*

---

## 2000

U.S. President: William J. Clinton

Best film: Gladiator, Chocolat, Crouching Tiger Hidden Dragon, Erin Brokovich, Traffic

Best actors: Russell Crowe, Julia Roberts

Best TV shows: Malcolm in the Middle; Survivor; Big Brother; Yes, Dear; Gilmore Girls; Ed

Best songs: Bye Bye Bye, American Pie, Everything You Want, I Knew I Loved You, It's Gonna Be Me, It's My Life

Civics: Cuban boy Elian Gonzalez at center of dispute, returns to Cuba; U.S. sailors killed on attack of Navy destroyer Cole in Yemen: America Online buys Time Warner, biggest merger in U.S. history; abortion pill RU-486 wins U.S. approval

Popular Culture: Kathy Lee Gifford quits Regis; Oprah Winfrey debuts *O* magazine; Ellen Degeneres and Anne Heche break up; Richard Hatch wins Survivor; Vermont is first state to offer civil unions to same sex couples; Sheila James Kuehl is first openly lesbian or gay person elected as a California senator.

Deaths: Steve Allen, Victor Borge, Alec Guinness, Hedy Lamarr, Walter Matthau, Tito Puentes, Jason Robards, Charles Schultz, Pierre Trudeau

---

*I'*m white. I figured that out when I was 53. You'd think after looking in a mirror for 53 years I'd have known I was white, but it took that long for me to really get it. I grew up in white North Miami Beach, before Cubans and Haitians and Viet Namese and others sought freedom there, when African Americans still lived primarily in the Liberty City area of downtown Miami. North Miami Beach was white and Jewish and no one thought twice—or much—about it.

183

My first actual encounter with African American people beyond Mary, my family's housekeeper, occurred in my residence hall at the University of Florida in the fall of 1965. There were a number of Jewish women from Miami who lived on the third floor of Rawlings Hall. Most of us were eighteen years old and away from home for the first time. One day three African American women who also lived in Rawlings saw two of us Jewish women in the study lounge. Without word or permission, they walked up to us and began sifting their fingers through our hair! I didn't know if I was more stunned from the boundary violation or that one of the women was really hurting my head.

"Where's your horns?!!?" she demanded to know.

"What??? What are you talking about? Let go of my head!! You're pulling my hair! Ouch!" I was furious! "Do you want me to do that to you???" I hollered at my hair-sifter.

She stopped, looking at me even more strangely than before she dove into my hair. "Where are your horns?" She asked again, though without fingers to head.

We had no idea what they meant, so we started to talk. We learned that the Black women had always been told that Jews had horns. They wanted to see our horns and were truly shocked that we had none. Once we talked it out, we were able to have discussions about our various cultures. What began as a serious violation of personal space became an ongoing fascination and friendship about differences and similarities. And so began my education on race and on being an ally, which helped tremendously when the National Guard planted itself and the curfews squarely in Gainesville in 1968 during what was called "the miniature Black Power invasion." Like many gay and lesbian people in the 1960s, it was easy for me to stand with my African American friends in the civil rights movement. But stand for myself as a lesbian? Never!

Almost forty years later I attended the Social Justice Training Institute (www.SJTI.org), founded and facilitated by my friends, Vernon Wall, Kathy O'Bear, and Jamie Washington, all openly gay or lesbian. Because of my work in higher education, I'm rarely a participant at seminars and trainings; I'm usually the facilitator. So I took a break, both for my mental health and for my need to reflect, and signed up for the weekend session with SJTI. I sent my check, bought my plane ticket

184

from Los Angeles to the dead-of-winter Massachusetts, and just went, without reading the brochure.

I arrived in Rockwellian-appearing Springfield on a snowy day in January and met my dear friend Judy Albin from Penn State. As the weekend began, I noticed that most of the participants were people of color, as are Vernon Wall and Jamie Washington. Of the 40 or so participants, Judy and I were two of just a handful of white people. For some reason, perhaps because of the facilitators, I thought I was attending a sexual orientation workshop. Turns out it was more of a racial immersion seminar. Nothing happens by accident, although it seemed like one initially, and I felt guilty for even thinking that. I should have been thrilled that the workshop was so diverse, but this was before I found out I was white.

I was supposed to be there that weekend. No doubt about it. I needed to learn about my whiteness. More importantly, I needed to learn about my privilege of being white. I always believed I was an ally for people of color, from that day in the study lounge in Rawlings Hall at the University of Florida those years ago when I had my first real and meaningful conversation with the three Black women, and when I stood with the African American community in Gainesville, Florida during the 1960s civil rights marches. But I never really thought about what it meant to be white and to have privilege because of my race until that workshop. I discovered—much to my surprise—that one of the privileges of being white was that I never had to think about it! That knocked the wind out of me!

And what about the privilege of heterosexuality? I'm aware that there has not been a day in my life since I was eleven and in love with Annette Funicello that I haven't thought about being a lesbian. Not one day. Yet heterosexual people never, or at least rarely, think about their sexual orientation. They just don't have to—that's the privilege of being heterosexual, of being male, of being wealthy, or able bodied or Christian. You just don't have to think about it until—if ever—you get whomped upside the head with a lack of privilege. I learned that weekend to be aware of my subordinate identities—lesbian, woman, Jewish, aging—and my dominant identities—white, educated, (mostly) able-bodied. Awareness. My head was spinning.

185

As I returned home from that weekend from SJTI, I was stunned at what I saw while traveling back to Los Angeles, what I allowed myself to see: passengers frisked at the airport because of their skin color; an African American man questioned about his first-class ticket; a white man in a business suit who received excellent service from the white female flight attendant; the white female sitting next to him who received little service; the man across from her who wore a turban and appeared to be of Middle Eastern descent who received no service. All around me, everywhere, examples of social *IN*justices that touched peoples' lives in both subtle and not-so-subtle ways. Awareness—once you have it, it becomes imbedded in your psyche and your heart. My awareness of my whiteness sure did.

Awareness is but the first step, then action. My awareness and my consciousness now guide me to right action. I have no choice. I'm aware, and I'm white. I must speak out for and with my sisters and brothers who are different from myself, just as I want them to do for me.

## 33.
## *Emotional Transformation, or*
## *Whomped Upside the Head*

### 2001

U.S. President: : George W. Bush

Best film: A Beautiful Mind, Lord of the Rings: Fellowship of the Ring, Shrek, Monsters, Inc., Moulin Rouge

Best actors: Denzel Washington, Halle Barry

Best TV shows: My Wife and Kids; The Fairly Odd Parents; Six Feet Under; The Amazing Race; Law & Order: Criminal Intent; Reba; Scrubs; The Bernie Mac Show

Best songs: Hanging By a Moment, All For You, Lady Marmalade, Fallin', I'm Real, Don't Tell Me

Civics: September 11th attack on the World Trade Center in New York; anthrax scare; global warming on the rise; artificial heart implanted in a man

Popular Culture: The Producers take a record 12 Tony awards; *John Adams* by David McCullough published; Federal judge upholds Florida law banning gays from adopting children; Netherlands is first country to grant full marriage rights to same sex couples; same sex marriage becomes legal in Canada

Deaths: Chet Atkins, George Harrison, Jack Lemmon, Anne Morrow Lindbergh, Carroll O'Connor, Anthony Quinn, Isaac Stern, Marc Bingham, Lance Loud

*R*ebecca and I met at UCLA shortly after I arrived in the fall of 1997. The University of California Board of Regents was about to vote on the recognition of domestic partnerships. The concept had been under discussion for a while, and testimony had been heard at the Regents' meeting the previous July. Rebecca was one of the esteemed faculty who

187

spoke. Her story was extraordinarily compelling: her long-time partner had to keep working after a serious cancer diagnosis to maintain her health insurance, creating tremendous stress that contributed to an early death. Rebecca was not allowed to add her partner to her UCLA insurance plan. Rebecca had testified in July and was invited to return to testify again before the Regents that October. We began dating the following January, and I moved into her house near campus eight months later.

Because Rebecca owned the house in which we lived and because her salary was easily twice mine, I deferred to her in all things—friends, restaurants, vacations, therapist—lest she reject me. My family was thrilled and impressed that my partner was a scientist. Once again, I felt I had made it into the stability of middle-class, but, as before, it was due to someone else's accomplishments, not mine.

As an experienced co-dependent, I was hypervigilent about Rebecca's thoughts and feelings, likes and dislikes, and made sure I had the same. Her friends were mine; I had none of my own away from UCLA. In fact the only place I felt strong and grounded and successful was at work. After two years, I was losing my personal self again. I knew if I didn't leave her, I would either fade into the woodwork forever, or explode. I left. Sadly, this was the usual script for most of my past relationships. Nothing changed. Same relationship, different face.

After Rebecca and I broke up, I needed to find friends in Los Angeles. I joined a lesbian social organization called Women On A Roll (WOAR) that was directed by an extremely creative woman named Andrea Meyerson. Andrea invited me to be on the board of WOAR which provided the connections and activities I needed to finally feel like a member of a vibrant social community.

Rebecca and I had been separated for just over a year when she called me. Though we both worked at UCLA we somehow managed to avoid each other for 13 months. We had parted after three years of struggling to maintain a relationship, struggling to pretend that everything was fine. Rebecca was extremely busy with her research and I was extremely busy directing the UCLA Lesbian Gay Bisexual Transgender Center, so we had little time together. Somehow, though, away from the realities and busyness of life, we managed to vacation well, whether snorkeling at Black Rock Beach in Maui or driving on the sheep-infested roads of New Zealand. But at home we were toxic for each other. When we broke up, I moved out of Rebecca's house to an apartment on campus at UCLA as a Faculty-in-Residence. I retired from UCLA to my retirement house in Palm Desert in October of 2010.

"Hi, Ronni. It's Rebecca. Just called to say hello. I've been thinking about you." Surprised and caught completely off guard I said, "Well hey there. How are you?" I was genuinely happy to hear from her.

"I'm actually very well. I was wondering if you'd like to get together for coffee sometime." We chatted a while longer and decided to meet for dinner that very evening.

Rebecca, who was always so tied up in her shorts about damned near everything, sounded calm for a change and, well, fun. I knew she had a great sense of humor, but it was always so tightly controlled, as was much of everything in her life. That evening, though, she was downright pleasant. I was happily surprised, and enjoyed our casual, familiar bantering. After dinner I walked her to her car. She was going to a meeting of some sort, something about codependency.

"Want to go with me?" she asked.

"Sure, why not?" I hopped into her car. If something she attended could help her get a grip, then perhaps I needed to be there, too, though I didn't really know why. Just something inside of me said I should go.

We entered the room in the church where the 12-step meeting for co-dependents had just begun. I observed perfectly normal-looking people saying some of the stupidest stuff I'd ever heard—about bad relationships, taking people hostage, controlling others by being silent or loud or selfish or a thousand other things. Control, unhealthy relationships, silence, pain—and then something about one day at a time, recovery, self love. I had no idea what was going on, the words swirling in my brain, but I knew without a doubt that I belonged there, no, *needed* to be there. That was ten years ago. I've hardly seen Rebecca since, but I continue to go to those meetings, and I always find truths about myself which I've learned to honor.

Over these past ten years I've come to understand how much of what I experienced in childhood set me up for so many failed relationships. I didn't trust or love myself so how could I possibly trust or love another? The underlying reasons were twofold: having colitis and being a lesbian.

With the diagnosis of colitis at such a young age, my body often failed me, to my extreme embarrassment. I was so angry with myself. I was fecally incontinent in high school and college, so I never knew if that gassy feeling was going to be a puff of air or diarrhea. It could be either, and it didn't matter where I was. The worst place, of course, was at school, but sometimes it happened in the car (I always carried a towel in the car just in case) or at the beach. I just never knew. I was too embarrassed to tell anyone. Not my parents. Not my doctor. Not a friend. I became hyper-vigilant about my body and felt so alone in dealing with issues of my health. (The colitis has been in remission for twenty years, thank God, but because of the diagnosis at such a young age, I'm at high risk for colon cancer, but I recently decided to banish that negative thought from my mind.) The colitis was the way my body betrayed me when I was young. My sexual orientation was the way my heart betrayed me.

Being a young closeted lesbian in the 1950s and 1960s was terrifying, so much so that I told no one, ever, like my secret about colitis. The Big Secrets of our lives. They cause such deep isolation for fear of discovery. I truly believed back then that if anyone, especially my family, knew about my sexual orientation, they'd lock me up and throw away the key. Those words were my deeply held belief. *They'd lock me up and throw away the key.* I made assumptions about how my family and friends would treat me based on my own internalized self-hate.

When I finally came out in 1979 and told my husband that I was a lesbian, I lost custody of my children. My greatest life-long fear was instantly validated: tell my truth and the people I love leave me. I told the truth and lost my children. And that was how I entered into every relationship I had with anyone. *If I tell you my truth, you'll leave me, so why bother?* I promised no one a rose garden, and I let no one into my heart. There was no such thing as real intimacy for me. Intimacy meant sex. If I was sexual with someone, I didn't have to talk. Perfect. When the sex waned, I created chaos of some sort or other, either by silence or drama, and left. It happened that way every time, with every person. Very predictable.

I've been single since March of 2001 when Rebecca and I broke up. I've dated a few women over these years but I've chosen to remain single, to build and nurture my friendship network, and to work on being my own beloved. I'm in a healthy place today. It took a great deal of work to get here, and it takes a lot of maintenance to stay in this place but it's worth it. Today I have wonderful friendships with women all over the country, and I'm lovingly connected with my family of origin, my children, and my grandchildren. I live life one day at a time and truly understand that my Higher Power, my God, is always with me. I'm never alone, and I'm unconditionally loved. As the saying goes, life is good. Truly.

## 34.
## *Extreme Makeover, 2003*

2003
U.S. President: George W. Bush
Best film: Lord of the Rings: The Return of the King, Finding Nemo, Mystic River, Lost in Translation, Seabisquit, Master and Commander: The Far Side of the World, Monster
Best actors: Sean Penn, Charlize Theron
Best TV shows: American Chopper; Queer Eye for the Straight Guy; Las Vegas; Two and Half Men; Cold Case
Best songs: Crazy in Love, Beautiful, Where is the Love?, Rock Your Body, When I'm Gone
Civics: Saddam Hussein captured by U.S. troops; Space shuttle Columbia explodes killing all seven astronauts
Popular Culture: Clay Aiken wins American Idol; Hubble telescope detects oldest known planet; The *Da Vinci Code* by Dan Brown, and *Harry Potter and the Order of the Phoenix* by J. K. Rowling published; U.S. Supreme Court overturns sodomy laws, Lawrence v Texas
Deaths: Johnny Cash, June Carter Cash, Althea Gibson, Katharine Hepburn, Bob Hope, Gregory Peck, John Ritter, Mr. Rogers, Morris Kight, Sarah Pettit

*I* sent a letter and a video to the television program *Extreme Makeover*. I wanted them to "do" me before I went back to Florida for my daughter's graduation from college, a feat that took her eight years to accomplish. I was so incredibly proud of her for keeping her commitment to her studies even though she had had two babies in the process, absolutely no money, and limited transportation. Not only did she graduate from the University of South Florida with honors, she received a full scholarship to continue with her graduate work there in history and religious studies.

192

Remarkable! So as I prepared to return to Florida to celebrate with her, I decided I needed an extreme makeover. The following is the application letter I sent to the producers of the show.

*I am going to Florida to celebrate my daughter's graduation and to host her celebration party. All of her family, including those crazy fundamentalists, meaning her father, his new family, and his parents, are cordially invited. I'm a lesbian, the frumpy kind, short hair and blotchy skin, and if my neck hangs any lower I'll trip over the damned thing!! None of this is good because I'm single, post-menopausal, and would like to attract a partner. The history is that when I came out as a lesbian in 1979, I lost custody of my children, then ages three and six. We became estranged when they were nine and twelve. I missed all of their events and rites of passage including their graduations from high school and my daughter's wedding. We recently reunited and she's graduating from college at the age of thirty. I want to look kick-ass good, both for her and, well, to look better than her father's new wife, though I don't really know why because I don't care about her. Nonetheless, I offer you both a physical and social challenge if I am a recipient of an Extreme Makeover.*

*I'm up for whatever you want to do to me: face lift, neck lift, body sculpting liposuction, laser eye work, tattoo, personal trainer. I want to have a tight muscular old bod—maybe I can't have six-pack abs any more but I bet I can muster up a four-pack! I want my granddaughters to look at their lesbian grandma and know that we as women can do anything we set our minds to, including re-work our bodies if we're not happy with them. It's our feminist prerogative!*

*Actually, I can't remember a time in my life when I was happy with my body. I always felt like a hot-female-jock-body-builder riding around in a fat, acne-scarred, bespectacled vehicle. For the past 10 years I have been the most self-conscious about my chicken neck, though the cystial acne and resulting scars were a big bummer. There have been times in my life when I simply did not want to be seen in public. My self-esteem was shot. It's better today, at least enough to allow me to complete this application. With an Extreme Makeover, my life will change in the most*

193

*primary of ways: my self-esteem will be elevated, I hope. I would like to look in the mirror and see the reflection of the beautiful woman that I know I am instead of the one I see.*

I had to write about family.

*My parents are terrific. Mom wears the pants in the family. Dad either doesn't know or just doesn't mind. Dad's very proud that he was the third American soldier into the Dachau concentration camp to liberate people during WWII. My parents are lovely people who cherish their children deeply. I have a great relationship with my siblings. My sisters are my best friends. My biggest— only—issue is that they're both so slim and beautiful. My brother is too. I remember relatives would visit us in Miami Beach from up north and say how beautiful my sisters were, how handsome my brother was, and what a great personality I had. I HATED having a friggin' great personality. I wanted to be beautiful like my sibs! My two sisters are tiny. I was 131 pounds in the 7th grade! By the way, they also have great personalities!*

*I am single. Since my husband and I divorced in 1979 and I came out as a lesbian, I've had many relationships. None took. It always felt like the same relationship, different face. I have lots of acquaintances and many close friends who are my family of choice*

I then had to address the issue of addictions. Did I have any?

*I am not addicted to anything except relationships. I'm codependent but I go to support group meetings, and I'm learning to love myself. Because my self-esteem has been so low, I tried to get warm fuzzies from others rather than accepting and loving myself exactly as I am. It's the neck thing!!! But I'm trying... Anyway, I drink only occasionally, don't smoke anything, and don't do drugs of any sort.*

Finally, a summary:

*My story is a good one, don'tcha think? Nice, smart, funny, intelligent woman with a great national reputation in higher education with a focus on sexual orientation and gender identity work, lost custody of children when they were very young due to her being a lesbian, estranged from children for years. Reunited when daughter was pregnant. Got to cut the cord when first granddaughter was born. Present when the second was born. Reunited with son when he needed to find me as he was searching for himself. Now very close with my children and want to look like a million bucks for my daughter's graduation. It's a heck of story. And it's true!!!*

That was my letter with my application to *Extreme Makeover*. I wasn't selected. A year later, I did the Los Angeles thing and "had work" on the chicken neck. (I wanted only to look age-appropriate, not like one of those Beverly Hills-type women with severe face lifts who look like they stood in a serious wind tunnel.) I'm 64 now and am finally comfortable in my own skin, which is a good thing because here's what happened recently: My two sisters and I had our photo taken together which I put on my *Face Book* page on the Web. I received an email from a friend who wrote, *Your sisters are so beautiful. You look so happy.* They are, and I was. I can smile at that comment now instead of resenting not being one of the *beautiful* sisters.

By the way, my ex-husband did not show up for his daughter's graduation. The reason? Because I was there! Too bad, because even without the extreme makeover, I looked damned good that day!

# 35.
## Moving Day—Again

Once Jake and I divorced in 1979 and I moved from the home I'd known for seven and a half years, my transient lifestyle began, though I certainly did not plan for that to happen. My first apartment was in a family complex only a couple of miles from Jake and the kids. It was affordable and safe, and I intended to stay there for a long time, but when I got fired from Burdines Department Store, I could no longer pay for a two-bedroom place. I moved into a studio apartment in Orlando.

As money became even tighter, I moved from the studio to a shack in an African American community near Winter Park. I was unemployed and on food stamps. Soon, though, a friend hired me to direct a women's clinic in Deland, Florida where I moved into an apartment in a lovely old Victorian house near Stetson University. I had been on my own for less than two years. I hated moving but I had no choice if I intended to keep a roof over my head.

I was hired by the Florida Task Force and lived with a woman who was an assistant school superintendent in that Baja-Georgia part of Florida. She was a very generous host (and became my lover) as I pursued a career as a legislative lobbyist for lesbian and gay issues. After I quit the Task Force, she quit the school board and we moved into a house with three other women near Orlando and in close proximity to my children. I lived there only a few months because we broke up. I moved in with my next girlfriend, the sex worker.

I didn't know her line of work at first. We lived in her mobile home about 40 miles west of Daytona. The property was lovely: five acres of old Florida scrub, secluded enough for wild lesbian parties which we never had because we were too isolated to have any friends. I was unemployed while she worked nooners with her A-list clientele: doctors, elected officials, business owners, scientists, and anyone from whom she needed a service, like the guy who delivered the 300 linear feet of cedar chips for her driveway. That's when I discovered her occupation.

196

"Sorry, she didn't leave a check for you," I said when he delivered the chips while she was in town on "business."

"That's okay. I don't need a check. She'll just pay in her usual way." He emphasized regular with a wink. *Usual way? Huh?* I suddenly got it. I couldn't stay with her.

Unemployed, I lived on the streets of Orlando and then Key West for a short time until some friends found me. They took me back to Orlando where I lived with a sales-person minister-to-be with a killer smile. She refused to discontinue her long-time affair with a "straight" married woman while we were together but I didn't really care. She hated it when my children came to visit, about *that* I did care. She and I split up and I moved aboard my boat.

My boat, the *Curious Wine,* was home to a cat, a dog, and two lesbians. We lived in Jacksonville, Key West, and Miami Beach. I had to sell the boat after I was fired from my job in Miami. We moved back to Jacksonville and I rented a house in the dilapidated Springfield area of Jacksonville. We were robbed twice so we moved to an apartment in a safer neighborhood, close to the St. Johns River to be near the water.

After we separated, I moved into a garage apartment in the San Marco area of Jacksonville, then a garage apartment in Avondale, then a small house in Riverside. Several months later I moved in with a middle-aged middle-class respectable executive director of a large social services agency who owned her own home. She loved to cook and was a celebrated hostess. But when the young man who lived with us died of AIDS, neither of us knew how to talk about it. All we could do was go to work. She had an affair. We split up.

I stayed with some friends until I got over the shock then moved in with a gorgeous-but-nuts mental health counselor who was too, too hot in bed. If we'd kept having sex without attempting conversation, we might have lasted a little longer than the eighteen months we were together. She tried to run me over with her car. I moved to yet another small, cheap studio apartment.

My next lover was waiting in the wings, Ms. Perfect Trophy Wife, who never left the bedroom in the morning without full makeup regalia and perfectly coiffed hair. We rented a house in the San Marco area of Jacksonville. A year later I was hired by the University of Michigan, moved to Ann Arbor, and lived in a shared apartment until I could buy a house and send for her and her sons. We separated after two years. I moved into a tiny apartment near the house. We got back together for about six months then separated again, which meant another move to yet another apartment.

I moved to Los Angeles to work at UCLA. I lived in a faculty apartment adjacent to campus for a year, then in my-girlfriend-the-scientist's house for two years, then back to campus as a Faculty-in-Residence. Thirty years and far too many moves, not counting the places where I lived or stayed for only a few days or weeks, places I've thankfully forgotten.

I share this experience of extreme transiency to emphasize and honor my resilience and my ability to survive. Ironically, though it doesn't appear to be so, I dislike moving and envy my family and friends who are so stable. As I reflect on all these moves, though, I realize that they served a very important purpose: each move kept me so busy, so emotionally occupied, that I had no time to feel my feelings nor mourn the repeated and ongoing losses in my life. I was too busy packing, unpacking, painting, and decorating, anything to not feel the pain.

Today I own my own little writing-and-golf retreat home in Palm Desert. I retired to this place, but who knows what's in store for me in the future. I'm always ready for that next adventure.

# 36.
## The Day My Uterus Fell Out

2006

<u>U.S. President</u>: George W. Bush

<u>Best film</u>: The Departed, Babel, Letters from Iwo Jima, Little Miss Sunshine

<u>Best actors</u>: Forest Whitaker, Helen Mirren

<u>Best TV shows</u>: ESPN Saturday Night Football; Monday Night Football; Men in Trees; Smith; Six Degrees; Heroes; Brothers and Sisters; Ugly Betty; 30 Rock

<u>Best songs</u>: Walk Away, Sorry, Talk, SexyBack, Unfaithful, Stupid Girls, Buttons, My Love

<u>Civics</u>: Hezbollah fires rockets in Israel; Bush renews Patriot Act: FDA approves Gardasil, a vaccine that prevents cervical cancer; Pluto loses status as a planet

<u>Popular Culture</u>: New Jersey legalized civil unions; Same sex marriage legalized in South Africa

<u>Deaths</u>: James brown, Gerald R. Ford, Betty Friedan, Ann Richards, Maureen Stapleton, Coretta Scott King

---

*My* golf game usually sucks. In fact my golf score and my bowling score are astonishingly similar. Neither is good. That October day was no exception. My scratch-golfer-very-patient brother and I were playing at the Knollwood Golf Course in Los Angeles. As I approached the 17th hole, I felt my tampax slip. *What???* I asked myself in my head while trying to look as if nothing was happening. *What was THAT!!?* I took inventory. No big deal, just a slipped tampax. I just need to push it back up, I thought, as I wiggled unnoticed, I hoped.

*WAIT! NO! WAIT!* If my tampax slipped, I'm REALLY in trouble! I've been post-menopausal for 10 years! A tampax hasn't been inserted

199

into my love-cavity since March of 1997! It was 2007! *What's going on down there???* Still trying to look bland.

The 18th tee, the green, the hole. Finally! I drove the golf cart like a crazy person up to the clubhouse and directly to the women's room. My brother almost fell out of the golf cart, but, bless his oblivious little heart, he asked no questions.

Feel. Giant squishy ball. Coming out of my vagina. Big tumor! Cancer! I'm dead meat! I'm a lesbian and I'm being punished for having sex with so many women. Now it's gonna kill me! I frantically called my doctor.


Later that afternoon, after a thorough examination, my primary care physician explained that I'm neither dying nor being punished. My uterus was prolapsing—that's medical talk for falling out, or at least trying to escape! It usually happens to women who have had large babies in the past and are now post-menopausal. I qualified. (Though both of my children are small adults, they were big babies at birth—Berit was 8 pounds 11 ounces, Erik was 9 pounds 11 ounces.) I probably needed surgery. A hysterectomy. My doc referred me to a gynecologist, Dr. Janine Rahimian, who specialized in robotic gynecological surgeries. I elected to undergo a full hysterectomy because Dr. Rahimian also found a tumor (it turned out to be benign) in one of my ovaries.

"You'll be the third person to undergo a hysterectomy with DaVinci, our surgical robot. No big incisions through muscle, no scars, and no six-to-eight weeks of recovery—probably. And if something goes wrong in the surgical suite, we can still do it the old-fashion slice-you-up-on-the-spot way." Well, maybe those weren't Dr. Rahimian's exact words but that's what I heard her say. Regardless, I was intrigued, and since I believe in donating my body to science while I'm still in it, I agreed to a date with DaVinci.

The UCLA surgical suite was prepared. DaVinci was cranked and I was ready to go. Dr. Rahimian was at the dash board of the computer while I was in an anesthesia-induced sleep. The surgery took place on a Wednesday. I went home the next day. Two days later, on Saturday, I went to a party though, admittedly, I was moving rather slowly. The

200

following Tuesday, less than a week after the surgery, I bought myself a sports car. Not one pain pill was needed, and I felt terrific! Truly amazing!

Two years later I had vaginal reconstruction—just *SO* Los Angeles though the reason was not Los Angeles-typical, meaning it wasn't cosmetic. My rectum and bladder, and then my small intestines, were prolapsing in and down and out, just as my uterus had done two years earlier. My guts were falling out again! We older women lose elasticity in the vaginal wall, so things cave in, or prolapse. Another gynecologist, Dr. Tarnay who specializes in vaginal reconstruction (some specialty!) did the repair. He put my organs back where they belong and then rebuilt the vaginal lining with a mesh bio-material—pig, to be exact. Oy! Such a deal for a Jewish girl. Regardless, at my advanced age, Kosher or not, at least one part of me looks like a twenty year old, even if you can't see it!

## 37.
## *Visiting Jacksonville*

*It* was April 2008. Jacksonville. My adopted home town. So many ups and downs of my life happened there, so many dear friends taken by AIDS. Much of Jacksonville and Northeast Florida still seemed beautifully uninhabited, with visible coast line, scrub forests, wild palms, and the spectacular St. Johns River. It felt good to be "home."

This trip, because of Lavender Graduation, was especially sweet for me. When I was at the University of North Florida (UNF) as a graduate student, from 1987 to 1996, nearly all of the lesbian and gay people there—students, faculty, and staff alike—were squished in a giant overcrowded closet. All except Tom Serwatka. As a student I was seriously out of the closet, so most gay folks I knew at UNF avoided me like the plague, fearing guilt by association. But not Tom. Brave Tom courageously came out as a gay man and as a person living with AIDS many years ago, and made it to the top as a vice president at UNF.

I gave the keynote speech at the University of North Florida's inaugural Lavender Graduation, the celebration that honors the lives and achievements of lesbian, gay, bisexual, and transgender (LGBT) students. I founded Lavender Graduation at the University of Michigan in 1995 because I wanted LGBT students' last interaction with the university to be a positive one. (Today many schools including UCLA host similar events.) The University of North Florida, my graduate school alma mater where I earned my masters and doctoral degrees, was initiating this wonderful celebration.

I waived my usual speaking fee that weekend because UNF is my alma mater and because I strongly supported the work of the talented young woman, Emily Rokosch, who founded and managed the UNF LGBT Center. Emily worked incredibly hard and at tremendous odds to grow that office, in the Deep South—*the golden buckle of the Bible belt*—in Florida where there are still no legal protections for LGBT

202

people. (I was so impressed with Emily that I hired her and brought her to work with me at UCLA. Sorry, UNF.)

Many old friends attended the Lavender Graduation that evening. Among them, Condom Commando partner Donna Zimmerman; my beloved friend Frieda Saraga, her husband Len, and their son Scott; Dr. Minor Chamblin, the UNF sex education professor; UNF Vice President Tom Serwatka; and lesbian-elder Vickie Wengrow. Many others from the LGBT community were there as well and it was wonderful to reconnect with so many beloved sweet faces.

The true highlight, of course, was witnessing the seven graduating students who participated in this first Lavender Graduation. What brave young people they were, to have the courage in redneck Northeast Florida to stand and be recognized for being out and proud at UNF. Only one student was accompanied by a parent, his mother. The other students said their parents would never attend such an event. And one young woman—Leni Akapanitis—who had been a tremendous help to Emily and the UNF LGBT Center, was the recipient of the inaugural *Ronni Sanlo Student Leadership Award*. I cannot begin to describe how deeply touched and honored I was that such an award was created in my name.


A few days after I returned to Los Angeles, I received this email from Vicki Wengrow:


*Ronni,*

*Your presentation, your presence, getting to benefit from your good work in support of our next generation, and being drawn to gather with others with whom we both share family ties, and more...Well, all I can tell you is that Saturday night was a HUGE gift of warm fuzzies to me. Thank you, thank you. You have been acknowledged as among the top 20 lesbian academics (in Curve Magazine) who are paid to work in academia on behalf of queers. Your energy is obviously powerful, and I'm sure, as you put it, you 'drive everyone crazy.' I've always admired you—and continue to—for putting your all into doing 'the work,' and in doing it your own way, with or without other people's approval or company, even at times when we had very different priorities. And I'm happy that you are led (driven?) to use the great energy and the great 'sechel'* (Yiddish for common sense) *you came in with, to do much more than one person's share of 'tikkun ha olam'* (Yiddish for the Jewish mandate to repair the world.).

*Many warm fuzzies back to you,*
*Vicki*


Thank you, Vicki. I've done this work over the years because I had no choice: I was called to do it, as were (and are) so many of us. I now understand the reason for all the challenges I've experienced throughout these years. Without the challenges, there simply would not have been the impetus for change. Our young people deserve our hard work and our attention. I am blessed to have been able to give them both.

## 38.
## *This Unintended Path*

*I* wanted to be a Rabbi when I grew up, but I was told that girls cannot be Rabbis. The best I could hope to be was a Rabbi's wife.

I was a music major at the University of Florida and intended to become a high school band director. I became a band director's wife instead.

When I came out as a lesbian in 1979 and lost custody of my children, I didn't know what I wanted to be. I was too enraged to make that decision! Nothing worked out as I had dreamed. I became a wild and risk-taking activist until I fell from exhaustion, from the anger that fueled my life.

My career path moved in a variety of directions. I was fired from many jobs in Florida because of my sexual orientation. Eventually I was hired by the State of Florida to work with people with AIDS. The pay was low but the benefits included continued education. I was able to earn a masters and a doctorate from the University of North Florida free of charge. In 1994, I was hired by the University of Michigan to direct their Lesbian and Gay Programs Office and became a new professional in higher education at the ripe old age of forty-seven.

May 1994

During my first month at the University of Michigan I was asked by a nurse to come to the UM hospital because a student had been admitted as a patient. He wanted to talk with me. As I entered the room, I saw a pale young man lying in the bed, covers up to his mouth. He looked as if he were ten years old. I walked over to his side and took his hand.

"Hi," I said softly. "I'm Dr. Ronni."

"Hi, Dr. Ronni," he said in a small quiet voice. "I'm Robert. I'm a sophomore and president of my fraternity, or I was until I tried to kill myself." He took a deep breath. "I read about you in the paper. I know you just got to Michigan but I need to talk to someone who will understand."

"What would you like me to understand, Robert?" I asked.

Another deep breath, tears welling up in his sky-blue eyes, Robert said, "I'm gay. God, I've never said that out loud before. I'm gay. I've been living in a horrible hell of secrets and silence for so long and I feel so alone. It just hurts my heart. I tried to stop the pain by stopping me." He was in the hospital because his suicide attempt had failed.

His parents were on their way to Ann Arbor. Although Robert was frightened, he had asked them to come. Robert's father was a retired military officer and former football player, his mother an elected official in the conservative state in which they lived. They were Republican and Catholic. Robert sobbed. "They'll hate me. I know it. I'm such a disappointment to them and I can't bear that." He cried, he talked for a while, and I listened, bearing witness to his pain along with the tiniest bit of courage he was beginning to muster.

Robert's parents arrived, both tall, well dressed, obviously powerful people. Robert's mother ran to him, held him, but said little through her tears. She made way for his father, a large man who appeared to be in nearly as much emotional pain as his son. With a gentle voice unexpected of a man his size, he asked, "What's going on, son?" Through his tears and with a deep breath, the young man said, "Dad, I'm gay and I don't want to embarrass or shame you and Mom." The big man scooped his son in his arms and held him close. Incredibly, and unexpectedly, he said, "Son, if you're gay, you get out of this bed and be the best damn gay man you can be."

I wrapped my arms around Robert's mother as we cried together. I suspect she was crying because the moment was both frightening and tender. I cried because I missed my own children so much, and marveled at how blessed this family was to have one another. I felt so privileged to be sharing this time with them.

Robert graduated from Michigan two years later. He went on to Harvard Law School and is a successful attorney today. When he graduated with his bachelor's degree, he dedicated his honors thesis to me. That cherished manuscript which Robert signed is in my office to this day as a reminder of one young man's courage to survive.

November 2004

I first met Tracy when I was the faculty guinea pig, I mean, chaperone, on a camping trip hosted by the UCLA Recreation Department's Outdoor Adventures program for new students. Twelve first-year students, three Outdoor Adventure staff, and this old Jewish dyke who detests tents, set out on a three day camping/kayaking trip to Santa Cruz Island off the coast of Ventura. I noticed Tracy right away. She reminded me of a hundred young lesbians with whom I've worked over the years. Tracy wasn't out to anyone yet, so she avoided me like the plague throughout the trip, until I was elected to take her to the airport when the adventure concluded. In my car for the ninety minute ride from Ventura Harbor to Los Angeles International airport, she chatted incessantly about my ineptness as a camper. *Hey! I'm Jewish, and I'm old. Gimme the Sheraton!* Tracy laughed at me, then hopped out of the car at the United terminal. Gone in an instant. Just like that. School wouldn't start for another month so she went back home to Napa.

During move-in several weeks later, as the new school year was about to begin, there was a knock on my apartment door. "Hi, Dr. Ronni. Remember me?" From that night on, Tracy was a frequent visitor. She would come to my office or my apartment, most often when she was either depressed or terribly excited about something. It didn't occur to me yet that Tracy was cycling up and down. I knew Tracy was on anti-depressants—when she remembered to take them. I'm not a therapist so I couldn't know that Tracy was probably suffering from bipolar disorder. I was a Faculty-in-Residence in the hall where Tracy lived. She often came to my apartment to study in the quiet of my space or to talk about the issues that affected her on any given day, including her depression.

During the times she felt down, Tracy's face would become pale, all color gone from her cheeks and even her lips, and she would say she was afraid of herself. During her upswings, she would sometimes seek quiet places that didn't feel like sensory overload. I realized that's when I saw her most often, when she was on an up-cycle. I connected her with a counselor in our Student Counseling and Psychological Services who provided excellent therapy for her, but it wasn't enough. She probably needed additional medication that only her psychiatrist at home could provide.

Tracy was an outstanding student despite having a reputation in the residence hall as a party girl. Strangely, and for as well as I knew her, I had no idea that she played—and drank—with gusto. Regardless, Tracy was adored by everyone with whom she came into contact. By the start of her sophomore year, she had come out to her parents and friends as a lesbian and had a crush on a new girlfriend who she planned to visit over the winter break. She had been accepted into the Study Abroad program for the following year, and in January she would begin the LGBT Studies minor. She was very excited about both. It was almost Thanksgiving and she told me she was looking forward to going home for the holiday and her father's birthday.

I was training for the December 2004 Honolulu marathon with the National AIDS Marathon Training Program. The final 22-mile training run was on Sunday, November 14th. I recruited students from the residence hall to staff water stops for us that day. Tracy volunteered. She showed up at 5:30 AM for the first shift and stayed the entire day. She said it was one of the most meaningful things she'd ever done because it was helping people with AIDS, and she cheered me on mightily as I ran by her station, making sure the water cup made it into my hand.

The following Thursday evening, November 18th, Tracy and I met at an on-campus theater for a film screening and to meet the director and actors. We walked back to the residence hall together around 10 PM. Tracy seemed to be in good spirits.

"What are you going to do now?" I inquired.

"I have an outline due in the morning. It's almost done. It won't take too long. Thanks for taking me tonight." I hugged her goodnight and went to my apartment to work on an article.

I sat at my desk near my living room window. About an hour later I noticed vehicles with flashing red lights pull into the driveway. There were too many emergency vehicles for the occasional drunk student lying in the grass so I went into the hallway to see what was going on. Quiet on my floor, so I went up to the next. I could see the Resident Assistant, my young friend Craig, down the hall, running towards me. He stopped in front of me, tears streaming down his face. He put his arms around me, sobbing.

"Dr. Ronni...It's Tracy." Stunned, I grabbed Craig. Holding each other, we slid to the floor. The remainder of that night—what I remember of it—was a living hell. *Another fucking loss. How on earth am I supposed to handle this???*

Tracy was one of those special students for me—the one who inadvertently makes their way onto your tidy stage before you even know they're there, and then you just want to adopt them. While I have felt very connected to many of my students time after time, there was always that one special child every now and then, who shows up and reminds me why I do this Student Affairs work. Tracy was such a student for me.

I miss Tracy. I was angry with her for a long time—for leaving me and her friends and her parents who will grieve for their only child for the rest of their lives. Why did she do it? For months I beat myself up, wondering what I missed. What could I have done differently? What should I have done to save her? For several years I would see her face in the nooks and crannies of the residence hall and campus. I still miss her. Surprisingly, I've received many gifts as a result of this unspeakable tragedy, and I'm deeply grateful. Because of Tracy, I allowed myself to open my heart to other students whom I never would have met. I keep Tracy's memory close to me like a cherished old friend, and her beloved Frisbee hangs in my office next to the beautiful Carol Peterson photograph of the candle-lit memorial that honored Tracy's presence at UCLA.


May 2006

Since the fall of 2001, I've taught a course at UCLA called *LGBT is Not a Sandwich: Straight Talk on Gay Issues in America.* For the past several years I've team-taught the course with my dear friend, Dr. Suzanne Seplow, director of the UCLA Office of Residential Life. The class is one of about 50 one-hour honors seminars, called Fiat Lux classes, taught in the living/learning environment of the residence halls. The purpose of this particular course is to provide a very general overview about LGBT people and issues. Topics include terminology, coming out, history, legal, political, and religious issues, and how to be an ally. Guest speakers share their experiences with the class in lively, frank discussions.

Only twenty students, mostly first years, are allowed to enroll for the course each quarter. In these small classes we are able to create a safe environment and build a trusting community where students get to know one another and the faculty. When we asked students why they registered for this particular course, they typically would say they wanted to learn more about the issues. Some say they've heard only negative things about LGBT people and want to hear different perspectives. Others say they have LGBT friends or family members and want to know how to support them. Yet others say they're coming out themselves or exploring their own identities and are in search of self. Occasionally someone, usually a male athlete who is slumped down in his chair with his cap over his eyes, says he just needs a one-unit course.

As Student Affairs professionals, Suzanne and I know a great deal about campus environments and the experiences of LGBT students in the residence halls. In weekly journal assignments, students are required to respond to two questions for each session: (1) What was this class like for you today?; and (2) share when, where, and what (not from who) you heard this week regarding anti- and pro-LGBT words. It's not unusual for students to say they heard words like *fag* or *faggot*, typically used by male students in groups, and the phrase *that's so gay* is common daily language by everyone. As our students become more aware, they admit to using such words themselves as well as language that might be offensive to other populations. During the last class session, students are asked how they think they might be allies for LGBT people and others who are different from themselves. Their responses are always heartfelt and genuine.

We've read many touching journal entries from our students, some sharing very personal experiences, some admitting for the first time that they're lesbian or gay or bisexual or transgender. The most unusual response we ever received in a journal, however, was from a Chinese male student. He wrote, "I never met any lesbians before, and now I know two. I didn't know what lesbians are supposed to look like, but you guys just look like women." *Guys? Us?* We'll save that for a different class!

December 2008

"Hi, Dr. Ronni!" He looked so grown up. Well, he was! Twenty-four years old now, in a suit and tie and a heavy overcoat because it was 34 degrees in Washington, D.C. Each time I go to Washington for a meeting or conference, I take a UCLA alumnus to dinner because there is always at least one there who stayed in touch with me. Last year and this, my dinner guest was Craig, the young man who had been the Resident Assistant in my hall at UCLA four years earlier when Tracy died.

"Hi, Craig," I hollered across the intersection of M Street and 19th as he walked towards me. We hugged tightly though I could barely feel his arms around me for my big fat down winter coat that Eddie Bauer said would keep me warm to thirty below. If I were knocked down, I would simply roll back up like a child's Weeble toy.

Craig and I had a deep bond because of the tragedy of Tracy's suicide. We were the ones who took care of our students through that long awful night as we ourselves struggled with our own shock and immense pain. Our bond, though, was established before that night. As a first year college student, 18-year-old Craig was just coming out as a gay man, and we often talked about it in the safety and confidentiality of my faculty apartment. Craig was a diver, a cheer-leader, an effective student leader, a good student, and a fine young man. I enjoyed spending time with him.

Craig was a junior when Tracy died. A year later almost to the day, Craig's beloved grandmother died in the same tragic way. Craig took an emotional nosedive but he managed to complete his senior year at UCLA, then headed to Chile where he lived with a local family and worked there with impoverished people. As he began to heal from his pain and sadness, he fell in love with the country. Craig decided to go to graduate school at George Washington University in Washington D.C., intending to go into the Foreign Service. He returned to Chile after an internship with the Obama administration.

We sat at dinner that evening as we had the year before, reminiscing about UCLA, about Tracy, about people we know. As we toasted one another with our wine, Craig said, "I've never told you this, Dr. Ronni.

211

You were always there for me and for so many. You were like my life-line at UCLA."

Dinner was over and we would go our opposite directions. As we hugged goodbye, Craig said, "I love you, Dr. Ronni" and ran off into the evening cold before I could respond. The snow began to fall as I watched Craig disappear into the December night. I'm grateful that I played a small role on his road to becoming such a beautiful young man.


These stories are among the very many gifts of being a Student Affairs professional. While I had no contact with my own children for many years, I have had the privilege of working with other people's children for periods of time. As a woman, a mother, a grandmother, as one who keeps students at the center of my focus, I cannot imagine working in any other field. It took me 47 years to find this profession. I have no doubt, though, that the profession found me, and I feel very, very blessed.

## 39.
## *Letter to Anita Bryant*

Dear Anita,

This is not the letter I would have written to you in 1979, but it is what I need to say to you today. In 1979 I was too angry. At the age of 31, in 1979, I acknowledged my lesbian identity. After 20 years of self-deprecation, of intense fear of discovery and deliberate, painful, deafening silence, I acknowledged my true self. After seven years of marriage and two beautiful babies, I came out. I didn't know about the laws that were passed by the Florida legislature following your 1977 anti-gay work in Miami. Your *Save Our Children* campaign led to the repeal of Miami's anti-discrimination ordinance. You said, "As a mother, I know that homosexuals cannot biologically reproduce children." Wrong, Anita. I reproduced. I'm a mother. I'm a homosexual and I reproduced.

I was naive back then about Florida's laws, about politics, about lesbian and gay history and civil rights, and even about you. Yes, I knew who you were. You were a popular singer and the spokesperson for the Florida Orange Juice Commission. In fact, my aunt was once your ex-husband Bob's secretary at the radio station in Miami. But in 1979 all I knew was that I could no longer live the "Big Lie." I didn't know that my decision to finally be honest about my sexual orientation would result in the loss of custody of my children.

Anita, were you ever aware of the ripple effects of your actions which were endorsed by then Florida governor Ruben Askew? Immediately following your hate-filled work in Miami, the Florida Legislature passed SB 354 which prohibited adoption by homosexuals. Senator Don Chamberlin tried to fight that law. He told the Florida Senate:

*There is no demonstrable social problem. Don't start a discrimination; don't pick a fight. At the heart of this bill is not the subject matter of*

213

*adoption—it is discrimination. This bill begins a state policy [of] selective, deliberate discrimination. It picks a fight. (Journal of the Florida Senate, 1977)*

The bill passed, and Senator Chamberlin was not re-elected. That was the state's first piece of anti-gay legislation, Anita, and it was to honor you. Today, thirty-three years later, Florida's adoption ban, the only one of its kind that remained in the United States, was finally overturned. The ban against homosexuals in Florida was the only categorical adoption ban on the State's books. Florida evaluated adoption applications from all other would-be adoptive parents, including those who have failed at previous adoptions and those with a history of drug abuse or even domestic violence. In Florida, the law was clear: Homosexuals were not fit parents.

You probably know that you weren't the first to actively fight to deliberately discriminate against homosexuals in Florida. Charley Johns beat you to it by about twenty years with the Florida Legislative Investigation Committee whose purpose was to find ways to identify and remove homosexuals from Florida's schools. Public school teachers and college professors were the primary targets of Johns' eight-year investigation. Many teachers—some gay and some perceived to be gay— were publicly named and forced to resign, wrecking careers, destroying families, and causing tremendous harm to many. *Homosexuality and Citizenship in Florida* (1964) was the resulting publication of the Florida Legislative Investigation Committee. *The Purple Pamphlet*, as the report became known, was the hottest item on the pornography market that year because of the explicit photos in it

I wish Florida's state-supported discrimination against homosexuals had ended in 1964 with the John's Committee disbandment, but then you came along in 1977, Anita. Following in your footsteps, Representative Tom Bush of Ft. Lauderdale and Senator Alan Trask of Winter Haven authored the Bush-Trask Amendment into the 1981 Florida General Appropriations Bill which was signed into law. The Bush-Trask Amendment read:

*No funds appropriated herein shall be used to finance any state-supported public or private post-secondary educational institution that charters or gives official recognition or knowingly gives assistance to or provides meeting facilities for any group or organization that recommends or advocates sexual relations between persons not married to each other (Laws of Florida. Chapter 81-206, p. 645).*

Tom Bush appeared on the Phil Donohue television program to explain that this amendment was specifically targeting "homosexuals in Florida's universities." Bush stated that he resented taxpayers' money going to support such "garbage" as campus gay groups. When Rep. Joe Kershaw inquired if gays were not taxpayers, too, Bush replied that while they might be, so are "murderers, thieves, and rapists."

During that time, I was the executive director and lobbyist of the Florida Task Force, Florida's lesbian and gay civil rights organization. The Task Force joined with other organizations and took this discriminatory law to the Florida Supreme Court. The Court unanimously agreed that "the proviso violates the freedom of speech under the First Amendment and article I, section 4 and is unconstitutional." Bush was not re-elected and Trask resigned. In fact, Trask was charged with violating Senate ethics rules and several federal rules as well.

When I came out as a lesbian thirty-some years ago, like so many of my contemporaries I was thrust into politics by a deep anger that was fueled by the loss of custody of my children. Passion and a need to create change were deeply ingrained in my soul, probably very similar to the feelings you had during that same period of time, and I remember how lucky I felt to be able to do lesbian and gay civil rights work. I also remember the 1998 reauthorization of the anti-discrimination ordinance against which you fought so hard twenty years earlier. Miami-Dade County now protects people on the basis of sexual orientation. Other cities and counties in Florida followed suit, but the state of Florida itself—like the federal government—still has no such protection.

I remember Tony and Richard, two young men who befriended me when I worked at Burdines Department Store in the late 1970s. They're

215

gone now. AIDS. But back then, they saved my life. When I was on the verge of coming out, they took me to Orlando's most famous gay bar, the Parliament House. I walked into that huge room where I saw men dancing with men, but far more important for me—because I knew no other lesbians yet—I saw women dancing with women. While I'm not much of a drinker and didn't know a soul there, I knew I was among my people. And so my journey out of the closet began.

I knew I was a lesbian by the time I was eleven years old, but I refused to accept being so different from my family and friends. I struggled hard to be like everyone else. By the time I was thirty-one, twenty years in the closet was long enough. I couldn't fight it any more. It was 1979. In a blink of an eye, in a heartbeat that thundered through my being, my six year old daughter and three year old son were taken away from me. I was "different"; I was a lesbian. Custody was granted to my children's father. When you and Bob divorced, Anita, you kept your children. I could not.

Although I was allowed sporadic visitation, my former husband and his fundamentalist parents maintained tight control over when and how I saw my children. By the time the children were nine and twelve, they didn't want to see me any more. They were told that all gay people have AIDS. Since I'm gay I must have AIDS, too. My children were told if they touched me or hugged me or kissed me, they would get sick and die. My children were afraid of me.

During the first few years after I had come out, I wondered every morning what my children were wearing to school. Were their clothes clean? Were their teeth brushed? Did they have a nutritious lunch? I wondered if they had any of the usual childhood diseases, if they wanted me to be there to hold them through a fever or a tummy ache. I occasionally wondered if I did the right thing by coming out when I did, but I knew that my only other alternative was death. I wondered how my children felt about me. Did they long to see me as I did them? I mourned for them, for my loss, but I felt confined and conflicted in my mourning: my children weren't dead, just out of my view, out of my reach. Where were your young children, Anita? As you railed against homosexuality in Miami and as laws were created out of your ranting, did you think about how your actions affected other parents and their children as you kissed

216

your own children good-night each evening? Probably not.

I remained in Florida until 1994. I believed that if my children needed me, I could get to them quickly. But by 1994, they were adults, eighteen and twenty-one. My staying in Florida was no longer a necessity. If my children wanted to contact me, they could do so no matter where I lived. I accepted a position as the director of the Lesbian and Gay Office at the University of Michigan and moved to Ann Arbor. The expectation of seeing my children any time in the near future was gone, but I always knew they would return to me. Someday.

I moved to Michigan in May of 1994. I had not heard from—or of—my children in many years. I had not been invited to their rites of passages such as their band recitals or their high school graduations or even my daughter's wedding. So it was with great surprise that I opened an email message on Christmas Day, 1994, that started out by saying, *Hi, Mom. I'd like to talk with you.* My daughter and her husband had just moved from Florida to Dayton, Ohio, only three hours south of Ann Arbor. They came to my house the next day. We began to get to know one another as mother and daughter, and as adults. In May of 1995 I witnessed the birth of my first granddaughter. My second granddaughter was born in 1998, and I was there to greet her at her birth as well.

I moved to California to become the director of the UCLA Lesbian Gay Bisexual Transgender Center. I was successful in my work and extremely happy with my life. All that was missing was my son, Anita, but I felt that one day he, like his sister, would also return to me. A year after I moved to Los Angeles, in August of 1998, I received a letter with my son's name on the return address. Slowly I opened it and read: *Dear Dr. Sanlo or Mom. I don't know what to call you but in trying to find myself I need to find you. I hope it's okay...*

I hope you would ask about my children, Anita. Though we were estranged for many years, we are now a close family and we've come together as adults to honor the love and history we share. While I missed many years of my children's youth, I am blessed that these two wonderful people are now friends and guides in my life. My son came out as a gay man several years ago and was disowned by his father and his fundamentalist grandparents. So much for Christian love. On Mother's Day recently he gave a card to me in which he wrote:

217

*Mom, I can honestly say that I can't imagine a more amazing mother than you. I am blessed and lucky to have you. You have shown me love and support even when I didn't know it. You have literally released me from so many chains. I owe you nothing less than everything I am. Happy Mother's Day!*

So, Anita, times have changed, thank God, over these thirty-some years. Your anti-gay work in Miami was overturned, but not without residual effects for both of us. You were shunned by the very fundamentalist Christians who pushed you into the anti-gay limelight, and, ironically, you helped jump-start a budding gay civil rights movement as no one else had ever been able to do. You even apologized later to the gay community for the hateful things you said and did.

I've come to understand that while your work and its fall-out back then destroyed people's lives, as the John's Committee did two decades before you, you were doing the best you could with what you knew. I believe that today. I was not in a place to understand that then. I don't know what my life would have been like had I been granted custody or even fair visitation with my children, but I can tell you that my life today is rich and full of love because of the experiences I've had, both positive and negative. Because you did what you thought was right, I made choices about the path I took, which became one of helping others survive in the face of great pain, both physical and emotional. My journey, though not without some tremendous bumps in the road, has been a blessing, and you, Anita, were instrumental in the way it occurred.

Because of the lessons I've learned—and perhaps this comes with the seasoning of age—as an educator, a mother, and a lesbian, Anita, I now let go of the last vestiges of anger. I forgave my former husband who kept my children away from me for all those years. I forgave his mother who choreographed the hate that filled their home. I forgave his father who stood by and did nothing to stop the madness as he secretly slipped money to me. I have even forgiven myself. In fact, I've forgiven the lawmakers of Florida for creating stupid, hateful, discriminatory laws, though I do believe that the Florida Legislature owes a tremendous public apology to lesbian and gay Floridians. And today, Anita, in honor of my children and grandchildren, and in memory of the many lesbian and gay Floridians we've lost, I forgive you

Sincerely,
Ronni Sanlo

## 40.
# To the Florida Legislature, Apologize!

If I returned to Florida as a resident, I would spend my days demanding your attention, demanding an apology for the hell you repeatedly brought upon your invisible citizens, your lesbian, gay, bisexual, and transgender tax-paying citizens.

Apologize!

For supporting the homosexual witch hunts in higher education in the 1950s and 1960s;
For allowing the Florida Legislative Investigative Committee to harass, antagonize, and even destroy lives of students and faculty;
For creating and publishing *The Purple Pamphlet* which showed a young man tied in leather, and prepubescent naked boys in various poses, and men having sex with other men in bathrooms (how DID you get those photos?);
And for daring to declare that those photos depicted Florida's lesbian and gay citizens!
Shame on you! Apologize!

Apologize!

For creating anti-gay adoption laws in 1977 as you praised Anita Bryant's hateful work in Miami in the name of God. There were no issues, no threats from lesbian and gay people. Why were those laws necessary?
Shame on you! Apologize!

Apologize!

For allowing Tom Bush of Ft. Lauderdale to call Florida's lesbian and gay citizens despicable names when he was on the national Phil Donahue

Show;

For creating a law in 1981 that threatened Florida's colleges and universities with the loss of state funding if they supported lesbian and gay students.

And for allowing that hateful law to pass.

Shame on you! Apologize!

Apologize!

For never including *sexual orientation* in the state's non-discrimination laws.

For continuing to discriminate against an entire population of people, of taxpayers, who are Floridians, and who simply wish to live in safety and in freedom, just like you.

Shame on you! Apologize!

Apologize!

Leave the old boys and the embarrassing old ways where they belong, in the past and long forgotten!

Have the guts to say the words and create new laws of inclusion!

It's time to stop being the most repressive state in the nation.

Your lesbian and gay and bisexual and transgender citizens and our families and friends and young people just coming out—perhaps some of your own children—deserve your loving attention.

Apologize!

Make amends!

Move into the 21$^{st}$ century with the light of freedom for *all* of your citizens in the Sunshine State.

Do it now!

Apologize!

## 41.
# TEAM SHERRY Takes the Walk for Hope

---

2008

<u>U.S. President</u>: George Bush
<u>Best film</u>: Slumdog Millionaire; The Curious Case of Benjamin Button, Milk, The Reader
<u>Best actors</u>: Sean Penn, Kate Winslet
<u>Best TV shows</u>: Lipstick Jungle; The Rachel Maddow Show; The Mentalist; SNL Thursday Night Live
<u>Best songs</u>: I Kissed a Girl, 4 Minutes, So What, Just Dance, Piece of Me, Touch My Body, Feedback, All Summer Long, No One
<u>Civics</u>: California Supreme Court ruled in favor of same sex marriage but voters passed Proposition 8 to ban same sex marriage
<u>Popular Culture</u>: Same sex marriage legal in California from June to November; New York recognizes same sex marriages from other states; Connecticut approves same sex marriage
<u>Deaths</u>: George Carlin, Bo Diddley, Bobby Fischer, Estelle Getty, Isaac Hayes, Heath Ledger, Bernie Mac, Mildred Loving, Paul Newman, Suzanne Pleshette, Tim Russert, Lawrence King, Del Martin, Eartha Kitt

---

*Breast cancer. Chemotherapy. Bald. Surgery. Radiation. Reconstruction.* Words she rarely spoke, and never in relation to herself or in the context of her family. And now these words were hers, in daily doses. My sister Sherry. Sherry's words. "Sher doesn't have cancer. *We* have cancer," said Barry, Sherry's husband. Barry's words.

The three sisters—Sherry, Bebe, and I—had mammograms in July of 2008. For Bebe and me, it was our annual check-ups. Results not good. We both needed biopsies and I needed a surgical excision. Thank God, both Bebe and I were negative. Sherry had her annual mammogram the previous January. It was clean then, but now, six months later, she

222

was experiencing some pain in her right breast that wasn't going away. "Well, at least it's not cancer," Bebe and I smartly stated because we'd always heard that breast cancer doesn't hurt.

"Ron, I have breast cancer." *What?* Did I hear her correctly? We were on the phone. I was vacationing in Florida when she got her results.

"Sher, what did you just say?" I was holding my breath. She can't have breast or any other kind of cancer. She's the one who didn't have an ounce of body fat, who worked out nearly every day of her life, who lived an exceedingly healthy lifestyle and always ate the right foods in just the right amounts.

"I had some tissue and lymph nodes removed, Ron. It's cancer. Stage 3. I start chemo next week." I heard her voice as it shook, thinking that her body was probably shaking, too, just as mine was, as she felt the surrealness of it all. I kept thinking *what in hell does one have to do to prevent this crap??? If Sher can get it, anyone can. This just sucks.* Any stupid thought to avoid the fear, the unthinkable. Please, God, not another loss.

It's not like there hasn't been cancer in our family. Mom's mother, my grandma Frances, had non-Hodgkin's lymphoma; Dad's father, a life long unfiltered-cigarette smoker, had lung cancer; Dad's sister, Aunt Rita, is a breast cancer survivor (She once told me that the good thing about her bilateral mastectomy was that it dramatically improved her golf game!); Dad had kidney cancer years ago; I'm a melanoma survivor; and most of us in the family have had basal cell carcinoma at one time or another. Yes, there's cancer in our family, and yes, we're all amazing survivors. But somehow, this felt different. More intense. More threatening.

Sherry is two years younger than I. Seven years separates the oldest (me) from the youngest (Bebe). Sherry and our brother Len are in-between. From the time we were born, we all have been one another's best friends. (Okay, maybe not as little kids because I thought my younger sibs were inconveniences. I would have much preferred to be an only child, until I went away to college and realized I missed them like crazy.) Miles and time and age and life experiences didn't separate us in our hearts. For the last decade, we sisters have lived within an hour of one another, spending time with each other as often as our busy schedules allowed. And we often visit Len and his family in Seattle. In fact, for the past 25 years, we've felt as close to Len's wife Carole as to Len himself. Carole is sister #4.

Bebe and I agreed that we wanted, needed, to visit Sherry as often as possible during her chemo ordeal. We all needed each other. As soon as Sher began chemo, Bebe and I went to see her every ten days or so. Sisters Lunches, we called them, but sometimes they were breakfasts or brunches or whole-day events. On those days, the sadness and fear we felt always gave way to the love and friendship and connectedness we have as sisters. The gift of Sherry's cancer was a deeper need and mightier love among the three of us. Bebe and I became Sherry's support network.

If Bebe and I were the support, then Barry was Sher's sustenance. Barry sat beside Sher as she underwent chemo every three weeks; he cooked for her, forced her to eat to keep her strength up. "I never knew about grocery shopping," said Barry who turned his business over to their son Kenny so that he could stay home to care for Sherry. "Now I know the names of all the check-out people at Albertsons, and today I'm pretty angry because orange juice just went up thirty cents!" We laughed at his indignation but marveled at his desire and ability to care for his wife, our sister. When Sherry went into the hospital for her bilateral mastectomy, Barry stayed with her the entire time, sleeping and eating within feet of Sherry's bed for all the days of her stay.

As Sherry began chemo, Bebe and I needed to feel some sense of control over Sher's cancer. We searched for a breast cancer event of some sort into which we could put our collective energies. Bebe found the City of Hope's Walk for Hope which took place that November, 2008, two days before Sherry's last chemo. I contacted the Walk for Hope people and TEAM SHERRY was born! TEAM SHERRY served two purposes: one expected, one not. The expected purpose was to raise money in Sherry's name for breast cancer research at the City of Hope. The unexpected purpose was that it gave Sherry a focus. She became very involved in the team and the fundraising. It took much of her time and concentration which was such a positive and exciting thing for her, despite her depleted energy and appetite, both zapped by the chemo.

The day of the Walk arrived. Our team was large: Sherry and Barry,

224

their son Kenny, his wife Jodi and their son Merex; Kenny's in-laws; our parents Sandy and Lois; sister Bebe; brother Len's daughter Ellie who flew in from Seattle and arrived with my son Erik; Roz, Sherry's best friend since they were 18, and her husband Jerry; the entire Otterman family, whoever *they* are, friends of Sherry's I didn't know; and my pal Regina and myself. TEAM SHERRY was present and accounted for! We had shirts and hats, white with pink TEAM SHERRY letters. Our pink silicon bracelets said TEAM SHERRY on one side and I LOVE SHERRY on the other. We looked damned fine and totally put together!

As the Walk began, I looked around. Thousands of people, each one there because someone in their life has or had breast cancer. I saw the beautiful shirts with women's photos and words like "We will always remember" or "She'll always be in our hearts." I felt myself get so angry. *NO!* I screamed inside. *NO! I will not be one of those people in one of those damned shirts!* I almost hyperventilated! My stomach tightened. I couldn't psychologically go there. Sherry was going to win. I knew it with all my heart. She had to! As I looked at this family that surrounded her, I saw the glow and the love on Sherry's precious face. Through her, I realized all would be well, whatever the outcome.

The Walk meandered throughout the campus of the City of Hope. Our mother made signs for us to carry and we also had the TEAM SHERRY sign supplied by the Walk for Hope folks, so every time we passed a person with a microphone, we heard, "There's TEAM SHERRY! Hi, TEAM SHERRY!" We hollered and cheered and gave ourselves permission to act completely silly. It was great fun.

The most wonderful thing about the Walk was seeing Sherry palpably feel the support and camaraderie of the many friends and family members who love her dearly. Sher sent an email to Bebe and me after the Walk.

*Dear Ron and Be,*
*How do I thank you both for all that you've done???? Today was such an emotional day for me and Barry. Just knowing how you put it all together from the very beginning with such love fills my heart with more love for you both than ever, if that was even possible! From the Team Sherry website, to all the generous donations, to the Team Sherry bracelets and*

*mostly to your support, encouragement and love, I feel so overwhelmed with love for you. Barry does, too. How do I thank you? Knowing I have two of the most incredible sisters ever has given me more strength than you will ever know. I want to spend many, many, many more years having our "sisters lunches"!!! You can't imagine how much I look forward to spending time with you. God blessed me with the two most amazing women for my sisters. I hope you both always know how very much I love you.*
*Sher*


Sherry completed the chemo which did not get all the cancer, but the bilateral mastectomy did. Sher decided to undergo radiation treatments for good measure. The cancer is gone and our prayers were answered. The family remains right here for Sher, with Bebe and me leading the charge. Sherry models for us what is means to have grace under fire, tremendous courage, and true deep-down strength.

For all the things both positive and negative that I've experienced in my life, Sher's fight with cancer put so much of it into perspective for me. Many of the challenges I've encountered over the years were merely inconveniences from which I was smart enough to learn some of the lessons offered. Sherry, my precious sister, I love you, and I walk with hope in my heart for you—and because of you—every moment of every day. Your battle with breast cancer was the challenge of a lifetime, and I feel so privileged to have taken that journey with you. I thank God for the outcome, and damn, girl, your hair is so cute!

# 42.
## The Purple Golf Cart

*I* sat in my purple golf cart, the one I bought for myself for my 60th birthday. The first time I polished it, I felt like a sixteen year old boy with his new hot rod. As I shined and primped my best old-lady toy, a memory landed on the hot pink upholstery. It was a quick flash of a memory, or maybe a wish, of my grandmother Frances, in 1958, sitting in her own golf cart, though probably not purple, just months before she died.

I felt a lump rise in my throat as my eyes moistened. My heart got heavy as I envisioned my grandma doing exactly what I was doing now, polishing her golf cart and then polishing her golf game. I miss my grandma, even now, more than fifty years later. My grandma was the only one, I recall, who hugged me like she meant it with those long Florida-tanned arms wrapped around my eleven year old self. I knew without a doubt that I was my grandma's beloved favorite, the first born of all the grandchildren, the special one, Grandma told me. *I love you, a bushel and a peck, a bushel and a peck and a hug around the neck!* She always sung that to me. She said I was splendid and smart and funny, and I believed her.

I wasn't allowed to go to my grandma's funeral. I had to stay home to help care for the younger children. Funerals weren't happy places and children didn't belong there. But I wanted to be there. I was so terribly, deeply sad and had no way to express my pain. My grandma just died and my heart was breaking. But I stayed home with the younger ones and to help prepare the house for the many relatives and Grandma's friends who would soon arrive.

I polished my purple golf cart with a vengeance, because even now, 50 years later, I still miss her, and my heart still hurts. As I moved the cloth in exaggerated circles, I reminisced about how death was handled in my family when I was young. For example, when a fish died, my mother flushed it down the toilet and bought a new one the same day. When one of those stupid parakeets died, a replacement appeared before dark, though sometimes of a different color which was a give-away of the change. My mother, who truly meant well and was just trying to protect her children from loss and sadness, never mentioned the death or the switch although the process was quite obvious when fifteen year old Rusty, our family sheepdog, was replaced with a chocolate poodle puppy the day after she died. So the confusing issue for my eleven year old self was this: *if animals who died were quickly replaced before the day was over, would there be another grandma by tomorrow?* I hoped not. I just wanted the original one to come back.

In my family, people weren't allowed to feel sadness or disappointment or anger. Nothing but happy—happy, happy, friggin' happy. Children weren't allowed to experience the passing of loved ones because the passing wasn't a happy thing, so I had no understanding of how to grieve a loss. Later, when I lost custody of my children and when my friends died of AIDS, I was emotionally unprepared for the feelings that swirled around and squeezed the life out of my heart.


I climbed into the passenger side of my purple golf cart, thinking about my grandma, feeling the sadness, still feeling the loss. I had to talk with her. I had so much to share, so much I wanted her to know. After fifty years, I still needed her. So I talked. I cried and talked and talked and talked. I told her about my children, about how proud she would be of them. I told her about Berit and what a terrific mom and scholar she is, and how she, too was *vaccinated with a Victrola needle*, as Grandma used to say about me with such pride because I was a non-stop talker as a child. I told her about Erik, what a fine young man he is and how he takes good care of his mother. I told her about my granddaughters and grandson, her great-great-grandchildren. I told her about me, about my life, about how crazy it's all been but that it's good now. I told her how much I love her and missed her all these years. And I told her that I know without a doubt that she's always been with me, taking care of me when I couldn't take care of myself.

With my tears landing on the hot pink upholstery, I scooted over to the driver's side and heard my own voice say, "C'mon, Grandma. This 60-year-old eleven year old girl is gonna take you for one hell of a ride!"

And I did! My grandma was with me. I felt her love enfold me as I cried a thousand tears. Suddenly, as I zoomed—as if one could really zoom in a golf cart—around the neighborhood golf course, I felt the sadness transform into joyous celebration. I felt the pain release its hold as I gave it over to the memories and to the joy of the moment. I began to feel a healing peace in my heart, perhaps for the very first time.

Later that afternoon as the sun was going down over the western San Jacinto mountains, I went into my house and saw the message light blinking on my answering machine. My heart, still full of emotion from the day, soared at the sound of the eleven year old voice of my own splendid, smart, funny granddaughter. "Hi, Grandma. I can't wait to come visit you and ride in your purple golf cart."

# 43.
## *What's Next?*

---

2009-2010

U.S. President: Barach Obama

Best film: Avatar; Precious; Up in the Air, Inglorious Basterds; The Hurt Locker

Best actors: Jeff Bridges; Sandra Bullock; Meryl Streep

Best songs: Halo; I Gotta Feeling; Poker Face; You Belong with Me

Best Television shows: 30 Rock; Glee; The Office; House; Big Love; Family

Civics: U.S. Jobless rate over 10%; H1N1 flu; attempted suicide bomber on Delta flight; large earthquakes in Haiti and Chile; Healthcare bill signed into law

Popular culture: Iowa, Vermont, New Hampshire, and Washington D.C. legalized same sex marriage; New York votes down gay marriage;

Deaths: Michael Jackson, Farah Fawcett, Ed McMahon, Gale Storm, Karl Malden, Walter Cronkite, Ricardo Montalbán, John Updike, Beatrice Arthur, Danny Gans, Dom Deluise, David Carradine, Walter Cronkite, Eve Kosofsky Sedgewick, William Saffire, Mary Travers, Patrick Swayze, Sen. Edward Kennedy, Les Paul, John Hughes, Frank McCourt, Robert McNamara

---

*G*ood question. I don't know what's next, and I'm okay with that. I'm open to whatever the Universe has in store for me. Maybe another book, a poem, a move, a partner, an improved golf game. (Please let it be an improved golf game!) Whatever, I'm ready for the next adventure, the next turning point.

My work changed at UCLA and I've chosen to retire. It's time for the younger generation to take over campus LGBT work. My vision has been fulfilled. Smart, energetic new professionals—like my mentees

230

Tom Bourdon, Molly Holmes, Jamelle Wilson, and many others—have new visions and new passions. They lived the lives their students are experiencing. They know without a doubt what to do and they have the courage to get it done.

Friends and acquaintances ask me how I feel about leaving campus work. After all, I've been a "gay activist" for over thirty years and now it looks like I'm putting away my rainbow gloves. First, I am the one who created this change. No one asked me to scoot over. I simply had the good sense to know and feel in my heart that it was time to do something different. When I began this LGBT work at the University of Michigan, my supervisor, Dr. E. Royster Harper, told me to remember each day to keep a student at the center of my focus, that we do our work in Student Affairs because of our students. I did. I had a student, though faceless, at the center of my focus every single day. When my son Erik came out as a gay man several years ago, suddenly that face was his. While many, many young people benefitted from my work, I realized I was called to do this work for my own child as well. He came out in safety and with love. I knew this part of my work was complete.

Second, I realized a couple of years ago that my personal identity had been completely wrapped around what I do, not who I am. My work was my identity. My *self* was an insecure women who needed to be propped up, bolstered by something because my personal life was such a mess. It's like the woman whose sole identity is her husband, that her own sense of self is buried somewhere in his underwear drawer. As I grew more comfortable in my own skin over the last few years, I discovered myself aside from my work. My identity, who I am, no longer needs the bolstering from what I do for work. I was able to let go of the work, pass it on to the talented young folks I've mentored over the years, and move on to grow further into myself as an educator and consultant, a woman, a grandma. Such freedom! Such love!

I've been so blessed with—and perhaps because of—the ups and downs life has provided. There is still much work to do, much *tikkun ha olam*—changing of the world—to accomplish, and many more stories to write, both mine and yours. I encourage you to write your stories, or at least talk to yourself in a small tape recorder. (We're old so we have the right to look and sound a bit crazy!) Who are you? What do you remember and how were you affected? Here are some prompts for you:

Green stamps (my favorite! I remember licking them into the books then going with my mother to the redemption center)
Dinah Shore: "See the USA in your Chevrolet!"
BurmaShave signs along the highways that weren't yet Interstates or freeways
Roadside drive-in motels
Marlin Perkins
Reel-to-reel tapes
45 RPM records
Brownie cameras
Flash bulbs
Chatty Cathy
Metal ice cube trays with the lift-up handle
Sky King
Rootie Kazootie
Transistor radios
Dial telephones and party lines
Studebaker
Fuller Brush (my mother was a Fuller Brush man!)
Topo Gigio
Television test patterns
Ringer washing machines

American humorist Erma Bombeck (1927-1996) once wrote:

> *Life is not a journey to the grave*
> *With the intention of*
> *Arriving safely in a pretty*
> *And well preserved body,*
> *But rather to skid in broadside,*
> *Thoroughly used up,*
> *Totally worn out,*
> *And loudly proclaiming*
> *WOW!!!! What a ride!*

232

Do it! Take the ride! Don't let those coming up behind you miss out on your life. Your stories are interesting to some and important to others. My email is ronnisanlo@gmail.com. Let's share our stories!

For me, this life has been one great adventure after another, and I hope it continues for a long time to come, But when I go, I plan to "*skid in broadside*" with gusto, into that great gay golf course in the sky! How about you?

Warmly,

*Ronni*

2012 (These are my personal selection)

U.S. President: Barach Obama
Best film: The Help, The Artist, Tomboy, Sarah's Key
Best actors: Meryl Streep, Glenn Close
Best songs: Just a Kiss in the Moonlight (for my sweet Kelly)
Best Television shows: Glee; Rachel Maddow; Today Show
Popular culture: New York and Washington State legalized same sex marriage
Deaths: Etta James, Whitney Houston, Don Cornelius

## ABOUT THE AUTHOR

Ronni Sanlo was a UCLA professor and director of the UCLA Lesbian Gay Bisexual Transgender (LGBT) Center. Formerly, she was an HIV epidemiologist in Florida. She earned her bachelor's degree from the University of Florida, and a masters and doctorate in education from the University of North Florida in Jacksonville. Dr. Sanlo's research and many publications and presentations focus on sexual orientation and social justice issues. While Ronni lives in her Palm Desert retirement community where she rides around in her purple golf cart and plays rotten but passionate golf, she also manages her publishing company, Purple Books Publishing.

Ronni invites your feedback, comments and speaking requests at ronni@purplebookspublishing.com. Please visit the Purple Books website at www.purplebookspublishing.com for other fine books and for the Discussion Guide for *Purple Golf Cart*.

23679004R00134

Made in the USA
San Bernardino, CA
27 August 2015

circumstances, I'm glad our paths crossed and our lives touched. I would have had a very different life experience had it not been for each one of them.

I'm 64 now. As I reflect back in these chapters, I realize that life has been good despite—or perhaps because of—the distant and recent crises: the loss of custody of my children; my poverty, transiency and homelessness; friends dying from AIDS; multiple failed relationships; depression; cancer; being fired from more jobs than I care to remember. Words in a Jimmy Buffet song describe how I feel today about my life's journey: "Some of it's magic, some of it's tragic, but it's been a good life all the way." Indeed...

I attended a workshop recently in which there was an ice-breaker that required participants to describe their very best day. "Are you kidding???" I proclaimed. "THIS is my best day. I woke up. I'm still here. It's good!" Today, this day, is my very best day. I have a large loving family including my parents who are in their 80s and still going strong; my children and grandchildren who fill my heart with deep pride and joy; my sisters and brothers, by birth or marriage to one another, who are my best friends; talented and passionate colleagues; and sweet loving friends. I have meaningful work at UCLA as a professor and Student Affairs professional, and I'm blessed to be surrounded every day by smart, excited, engaged students. I have good health and a happy heart, and I have my purple golf cart.

I invite you to come along on this journey with me. It is a journey of reflection and resilience, of sharing stories about my life, of remembering from where I came. Perhaps something will resonate with your life experiences and you, too, will be motivated to write your story. My email is ronnisanlo@gmail.com. I hope you'll let me know what you think. In the meantime, hop aboard my purple golf cart and let's ride!

*Ronni*